American Will

Will

THE FORGOTTEN CHOICES THAT
CHANGED OUR REPUBLIC

BOBBY JINDAL

THRESHOLD EDITIONS

New York   London   Toronto   Sydney   New Delhi

Threshold Editions
An Imprint of Simon & Schuster, Inc.
1230 Avenue of the Americas
New York, NY 10020

First Threshold Editions hardcover edition October 2015

THRESHOLD EDITIONS and colophon are trademarks
of Simon & Schuster, Inc.

For information about special discounts for bulk purchases,
please contact Simon & Schuster Special Sales at
1-866-506-1949 or business@simonandschuster.com.

The Simon & Schuster Speakers Bureau can bring authors
to your live event. For more information or to book an event,
contact the Simon & Schuster Speakers Bureau at 1-866-248-3049
or visit our website at www.simonspeakers.com.

Interior design by Akasha Archer

Manufactured in the United States of America

10 9 8 7 6 5 4 3 2 1

Library of Congress Cataloging-in-Publication Data is available.

ISBN 978-1-5011-1707-7
ISBN 978-1-5011-1710-7 (ebook)

To my best friend, Supriya, and our kids,
Selia, Shaan, and Slade.
Thanks for putting up with me.

CONTENTS

INTRODUCTION

AMERICAN WILL

It may seem odd for a governor to write what is, in a sense, a history book. But that's because so many history books recite names and dates with little meaning or message. Many of them are dreadfully boring. Others oversimplify. Most tell stories with no impact on the present and no lesson for our times.

I don't like reading those kinds of history books, and I certainly have no interest in writing one. But there's a different kind of history that I've always cherished. The kind that brings the past to life by capturing the human condition, in all its dynamics and dimensions. The kind that speaks to who we are, what our culture means, and why, in this blip on God's infinite calendar, we matter. The kind that witnesses to a larger truth and a higher power. The kind that makes us stop and think. The kind that is a call to arms. The kind that shows the power of American will and individual choice. One person, one decision, truly can change the world.

It was that kind of history that came to mind as it became increasingly clear that our country is arriving at one of its most consequential crossroads. Not long ago, as recently as the 2000 presidential election, it was fashionable to believe that elections didn't much matter. "New Democrats" and "Compassionate Conservatives" had migrated so far to the political center that many believed they were about to meet in the middle. But since then, left-wing Democrats have regained control of their party, and challenges at home and abroad have underscored the limitations and liabilities of both liberalism and any compromised version of conservatism. Each recent presidential election has seemed to matter more than the one before it, and I believe none will be more decisive than our next.

In 2016, we can continue down the path of bigger government, emboldened enemies, diminished liberties, and hostility to religious faith. Or we can embrace the hallmarks of our history and the themes of this book: limited government; the power of free people and free markets; American strength and exceptionalism; and the indispensable role of faith in America's intellectual and political arena.

To be sure, I could have published a series of policy papers about each of these principles. In fact, I did. Through a think tank I chair called America Next, our team has explored and articulated a conservative policy agenda to unleash enormous opportunities for America's future. But if conservatives' most common error is criticizing liberalism's failures without offering solutions of our own, then our second most common mistake is tossing around solutions as if their merits are self-evident, without connecting them to our history, our heritage, and our culture.

The challenge for conservatives is to remind skeptics that our philosophy did not arise from a vacuum. It is the product of centuries, even millennia. It is the legacy of our forebears, the foundation of our experiment in self-governance, and the result of lessons learned—sometimes painfully—from choices made by men and women who blazed an imperfect path of progress that was neither accidental nor inevitable. I decided that I could not fully communicate my beliefs unless I shared some of the stories from our country's past that inspired and illustrate them.

There is, of course, some precedent. Aesop taught lessons through fables. Lincoln through homespun yarns. Christ through parables. I don't pretend to possess an iota of their wisdom or eloquence. But I hope my stories, like theirs, have more than a narrative. I hope they have a message. I hope they say something about what our nation means. And I hope my selection of them also says a little bit about me—and what I believe our past can teach us about our future.

In bringing the history of these times to life, I have taken some literary license in setting up some of the scenes in this book. Though we worked hard to meticulously footnote any meaningful dialogue or events, I also added occasional details to better reflect the vividness of the moment when the historical record was incomplete. My hope is that this would allow readers a more enjoyable reading experience of a book that is as entertaining as it is enlightening.

Imagine a man nearing the end of a long life. He looks back on his many years with pride. To be sure, he has a few regrets, a few decisions he would change if he could. But when he thinks of his life, the memories that stand out are those that made him the man he has become. Some are obvious, like the day he married the love of his life, and the births of his children. But some of the moments that defined him are known only to the man and his closest friends. A few are shared only with God.

Nations are no different—whether old or, like ours, young. They are the product of the great—and not so great—choices their citizens make. For the United States, some of those crossroads are famous: whether to defy a king and declare our independence; whether to elect a country lawyer who saw in slavery a "monstrous injustice"; whether to order history's mightiest armada to the beaches below a führer's Atlantic Wall. But other crossroads that defined our republic—from the antifederalists' fight for a Bill of Rights, to a plain-talking Texan's stand against socialized medicine—are largely forgotten. This book is the story of those moments.

At the heart of these stories are three types of characters. The first are the unsung—or seldom sung—heroes of our history. They have emerged in every era, from every walk of life, and if we look around us, it's hard to go through a whole day without meeting at least one of them. They are grandparents who bled in the snowy mountains of Korea and the sweltering jungles of Vietnam, as well as the sons and daughters who drove the Taliban from Mazar-i-Sharif and Al Qaeda from Fallujah. They are the neighbors who build our businesses and fight our fires and teach our kids. They are the rabbis who read in the language of Moses the laws he received from the Lord on Mt. Sinai, the priests who bring sacraments of salvation to quiet hospital rooms forgotten by all but those dying there, and the country preachers who reveal the Good Shepherd to His lost sheep.

In one chapter, you'll meet an unsung hero named Melancton Smith, a simple man with an unusual first name and an unshakable belief that no constitution is complete without a Bill of Rights. To defend his principles, he challenged the most famous men of the founding generation, and to save the union, he sacrificed his career. In other chapters you'll meet slaves fighting for their freedom, born-again Christians leading a social movement for justice; a stubborn minority of legislators who stopped our Constitution from being amended with the words of intolerance; and an economics-professor-turned-conservative-firebrand who said Hillary Clinton's health care legislation would pass over his "cold, dead political body."

Another group of characters in this book is famous, but not for the genius they display in the pages of this book. Most school-children know that Thomas Jefferson wrote the Declaration of Independence. Many of us also know that he purchased Louisiana. But few histories explain how his purchase was inspired by his vision of American exceptionalism or why his purchase was the product of a foreign policy that refused to surrender American interests and ideals, even in the face of the most famous conqueror since Caesar. Similarly, most conservatives know that Ronald Reagan's presidency made history, but many are less familiar with how his courage as a governor lit a spark that would one day revolutionize welfare in America.

Another group of characters is also somewhat famous, but they're featured in these pages for their failings, rather than their sometimes considerable virtues. Napoleon Bonaparte, for example, was brilliant on the battlefield, but he was no friend to freedom or to the United States. He met his match in America's third president, and the lesson Napoleon teaches Americans is that our enemies can be contained and ultimately defeated only if we do not provoke them with weakness.

Others in this book teach additional lessons. The foreign policy of Henry Wallace—now an obscure figure but once one of the most powerful men in America—shows the dangers of looking at adversaries while wearing rose-colored glasses. Richard Nixon's welfare policy shows that one of the greatest threats to the conservative movement is a powerful Republican who betrays his conservatism. And Hillary Clinton's health care policy shows the perils of hubris and the innate hostility of the American people to higher taxes, fewer freedoms, and bigger government.

In fact, all of the men and women whose stories I tell in this book—the heroes through their virtues, the foils through their faults—illustrate the folly of looking to the government for the solution to all of our problems. In their experiences, government was often an obstacle to liberty and opportunity. Their stories testify to the five fundamental principles that I wanted to convey when I conceived of this book—which I hope will be the primary principles candidates discuss during the 2016 campaign.

The first principle is the Jeffersonian maxim that "the government which governs least governs best." The proposition that there are simply some things that the government should not do—and cannot constitutionally do—sounds quaint today in some liberal quarters. Frankly, it sounds almost as strange to some so-called moderate Republicans. But to the heroes of *American Will*, liberty was impossible without limited government. It's why in one chapter the antifederalists insist on a Bill of Rights listing, point by point, the most important things our federal government must not do. It's why in another chapter Governor Reagan stops the expansion of welfare dead in its tracks, even though it's not a popular position within his own party. It's why Phil Gramm does the same to Hillary Clinton's disastrous health care initiative, even though, like Reagan, he faced significant skepticism from his fellow Republicans.

The second principle, not unrelated to the first, is that, as President Reagan once said, "No power of government is as formidable a force for good as the creativity and entrepreneurial drive of the American people." Our history is the story "of free men and free markets, and of the extraordinary possibilities that lie within seemingly ordinary men and women." Among the most famous of those men and women are entrepreneurs like Estée Lauder, Walt Disney, and the giants of Silicon Valley who made the web worldwide and the cellphone smart. But in other chapters you'll meet a less famous—but no less audacious—entrepreneur. Edwin Drake found a jar of rock oil on the shelf of a general store in a quiet corner of northwestern Pennsylvania, and he saw in it the makings of an energy revolution. Americans such as Edwin Drake—and millions like him—bet everything on those most precious of treasures: ideas. Theirs is a contribution to the American experiment that could not have been replaced—and that the Progressives described elsewhere in this book could not understand.

The third principle is the Latin adage *si vis pacem, para bellum*—if you want peace, prepare for war. It is, unfortunately, a principle that our current president does not understand, and the world is more dangerous because of it. The problem with "leading from behind" is that it's just another phrase for not leading at all, and the vacuum left by America's retreat is being filled every day by such enemies and adversaries as Iran's ayatollahs, ISIS's terrorists, and Russia's czar-in-the-making. If we want peace—not just in the neighborhoods of our allies but in our homeland as well—we must prepare for war by recognizing our enemies, rebuilding our military, and making clear to allies and adversaries alike that the United States will negotiate, but when it comes to our interests and our ideals, we will never surrender—or apologize for our strength. Because one of our protagonists, Thomas Jefferson, understood this principle, a war with Napoleon was averted, and the size of our nation was doubled. Because one of this book's antagonists, Henry Wallace, failed to understand it, the Cold War was almost lost before it even began.

A corollary to this principle of American strength is my belief in American exceptionalism—the notion that America, though capable of grave mistakes, has a destiny unique among history's empires. I believe that when the God of all ages put a continent between the Atlantic and Pacific, He had a plan for the territory we now call home. There, He hoped, men and women would be able to come from every corner of the globe to build a better life for themselves and their families, free from the religious tests and property seizures and secret police that have defined so much of the human experience in so much of the rest of the world.

My belief in American exceptionalism is the product of my own family's experiences, because my father was one of those men who came to this nation in search of a new life. He was raised in rural India in a home without electricity or running water. None of his eight siblings spent a day in school beyond the fifth grade. When my dad and my mom, who was pregnant with me, arrived in Louisiana nearly half a century ago, he started his job search by calling the numbers he found in the Yellow Pages. As my parents raised my brother and me, Dad reminded us every day that we were lucky to live in the United States of America. "Bobby," he would say, "you should give thanks to God every day that you were blessed to be born in the greatest country in the history of the world." That's why, for me, *American Will* is not just a title; it's a philosophy.

The fourth principle of this book is that, in the words of our First Amendment, Congress must make no law "prohibiting the free exercise" of religion. Unfortunately, today's world is increasingly hostile to matters of faith. Whether we know it or not, we are mired in a silent war that threatens the fabric of our communities, the health of our public square, and the endurance of our constitutional governance. It is a war against the same Bill of Rights that the antifederalists demanded. It is a war against the spirit that motivated the abolitionist movement. It is a war against the parochial schools targeted by the little-known Blaine Amendment. It is a war against the faith that motivated the civil rights struggle, against the soul of countless acts of charity, and against the heart that binds our neighborhoods together. In short, it is a war against America's best self, at America's best moments—a silent war against religious liberty.

This war is waged in our courts and in the halls of political power. It is pursued with grim and relentless determination by a group of like-minded elites, determined to transform the country from a land founded and sustained by faith into a land where faith is silenced, privatized, and circumscribed. Their vision of America is one in which an individual's devotion to Almighty God is accorded as much respect as a casual hobby—and with about as many rights and protections.

In the wake of a presidential administration that has tried to deny churches the right to choose their ministers and force religious employers to buy abortifacients for their employees—not to mention the countless crosses borne daily by men and women of faith working and worshipping among a media and a politically correct thought police determined to silence, shame, and ridicule them—the temptation in some corners is to ask for a truce. But in practical terms, a truce would only amount to those who value religious liberty laying down their arms. As is evident to any American who has ever opened an honest history book, our religious freedom was won over the course of centuries of persecution and blood, and we should not surrender it without a fight.

Finally, the fifth principle of *American Will* is one that I suspect at least a few of our political opponents would agree on. It is that there was nothing inevitable about the great turning points of our past, nor is there anything predetermined about our future. The difference between success and failure is the difference between courage and cowardice, between insight and ignorance, and between the servant's faith and the proud man's hubris. Progress depends on the spirit of our great people, which never falters, and on the wisdom of our leaders, who sometimes fail.

This principle, like each of the others, is not abstract for me. It's personal. I know that the choices we make have consequences. I know what it means to come to a crossroads in the journey of life—a crossroads I described in my first campaign for public office, when a debate moderator asked me, "What is the single most important moment in your life?"

I knew what my campaign advisors likely wanted me to say.

They were probably hoping I would appeal to female voters by offering a touching story about when I asked my wife, Supriya, for her hand in marriage, or about the birth of our first child, a beautiful baby girl. And yes, those were amazing moments. But instead, I decided to do something unusual in politics: I told the audience the truth—that the most significant moment of my life was when I turned it over to Jesus Christ and acknowledged Him as my Savior.

I'd love to say I'd had a sudden epiphany, but it took me seven long years to become a Christian. My best friend gave me my first copy of the Bible one Christmas, but it wasn't the gift I wanted at the time, so I put it aside. The first time I thought seriously about matters of life and death was when my grandfather died. I picked up the Bible and started reading God's words, often in my closet, not sure how my Hindu parents would respond. I spent many years reading books by Christian authors like C. S. Lewis and Chuck Colson. Finally, years later, my best friend invited me to hear him sing at a church on LSU's campus, and they showed a movie there. When I saw the actor playing Jesus hanging from a cross at Calvary, it hit me that He was on that cross because of our sins—because of *my* sins. How arrogant for me to do anything but get on my knees and worship Him.

Since then, I've sometimes made the mistake of saying that I have found God. The truth is, He found me. And it happened because people were brave enough to plant the seeds of the Gospel in my life. The choices they made mattered. They were the unsung heroes in my life's story.

I do not know what the next great crossroads will be for me in my personal life, but I have no doubt that the next great crossroads for our country will be the presidential election of 2016. Will we elect a cynic or a statesman? Will we choose a politician or a problem solver? Will we pick a president who embraces the fundamental principles of our history, or one who does not understand our culture, our people, and our exceptional destiny?

I hope the heroes of *American Will* illuminate the courage, faith, and vision that the United States needs in 2016, and I hope its antagonists illustrate the liberal dogmatism, naiveté, and folly that so jeopardize our nation's future.

PART I

★ ★ ★

AMERICAN VISIONARIES

1

★ ★ ★

INDIVIDUAL LIBERTY

The Antifederalists and the Fight for a Bill of Rights

Americans will elect a new president in 2016. We will choose from candidates with different backgrounds, records, and ideologies. But there's one thing you can bet they'll all have in common: Every single one of them will praise, with great feeling and fervor, American freedom.

We hear the word "freedom" tossed about so frequently by politicians that it rarely means what it once meant to the patriots who declared the right to it inalienable in 1776 and who secured it on bloody battlefields from Lexington to Yorktown. The next time you hear politicians invoking American freedom, ask yourself: Do they mean what our founding fathers meant? Do they even understand what the founders meant? Do they care? Leaders cannot be expected to defend principles they do not understand.

It is the job of each of us, particularly those of us in public office, to remember, first, where our freedoms come from, and, second, how and why the most sacred of those freedoms were written into the Bill of Rights of our Constitution. For a story of the former—where our freedoms come from—I would recommend the Bible, because we were endowed with our inalienable rights "by our Creator." But for a look back at the latter—how and why those freedoms found protection in our Bill of Rights—read on. It's the topic of this chapter.

There's an old saying: Winners write the history books. And because the men who wrote and advocated for the Constitution succeeded in securing its ratification, history tends to remember them as white knights, and their opponents, dubbed the "antifederalists," as the villains. But that is an oversimplification. Many antifederalists wanted to ratify the Constitution, but only if it included a Bill of Rights to provide explicit protection for liberties such as free speech, the free exercise of religion, the right to keep and bear arms, and the enduring role of states and state governments.[1] Arrayed against the antifederalists' demand for a Bill of Rights were such federalists as George Washington, James Madison, and Alexander Hamilton.

I have great respect for the federalists. In a way, they were the more idealistic of the two groups. I wish they had been correct in their belief that the structural protections of the Constitution would prevent the excessive growth of federal government at the expense of individual liberty and states' rights. But I have a soft spot in my heart for the antifederalists. In the end, they were the side that was right. From a modern-day perspective—with the EPA threatening the economies of Louisiana and most other states by imposing job-killing regulations on our industries, with the Justice Department suing Louisiana to block school choice, and with the Obama administration waging a war on the free exercise rights of religious Americans—anyone can see that the federal government has grown beyond what anyone in the founding generation could have imagined. It is the realization of the antifederalists' worst fears.

The antifederalists' concerns about government remain our

concerns. Does the federal government have too much power? Will leaders hundreds and thousands of miles away from constituents truly represent their interests? How secure are our God-given civil liberties?

What follows is the unlikely story of how a band of largely forgotten Americans fought for a Bill of Rights; how they won far more than they lost in the struggle over the Constitution's ratification; and how they are responsible for the protection of the rights that have defined the American experience for more than two centuries.

This is their story.

July 17, 1788—State Ratifying Convention, Poughkeepsie, New York

One month into the state of New York's convention to consider the ratification of the United States Constitution, Alexander Hamilton rose to deliver the most important speech of a life that had begun on a distant island in the Caribbean. There, he had seen the cruelty of slavery, and he had in turn developed a hatred of oppression. But it was also on the island of St. Croix that young Hamilton had been orphaned, and he had, perhaps as a result, learned to long for order, the kind of order children take for granted when their loving parents protect them. So, when Hamilton rose to address New York's ratifying convention, he brought with him a love for freedom from slavery *and* from chaos; for liberty *and* order; for independence *and* union.

Union was very much on his mind this day. With so many states having already ratified the Constitution, Hamilton was sure that if his home state of New York voted not to ratify, it would be voting itself out of the Union. But could one of the most forceful advocates for a new, stronger federal government and an architect of the Constitution persuade his colleagues? In the first month of the convention, all evidence suggested that his opponents at the convention outnumbered him by more than two to one.

Hamilton began his speech by blasting the Constitution's opponents for claiming to represent "our spirit of '76." He reminded them of the dark days that preceded America's independence, when it was ruled by a king "three thousand miles off," when Americans "had no share in the representation," and when the British "claimed absolute power over us." How could anyone compare that tyranny to the government proposed by the Constitution, which was "built on all the principles of free government"? His opponents were looking at the Constitution "only to find out the defects and not to discover its securities—and beauties."[2]

This, however, was familiar ground. Hamilton had been tirelessly defending the Constitution's "beauties" at the convention and in New York's editorial pages (under his *Federalist Papers'* pseudonym, Publius). Thus far, at least in upstate New York, those arguments had largely fallen on deaf ears.

Hamilton knew he needed to play his ace in the hole. Rather than defending the Constitution's merits, he would paint a vivid picture of the chaos and disorder that would follow a vote against ratification. New York would be "out of the Union." The state would be alone, with the nation's "power of government" and "the wealth of the whole country against us." New York City, whose inhabitants supported the Constitution and the trade that would come with it, would "warmly attach" to the federal government, depriving the state of "our port—the chief source of wealth." Upstate New York's isolation would require, ironically in light of opponents' invocation of the "spirit of '76," an "alliance with Britain." But even if Britain agreed to an alliance, "Who would wish again to come under her dominion?" New York could bid "adieu to liberty." Only "despotism will follow."

There was, though, an alternative, and supporting it were "distinguished patriots" who commanded far more admiration than the controversial Hamilton could ever hope to. "Hancock," for example. The first man to sign the Declaration of Independence. And "Adams," who "first conceived the bold idea of independence. He is for it." So was "Franklin—this old grey-headed patriot looking into the grave." These surnames—there was no need for first names, not with men as famous as Hancock, Adams, and Franklin—carried with them the history of an infant nation's audacious defiance of taxes and tyranny. To oppose the Constitution was to oppose them—and that history.

But Hamilton saved the best for last. There was another advocate for the Constitution. A man whom "all parties . . . admired and put confidence in." A man who "at the close of the war" was "at the head of a discontented Army" that would have made him a dictator if he had only said the word. But "did he take advantage of the situation of the army or country? No. He proved himself a patriot" by retiring to Mount Vernon. And last year, "This man came forward again and hazarded his harvest of glory," because "he saw the work he had been engaged in was but half finished." His name, of course, was "Washington."

Having invoked the names of America's most treasured patriots, as one might invoke saints in prayer, Hamilton asked, "Is it in human nature to suppose that these good men should loose [sic] their virtue and acquiesce in a government that is substanically [sic] defective to the liberties of their country?" To consider the question was to answer it.[3]

When Hamilton finished, according to The Daily Advertiser, "tears" filled the eyes of "most of the audience."[4] That audience included spectators who had, for a month, hung on Hamilton's every word. But it also included antifederalist delegates, and The Daily Advertiser did not report on the tears—or absence of tears— in their eyes. They were still as opposed to Hamilton and the

Constitution as they had been when he began. Or at least, they appeared to be.

There was, however, at least one opponent, the most prominent antifederalist, in fact, who was having second thoughts. This delegate may well have found Hamilton's words as moving as did the teary-eyed spectators in the galleries. It was now clear they could no longer stand in the way of a new Constitution to govern a new nation. But it looked as if they would get a Bill of Rights that would alleviate their concerns about the need to preserve individual and state rights. The delegate was the *leader* of the opposition: a simple man with a funny name, largely unsung by history, with a crucial role to play in the destiny of the American republic.

With Hamilton's eloquence still ringing in his ears, Melancton Smith rose, looked out across the convention floor, and spoke words as critical to the fate of the American union as any in the next seventy-three years, until a prairie lawyer from Illinois delivered his first Inaugural Address. If the man looked tired, his eyes rimmed with dark circles and his long hair unruly, it was understandable. The fight for liberty had taken its toll on Smith and his fellow antifederalists.

Ten Months Earlier, September 29, 1787— Philadelphia, Pennsylvania

The nation's ratification debate began ignominiously, when four men burst through the doors of Major Alexander Boyd's boardinghouse. The targets of their pursuit were two men—James M'Calmont and Jacob Miley. They were dragged from the house by force and taken through the Philadelphia streets. Their clothes were torn and their temperatures boiling.

These men were not petty criminals, but Pennsylvania legislators. And their pursuers weren't police officers, but with the legislature's sergeant-at-arms, who was ordered to apprehend M'Calmont and Miley at any cost. Both men were skeptics of the proposed U.S. Constitution—part of a group derisively named the "antifederalists" by their opponents. Their absence from the proceedings of Pennsylvania's legislature was intentional; the men hoped that there would not be a sufficient number of legislators present—a quorum—to allow a vote to go forward on creating a state convention for the Constitution's ratification.

Two weeks earlier, in this very city, delegates to the Constitutional Convention had finished their work. After a summer of debate and division, they had signed their names to a Constitution that replaced the Articles of Confederation, a governing structure put in place after the Revolutionary War that had proven disastrous.

Under the Articles of Confederation, state governments had wrecked the American economy with policies that caused inflation (by printing their own paper currencies) and frightened investors (by refusing to require debtors to abide by the conditions of their contracts). With no president, no federal courts, and no power to pass laws directly binding on the American people, the national government had no ability to correct these catastrophic policies or to quiet violent rebellions by desperate and destitute farmers ruined by the anemic economy.[5]

What had happened at the Constitutional Convention that summer promised salvation from the chaos and near-anarchy of the Articles of Confederation—but only if the required nine of thirteen states agreed to ratify the draft Constitution. And largely because many liberty-loving citizens were hesitant to adopt a Constitution whose framers had failed to include explicit guarantees of Americans' most sacred civil liberties to protect them from an all-powerful central government, ratification was far from certain.

This was what motivated M'Calmont and Miley—they feared approval of a document that might very well bring another George III to power in America.

When they arrived at the State House, M'Calmont demanded to "be dismissed from the house."[6] But the other forty-four legislators gathered there wouldn't hear of it. They needed forty-six legislators to make the quorum. These two men weren't going anywhere.

Suddenly, M'Calmont made a bolt for the exit. "Stop him!" spectators in the legislature's gallery called out.[7] After the crowd at the door physically blocked M'Calmont's attempted escape, the majority voted to hold elections for the state's ratifying convention as soon as possible—on the first Tuesday in November—with the convention itself to begin two weeks later. And with that, the final action on the final day of the Pennsylvania legislature, the fight to ratify the United States Constitution had begun.

It had not been pretty.

It had not been fair.

But it was a harbinger of things to come.

Nine Days Later, October 8, 1787

In the autumn of 1787, the nation's big cities had already rendered their verdict on the Constitution. They loved it. Their rich merchants expected to make a fortune in a revived economy. Their wealthy bankers stood to collect sizable debts from farmers, while its bondholders would collect considerable interest from war bonds bought from those same farmers at rock-bottom prices. Even the workers in cities couldn't wait for the increased trade and investment that would provide new work for countless sailors, blacksmiths, bakers, carpenters, and other mechanics.[8]

But elsewhere, rural and small-town Americans had reason to

be far more skeptical. Farmers did not enjoy the prospect of their creditors' gaining more power. And their neighbors were nearly as disenchanted as was much of the nation with the Articles of Confederation. Why should they hand over new powers to a distant federal government?

Somewhere between the extreme positions beginning to emerge in the ratification debate was an anonymous essayist. He knew he was up against formidable opposition in the form of the well-argued and prolific federalist essays, most of which were written anonymously, and which were appearing in newspapers around the country.[9] They were clear on the merits of ratification of the new Constitution—but what of the dangers? What of the risks to liberty and the very principles thousands of Americans had fought, bled, and died for? The future of the infant republic depended on the outcome of the ratification question. It was the only topic many Americans wanted to read about in their newspapers or talk about at their dinner tables. And so he decided to write a series of essays about the Constitution's ratification.

He began by acknowledging that "our situation is critical" and that a "federal government of some sort is necessary." But the Constitution drafted in Philadelphia failed to guarantee the rights of individuals or the role of the states. Instead, it appeared "calculated ultimately to make the states one consolidated government," because it did not make clear that the powers granted to the federal government were few, narrowly defined, and confined to those expressly provided in the Constitution.[10]

At the end of his essay, he wrote that "several principles should be considered and facts ascertained" before we "consolidate the states into one entire government." That was a promise of more essays to come.

Following the practice of that era of anonymous essayists, he signed his work with a pseudonym: "Yours, The Federal Farmer."

Four Days Later, October 12, 1787

When the prolific Federal Farmer began working on his fourth "Letter"—his fourth in five days—he chose as his topic the set of amendments that he believed would go a great way toward curing the flaws of the Constitution. They would come to be known as a Bill of Rights.[11]

Without a Bill of Rights, the Federal Farmer believed, there wasn't a sufficient protection of the people's liberties, because "men who govern, will, in doubtful cases, construe laws and constitutions most favourably for increasing their own powers." Therefore, "all wise and prudent people, in forming constitutions, have drawn the line, and carefully described the powers parted with and the powers . . . reserved in the people."[12]

"On the whole," wrote the Federal Farmer, "the position appears to me to be undeniable, that this Bill of Rights ought to be carried farther, and some other principles established, as a part of this fundamental compact between the people of the United States and their federal rulers." Among those principles were the free exercise of religion, trials by jury, and other "essential rights, which we have justly understood to be the rights of freemen."[13]

The Federal Farmer conceded that "we are not disposed to differ much, at present, about religion." But they were not debating a Constitution for only the present era. They were "making a constitution, it is to be hoped, for ages and millions yet unborn." Such a constitution required a Bill of Rights.[14]

Five Days Later, October 17, 1787—Philadelphia

The drum-beating for the Constitution in the federalist newspapers continued. On this third Wednesday in October, *The*

Pennsylvania Gazette—perhaps the most respected newspaper in America[15]—reported that Patrick Henry supported ratification. Among the most popular men in America, he was in fact one of the Constitution's fiercest opponents.[16]

The lies were piling up, but antifederalists would soon see that not only were federalists unwilling to play fair in the war of words; they were unwilling to limit the war to words.

Three Weeks Later, November 6, 1787—Philadelphia

The federalist mob came carrying heavy rocks, which they threw at the door of Alexander Boyd's boardinghouse—the same building from which James M'Calmont and Jacob Miley had been dragged in late September. This time, they shouted that the leading anti-federalists who resided there were "damned rascals" who "ought to be hanged," before breaking the front door's sash and then running away.

In a city where—as in all the big cities—federalists controlled almost all the newspapers, not a single article reported the riot.[17]

Seven Weeks Later, December 25, 1787 through January 4, 1788

On Christmas Day, while most of his four million fellow Americans were praying at their churches and feasting with their families, the Federal Farmer began an eleven-day stretch of writing that would surpass even his previous essays, and that would prove as profound, and as profoundly prophetic, as the words of any American political scientist before or since.

At the heart of the Federal Farmer's Sixth, Seventh, Eighth, and Ninth letters were the virtues of decentralized government—government that is as close to, and as representative of, the people as possible. In the state legislatures, there was an average of one representative for "each 1,700 inhabitants."[18] But under the Constitution, there could be as many as thirty thousand inhabitants for every representative.

Large electoral districts would, the Federal Farmer predicted, lead to the election of wealthy aristocrats. When "we call on thirty or forty thousand inhabitants to unite in giving their votes for one man," he wrote, ". . . it will be found totally impracticable for men in the private walks of life . . . to become conspicuous enough to attract the notice of so many electors and have their suffrages."[19]

By the Federal Farmer's reasoning, these "conspicuous" men—the rich, the famous, the already powerful—would be unable to represent the interests of the people, because they would not understand the interests of the people. They would not "possess abilities to discern the situation of the people and of public affairs, a disposition to sympathize with the people, and a capacity and inclination to make laws congenial to their circumstances and condition."[20]

In other words, a national government would likely be led by people out of touch with the common man. And because they couldn't be completely trusted with the liberty of citizens they were disconnected from, a Bill of Rights was necessary. True, the Constitution "affords, all circumstances considered, a better basis to build upon than the confederation," which had led to lawlessness and economic chaos. But "amendments are essential and necessary," because Americans need "constitutional barriers for their permanent security" that "are well fixed between the powers of the rulers and the rights of the people." Those "visible boundaries" would "serve as centinels [sic] for the people at all times."[21] They included guarantees that no one "shall be molested on account of his religion or mode or worship" and that no law would prohibit free expression—the "right to assemble," to "petition the government for a redress of wrongs," and the "freedom of the press."

Five Days Later, January 9, 1788— State Ratifying Convention, Hartford, Connecticut

By early January, a wide range of antifederalist essays had been written under such pseudonyms as Centinel, Brutus, Cato, Agrippa, an Old Whig, and, of course, the Federal Farmer. But antifederalist arguments could persuade people only where newspapers were willing to print them. Nowhere was that a greater obstacle to the exchange of ideas than in the state of Connecticut.

Connecticut's press was dominated by federalist publishers, and the Constitution's supporters in the Nutmeg State "forcibly blocked the circulation of literature critical of the Constitution."[22] Of the nearly one hundred essays written by antifederalists, only six were published in Connecticut—three fewer essays than there were total newspapers there. One of the six essays was more than likely a fake straw man, written by a federalist, so that he could then criticize it. Two others were printed only at the request of a local federalist, so that he could rebut them by accusing antifederalists of being British loyalists, dishonest debtors, or local officeholders worried about losing their local power. When newspapers reprinted "squibs" from other states' papers, the news items "praised Federalists, claimed the Constitution's critics wanted to destroy the union, and suggested that ratification was a sure thing."[23]

It likely came as no surprise to the Federal Farmer when he learned that Connecticut became the fifth state to ratify the Constitution, without amendments, after just eight days of debate at its convention. The real surprise was that 40 of 168 delegates had voted *not* to ratify, 17 more votes than in the previous four states—Delaware, Pennsylvania, New Jersey, and Georgia—combined. If antifederalists could garner that much support in a state where their arguments were stifled and their characters assassinated, there would seem to be real potential for them to beat the odds in states where antifederalists had access to at least a few printing presses. Among the states where antifederalists believed they had a real shot at prevailing was New York, where allies of the Federal Farmer were determined to secure access to sufficient newspapers—if possible, by persuading publishers; if not, by paying them.

Five Weeks Later, February 16, 1788— State Ratifying Convention, Boston, Massachusetts

By a vote of 187 to 168, Massachusetts became the sixth state to ratify the Constitution. Through a series of arguably dirty tricks—including a sweetheart deal for the support of John Hancock, and rumors that convention delegates would not be paid for their six weeks of work if the convention did not ratify—the urban, federalist minority at the convention had prevailed over what for many weeks of debate appeared to be a rural, antifederalist majority.

But the news for the Federal Farmer and antifederalists in New York and elsewhere was not all bad. First of all, unlike the contests in the previous five ratifying states, the fight in Massachusetts had been hard-fought and in doubt. With access to at least a few Boston newspapers—one of which went out of business because its federalist readers canceled so many subscriptions—antifederalists had been able to air their arguments in the pages of the state's press, as well as in the six weeks of heated debate at the ratifying convention.

More important, unlike the previous ratifying states, Massachusetts had ratified with a call for amendments to the Constitution. True, Massachusetts did not make ratification contingent on the amendments, which antifederalists believed necessary to guarantee their adoption. But the Bay State had made clear that its support for the Constitution was not unqualified. The newly proposed government, promising as it might be, was in need of alterations. And now, behind the call for the amendments the Federal Farmer desired was the moral authority of the Commonwealth of Massachusetts, where the very names of cities—such as Plymouth, Lexington, and Concord—stood for some of the most hallowed chapters of the American story.

Five Weeks Later, March 23, 1788—Albany, New York

Among the antifederalists most passionate about the need for those amendments was a merchant from Poughkeepsie, New York, who had moved to Manhattan just three years prior. He was undistinguished in appearance, with disheveled hair and a plain face, but he had developed a way with words. A powerful way. Melancton Smith knew how to communicate complicated concepts in essays and speeches that were clear, concise, and persuasive.[24]

Named for a leader of the European Reformation named Philipp Melanchthon, Smith had been a merchant, a lawyer, and a politician, but beginning with his service as a soldier in the Revolution, he had been, was, and would always be first and foremost a patriot. Every time he had seen an opportunity to contribute to his country, Smith had answered that call, and today was no different. The future of the infant republic depended on the outcome of the ratification question, and Melancton Smith was determined to do everything in his power to ensure that the outcome of that debate would protect the liberties that his fellow Revolutionary War veterans had fought so hard to obtain.

With elections for New York's ratifying convention barely more than a month away, Melancton Smith had reason to feel optimistic. Even though six of the required nine states had already ratified the Constitution—and two more, Maryland and South Carolina, were expected to ratify before summer—their votes were a testament not to the merits of amending the Constitution but rather to the strategic advantages the federalists had enjoyed up to that point.[25] In state after state, even in Massachusetts, the federalists had dominated the media, because their support was strongest in the big cities where most newspapers were found. Federalists had also been better and faster at organizing coalitions, had spread falsehoods about the antifederalists' supposed lack of support, and delayed the distribution of antifederalist literature, including the delivery of private mail and newspapers.[26]

In five of the remaining states, however, the antifederalists' prospects appeared likely to be quite different. In those states—Rhode Island, North Carolina, New Hampshire, and, most important, Virginia and New York—the ratification question was moving into areas where voters were inclined to view increased federal power with tremendous skepticism. There were indications that antifederalists enjoyed a majority among the population of Virginia, a three-to-one majority in New York and North Carolina, and an even larger majority in Rhode Island, which had already voted ten to one in a referendum not to even call a ratifying convention.[27]

Moreover, at least in Melancton Smith's New York, antifederalists were finally going to enjoy an organizational advantage. The most popular man in the state, Governor George Clinton, was fiercely opposed to the Constitution, and his political machine was already nominating candidates, educating voters, and mobilizing for the ratifying convention scheduled to open in June. The antifederalists' organization had even sent the "Letters by a Federal Farmer" to every town and city in the state.[28] Those Letters reflected Smith's beliefs with such precision that many scholars would later believe he was their author—though Smith himself had never confirmed or denied authorship.

There was, however, one more organizational matter that the antifederalists believed was absolutely necessary to resolve before the election of delegates in late April. They needed an upstate newspaper to print their essays and campaign papers. They already had access to one of New York City's seven newspapers, but each of the state's other five newspapers was run by federalists unwilling to provide access to their presses.[29]

Even if all five of those newspapers were going to publish federalist literature, antifederalists needed at least one of them to also publish antifederalist literature, and on March 23, they found their man. Charles Webster, the owner of two Albany papers, opened his presses to the antifederalists—shortly after they opened their wallets to him. For the antifederalists, there was nothing free about the press, but they believed access to Webster's pages was worth the cost of paying him to print their essays. They were not going to repeat the mistakes of antifederalists in the first ratifying states. In the Empire State, both sides would be heard. And none of those voices would prove more powerful or persuasive than that of Melancton Smith.[30]

Three Months Later, June 21, 1788—
State Ratifying Convention, Poughkeepsie, New York

There were few days at the New York ratifying convention when important antifederalist arguments were not led, at least in part, by Melancton Smith, and that day, the convention's fifth day, was no different.[31] Clearly, calmly, and with power and precision, Smith articulated the Constitution's flaws. Without an amendment guaranteeing to the states powers not expressly granted to the federal government, the people would not be adequately represented on matters that threatened their most important liberties.

Smith worried that Congress would be a "mere shadow of representation." True representatives must be acquainted "with the common concerns and occupations of the people, which men of the middling class of life are, in general, more competent to than those of a superior class." But because of the size of congressional districts, Congress was likely to be filled only with people famous enough to win a district-wide election—"the natural aristocracy." Rather, a "representative body, composed principally of respectable yeomanry, is the best possible security to liberty."[32]

When Smith spoke those words, he saw before him the middle class he imagined. The majority of delegates came from the state's small farms and small towns, where Smith had lived most of his life. True, the landed gentry and New York City tycoons were also represented there, but they were a minority. Due in part to Smith's essays and his allies' organizational prowess, forty-six of the convention's sixty-five delegates were antifederalists, all of them elected outside of New York City.[33]

The forty-six antifederalist delegates were the embodiment of the citizen servants who led state and local governments from New Hampshire to Georgia, and Smith feared for the liberty of his nation if a federal government without this degree of almost direct representation were granted broad powers unconfined by a Bill of Rights.

Three Days Later, June 24, 1788— State Ratifying Convention, Poughkeepsie, New York

For the first week of the convention in Poughkeepsie, Smith and Hamilton—each equally eloquent; each equally passionate about his own approach to the great questions of that, and every, era—fired broadsides against each other over the merits of representative government, local control, and checks on federal power. It was a fight that the antifederalists appeared sure to win. After all, they outnumbered federalists two to one.

The Smith-Hamilton debate that defined the first week of New York's convention was the high-water mark for antifederalists in New York—and beyond—because while the two titans debated, other delegates were debating, and voting, in other states. A week after the New York convention began, news arrived in Poughkeepsie from New Hampshire. The Granite State had ratified the Constitution.[34]

The vote had been the closest of any state so far—fifty-seven to forty-seven—and the convention had called for amendments. But like the eight ratifying states before it, New Hampshire had not made its ratification contingent on its proposed amendments, which meant that the Constitution had now been ratified by the number of states required by its terms in order to make it the highest law of the land.

One might have expected Melancton Smith and his fellow antifederalists in Poughkeepsie to be dejected. They weren't. Smith went so far as to say New Hampshire's ratification had "no effect" on him. His reason was simple: Virginia had not yet ratified.

With a quarter of the nation's population, Virginia and New York held a de facto veto on the Constitution. Sure, it might be possible for the Constitution to go into effect without states like "Rogue's" Island, which was home to less than 2 percent of the nation's population. But a Union without the population and prestige of Virginia and the wealth and commerce of New York was unthinkable. If only Virginia—where around half the convention delegates were antifederalists and where a final vote on ratification was expected any day now—ratified *on the condition* that a Bill of Rights be amended to the Constitution, New York could do the same. The antifederalists could then expect the Confederation Congress, or even a Second Constitutional Convention, to propose a Bill of Rights before the Constitution went into effect.

In short, there were good reasons why New Hampshire had "no effect" on Melancton Smith.

But the same could not be said for the then-uncertain outcome of the ratifying convention in Virginia.

Eight Days Later, July 2, 1788—
State Ratifying Convention, Poughkeepsie, New York

A week later, as abruptly as the sergeant-at-arms had burst through the doors of Major Alexander Boyd's boardinghouse nine months before in Philadelphia, at the dawn of the ratification debate, an express rider named Colonel W. S. Livingston suddenly interrupted the afternoon's debate in Poughkeepsie with news from Richmond, Virginia. The convention there had concluded. The vote had been close. The federalists had won.

In a compromise with their opponents, the federalists had embraced a call for amendments, phrased in unprecedentedly strong terms, but had not conditioned ratification on them. Virginia had just become the tenth state to adopt the United States Constitution.[35]

Inside the stone courthouse that was home to the Poughkeepsie convention, the federalist delegates erupted in cheers. There was now no doubt that a new government would convene next year under the provisions of the new Constitution. Virginia would be there. So would the representatives of almost all American voters outside of New York. The choice for the Empire State was now no longer between endorsing the Constitution, rejecting it, or requiring it to be amended. The choice was between union and disunion. The convention could still call for amendments, but if it made ratification contingent on those amendments being adopted before New York's entry into the new government, its ratification instrument would be invalid. In other words, if it ratified with conditions, it would not ratify at all. The people of at least ten states would elect a Congress and a president to govern a nation that would not include New York.

Two Days Later, July 4, 1788—Albany, New York

A federalist city surrounded by an antifederalist county, the capital of New York was a powder keg, and on the thirteenth celebration of America's Independence Day, Albany exploded in violence. Federalists began the day by firing a ten-gun salute to the ten states that had ratified the Constitution. Antifederalists responded by marching from Hilton's Tavern to the site of what was once a British stockade—Fort Frederick—and burning a copy of the Constitution. When federalists heard about the improvised parade and ceremonial burning of their cherished Constitution, hundreds of them marched to Fort Frederick, "raised a thirty-six-foot pine tree with the Constitution at its top on the very spot where the 'Antis' had burned it that morning, played music, shouted huzzas, shot more cannon, then took the tree and the Constitution down and paraded them through town."[36]

By this point, and probably well before this point, both sides of the celebration were drunk on rum, and when the federalist parade approached the antifederalists' Hilton's Tavern, the antifederalists charged the parade. Wielding weapons that included rocks, bricks, and clubs, they plunged themselves into a bloody brawl that left eighteen men injured and several antifederalists taken prisoner.[37]

By the end of the day, calmer heads prevailed, and the prisoners were released.

Whether calm heads would prevail at the convention in Poughkeepsie remained to be seen.

Eleven Days Later, July 15, 1788—Poughkeepsie, New York

"My dear Sir," wrote Melancton Smith to his friend Nathan Dane. "I have received your [letters] and thank you for them."[38]

Dane shared Smith's desire to amend the Constitution. "I retain my opinion," Dane had written, "restricting the feeble features, the extensive powers, and defective parts of the System." But with passion, Dane now urged Smith to drop the antifederalists' demand that amendments to the Constitution precede its ratification. Because ten states had already ratified unconditionally, "the new system must soon go into operation," wrote Dane. Because no previous state had endorsed a conditional ratification, there was now no chance Congress would accept a conditional ratification by New York.

Moreover, Dane was sure that several of "the most important laws" would "be made in the first Congress," including at least some of the "amendments" that Dane and Smith considered "essential." If New York "comes into the Union armed with the declared Sentiments of her people"—not to mention the similar sentiments of such powerful states as Virginia and Massachusetts, which had both called for amendments—New York "will immediately have a voice in the federal Councils." The state's congressional delegation would be able to "avail herself of all her influence" and secure the guarantees of liberties that antifederalists wanted amended to the Constitution.[39]

The alternative, Dane wrote, would be disastrous. If states like

New York did not ratify, "men who wish to cement the union of the States on republican principles will be divided, and have but a part of their Strength in Congress, where they out to have the whole." In other words, because "the ground" had "totally shifted" when New Hampshire and Virginia became the ninth and tenth states to ratify the Constitution, the best way to add a Bill of Rights under the new circumstances was to ratify the Constitution, send New Yorkers to the new Congress, and use New York's influence in that Congress to insist on a strong Bill of Rights.

Melancton Smith did not know whether his fellow New York antifederalists would embrace this change of strategy that circumstances had dictated. But he knew what he had to do. "I entirely accord with you in opinion," he wrote Dane. For the patriot from Poughkeepsie, the choice between union and disunion was no choice at all.

Two Days Later, July 17, 1788—
State Ratifying Convention, Poughkeepsie, New York

By July 17, a month into New York's ratifying convention, the antifederalists had gained much of what Melancton Smith and his allies had wanted from the day they first read the proposed Constitution, nearly ten months ago. They had battled countless obstacles to persuade the American people that the Constitution required a Bill of Rights, and it was now clear to Melancton Smith that so many Americans had joined them in that demand—and so many ratifying conventions had echoed that demand—that the first Congress to convene under the Constitution next year would have no choice but to send a Bill of Rights to the states for their certain ratification.

The open question was whether New York would be, on the one

hand, a part of crafting that Bill of Rights in the new Congress, or, on the other hand, a mere spectator, opposed to immediate union, and risking permanent disunion.

Early on that day, Alexander Hamilton made a powerful case for union, laying out, step by step, the consequences of a conditional ratification. But more powerful than his words were his actions. Although he had never seen the need for a Bill of Rights as a legal matter, even Hamilton now recognized the need for it as a political matter. In state after state, the people had spoken, and they had spoken forcefully in favor of amendments to the Constitution guaranteeing free speech, the free exercise of religion, the right to bear arms, the principle that powers not expressly given to the federal government belong to the states, and other essential safeguards of American liberty. And so Hamilton had proposed ratifying the Constitution with "recommendatory & explanatory" amendments, many of them modeled on those called for by Virginia. His proposed amendments stated that "no right of any kind . . . can be cancelled, abridged, restrained or modified by Congress, or by an Officer or Department of the United States, except in conformity to the powers given by the said Constitution."

Later in the day, when Melancton Smith rose to speak about the conditional form of ratification he himself had previously proposed, many delegates and the spectators in the gallery expected a hearty defense. He was not only an antifederalist; he was an antifederalist leader—*the* antifederalist floor leader. No delegate had spoken more eloquently—and perhaps not as often—in defense of antifederalist principles than had Melancton Smith.

But in a remarkable turnabout, Smith announced that he would be voting for ratification unconditionally. The thought of an independent New York outside of the Union was unbearable to the patriot. His case had already persuaded America that amendments to the Constitution would be necessary; he had "the firmest confidence that an opportunity will speedily be given to revise and amend the Constitution."[40]

Six Days Later, July 23, 1788—
State Ratifying Convention, Poughkeepsie, New York

Smith's switch landed like an earthquake, and six days later, its effects were still being felt, although the extent of those effects remained uncertain. Had Smith persuaded enough of the forty-five other antifederalists to follow his lead? Many of them had reacted to his compromise proposal with, in the words of one contemporary, "indignation & suspicion."[41] Would they vote for unconditional ratification? Would the union be preserved?

Before the critical procedural vote to strike the words "upon condition" from the ratifying instrument, Smith rose one last time to attempt to persuade dozens of skeptical delegates. The antifederalist leader assured them he remained "consistent" in his "principles and conduct." The "object" of Smith's "pursuit" had been, and remained, "amendments." But after "Virginia came in," he realized that amendments could not be "obtained previous to the operation of the Government." The dictates of "reason and duty" required antifederalists to "quit" their original strategy, so that New York "might be received into the Union." After ratification, he would lead them in pursuing their "favorite object of amendments, with equal zeal as before, but in a practicable way."[42]

When the voting began, Smith knew he could count on the convention's nineteen federalists. He could also count on the support of four antifederalists—Samuel Jones, John Schenck, Jonathan Havens, and Zephaniah Platt—who had either spoken or voted for compromise and conciliation in the past week. With Smith's vote, that meant only twenty-four safe votes for unconditional ratification. But he needed seven more votes.

The popular and powerful Governor George Clinton, the convention's president, would not cast one of them. He had always been among the more extreme of the antifederalists, and he had made clear that so long as the Constitution lacked amendments, his vote would be no. His prestigious allies Robert Yates and John Lansing—delegates to the Constitutional Convention in Philadelphia who had left early in protest—were sure to stand by him.

The spectators in the convention's gallery sat in anticipation as one by one, the representatives of the people of the Empire State cast their votes, and when the votes were counted, there were thirty-one in favor of unconditional ratification—and twenty-nine against. If but a single delegate in the majority had switched his vote, New York would have been out of the union. On the question of the Constitution's ratification and the fate of an undivided union, every vote mattered that day, and by the narrowest of margins, the Constitution won.

When the First United States Congress met in 1789, Melancton Smith was not in it. Though he was a popular congressman in the Confederation Congress and a candidate for the new Senate created by the Constitution, Smith's campaign in the fall of 1788 was sabotaged by Governor Clinton, who could not forgive him for voting in favor of ratification. Aside from a brief stint in the state legislature, the antifederalist leader would never again hold public office. In a sense, Smith stands for the proposition that political leaders should always be willing to put their country ahead of their careers, a principle I vowed never to forget when I was first elected to office in 2004.

In a larger sense, however, Melancton Smith won. He had

wanted more representatives in Congress, and in the early 1790s, Congress increased the number of its members from 65 to 105. He had wanted a guarantee that the federal government would not consolidate unenumerated powers that belonged with the states, and for the next century and a half, the "states remained the most powerful component of American government"—as provided for by what became the Constitution's Tenth Amendment. And most important, he had wanted guarantees of Americans' most prized freedoms from government interference, and in the first year of the first Congress created by the Constitution, Congress adopted, and the states soon ratified, a set of amendments providing the United States with exactly that.[43]

The fact that those amendments were drafted in Congress by none other than James Madison was a testament to the power of the antifederalists' efforts throughout the ratification process. When the fight for ratification began, Madison had called a Bill of Rights unnecessary. His federalist allies had almost unanimously done the same. And yet, despite a long line of federalist shenanigans such as spreading false rumors, obstructing antifederalist mail, and keeping calls for amendments away from as many newspapers as possible, the antifederalists had persuaded so many Americans to demand a Bill of Rights that James Madison, federalist leader and father of the Constitution, believed Congress had no choice in 1789 but to make the Bill of Rights among the first priorities of the new government. Even in Pennsylvania, where ratification had been achieved so quickly by dragging James M'Calmont and Jacob Miley from Boyd's boardinghouse, an unofficial second ratifying convention had met and called for "very considerable amendments and alterations."[44]

On the question of whether the Constitution would be amended before ratification, the antifederalists had failed. But on the larger question of whether it would be amended at all, they not only succeeded; they did so in one of the most profoundly important victories for liberty in the history of this—or any—nation.

For more than two hundred years, the Bill of Rights has been the backbone of liberty in the United States. With that liberty, Americans have shown that a free people can to do anything and go anywhere their imaginations take them, from Manhattan's skyscrapers to the moon's Sea of Tranquility. But today, as never before, the Bill of Rights is under assault, by a president with little understanding of American history and little regard for the spheres of individual liberty our first ten amendments protect.

The Bill of Rights begins by protecting "the free exercise" of religion. But with no regard for the First Amendment, President Obama has waged a war on the consciences of American Christians. His health reform law attempted to coerce religious individuals and religious institutions into offering and subsidizing contraceptives, including abortion-inducing drugs and devices, that their faiths consider immoral. When Archbishop Timothy Dolan of New York raised concerns about the contraceptive mandate in a face-to-face meeting with Obama, the president promised to seek a compromise solution that would respect the religious freedom of the American people—a promise that he, after fierce lobbying from Planned Parenthood, promptly broke.[45]

The president has also attempted to repeal the First Amendment's guarantee of "freedom of speech." In addition to his IRS targeting conservative nonprofits because of their speech, President Obama has proposed to amend the First Amendment in order to exclude from its protections certain political speech, including speech that is expressed by groups of people, such as the National Right to Life Committee and the National Rifle Association, who have organized themselves as nonprofit corporations. President Obama and his allies call this abridgement of the First Amendment campaign finance regulation.

President Obama has also taken aim, pun intended, at the Second Amendment. Time and again, he has tried to exploit national tragedies and gun violence in order to take away Americans' "right to keep and bear arms," including commonly possessed rifles that fire only a single bullet with each pull of the trigger and that are less dangerous than most handguns. Many of his allies have also advocated for an interpretation of the Second Amendment that would confine it to the protection of militias, rather than the protection of individual citizens who want to protect their homes and their families from violence in cities like Obama's hometown of Chicago, which has one of the nation's highest crime rates, in spite of—or perhaps because of—the fact that it is home to some of the nation's harshest gun prohibitions.

The Fourth Amendment has also taken a beating in the past seven years of the Obama administration. It provides that the people's right "to be secure in their persons, houses, papers, and effects, against unreasonable searches and seizures, shall not be violated." But President Obama's National Security Administration has engaged in countless unreasonable searches and seizures, even though the government had no warrant or probable cause to believe that the targets of these searches had committed a crime. These overreaches have been justified in the name of fighting terrorism—a fight in which the president's record is far from successful—but violent Islamic fundamentalists are best fought by acknowledging the nature of the enemy, which President Obama has refused to do, rather than violating the privacy rights guaranteed to Americans in the Fourth Amendment of the Bill of Rights.

Finally, President Obama's arguably most significant—and certainly most successful—assault on the Bill of Rights has been his attack on the Tenth Amendment. It provides, in words that the Federal Farmer's writings and Melancton Smith's speeches echo repeatedly, that "the powers not delegated to the United States by the Constitution, nor prohibited by it to the States, are reserved to the States respectively, or to the people." In other words, it says that the federal government cannot create a law unless the Constitution gives it the power to create that law. Of course, nowhere in the Constitution is Congress given the power to make Americans buy health insurance—or to make Americans buy *anything*. Congress can regulate interstate commerce, but it cannot *compel* commerce. Yet that is precisely what ObamaCare's individual mandate does, thereby "chang[ing] the relationship of the Federal Government to the individual in [a] very fundamental way," as Justice Anthony Kennedy told the president's solicitor general during the oral argument over the constitutionality of the individual mandate.

As one of the nation's most consistent and relentless defenders of religious liberty—which I elaborate on in my chapter about the Blaine Amendment—it pains me to see what President Obama has tried to do to the "free exercise" clause, as well as to free speech, gun rights, and the Tenth Amendment's principles of federalism. I don't believe the president ignores and belittles the Bill of Rights because he is a bad man. Rather, he does so because he has too much faith in big government and too little faith in the American people.

Antifederalists like Melancton Smith understood the perils of big government. They had lived under the reign of a monarch. They had seen their taxes raised, their guns seized, and their privacy invaded. After waging a revolution against King George III, they waged a political war against the likes of Alexander Hamilton, not because they distrusted federalists like him, but because they distrusted unchecked government power in the hands of the men who would come after them.

Against the most powerful of political opponents, antifederalists fought to amend the Constitution so that it would protect civil liberties and the role of local governments. Because of the courage they showed and the choices they made, the United States remained a free nation. And just as it did in the 1780s, our liberty depends today on millions of Americans with the wisdom to understand the dangers of unlimited government and the courage to fight against it.

2

DEFENDING AMERICAN SOVEREIGNTY

Napoleon, Jefferson, and the Louisiana Purchase

Nearly fifty years ago my parents came halfway across the world to Baton Rouge, Louisiana. They had never been on a plane. They had never been to the United States. But they knew in their bones that if they could get to America, and if they worked hard, they could create incomparable opportunities for themselves and their children. Years later, my dad used to tell us, "Sons, you need to thank God every night that you are blessed to be born in the greatest country in the history of the world." He understood that America is an exceptional place, and that the United States has an exceptional role to play in the realm of global leadership. That leadership role is in many ways the product of the story described in this chapter.

American leadership begins by humbly acknowledging that American power is precious. It ought not be thrown around lightly. But it also must not be hidden, squirreled away, or apologized for. Our vital interests and our closest allies depend on American leadership. And when we abandon our responsibility to lead, we betray our interests, our allies, and our future.

No president understood the importance of American leadership better than Thomas Jefferson. In his first term, he faced a crisis caused by a foreign dictator who was undefeated on the battlefields of Europe and covetous of an empire in North America. President Jefferson believed that war with that dictator—indeed, war with any adversary—should be an absolutely last resort. But he also believed that the United States could not deter the dictator's aggression by leading from behind. There was strength in the infant republic he had helped create, and only through the strategic projection of that strength could Jefferson defeat his adversary, protect America's interests, and ensure that the United States would remain a haven for men and women, not altogether unlike my parents, determined to explore the unknown and build for their families a future out of the frontier.

The dictator was Napoleon Bonaparte.

This is the story of how he lost Louisiana.

1778—Monticello, Virginia

The shy Virginian with the reddish hair and the unkempt clothes was never more comfortable than when he was holding an open book, and today he peered through his hazel eyes with delight at the pages of a memoir by a Massachusetts-born trailblazer named Jonathan Carver.[1] The volume told of faraway places along the northern stretches of the Mississippi River, and beyond it, to a West of amazing beauty and infinite possibilities.

"There is no doubt," Carver wrote, "that at some future period mighty kingdoms will emerge from these wildernesses, and stately and solemn temples with gilded spires reaching the skies supplanting the Indian huts."[2]

Thomas Jefferson's vision for the West didn't include "gilded spires," though he did share the author's faith in its potential. The thirty-five-year-old Jefferson, currently serving in the Virginia House of Delegates and living at his Monticello estate, believed that the "life, liberty, and the pursuit of happiness" he had written of in Philadelphia depended on a man owning his own land, working with his bare hands, and remaining independent from the clutter and filth of big cities.[3]

Carver's book described a place where there was enough land for *every* American citizen to stake a claim and build a better life. It included a map of North America unlike any Jefferson had ever seen, with mighty rivers flowing from the waters of the Mississippi and the peaks of the Shining Mountains, across a land mass far wider than the Sage of Monticello had ever imagined.

His godfather had crossed and recrossed the Cumberland Gap many times and as a boy, Jefferson had often heard about, read about, and thought about the frontier beyond the Blue Ridge Mountains, where lakes stretched on for hundreds of miles, and enormous forests remained untouched by a single settlement.[4] But the years between then and now had brought other pursuits and intellectual interests, and Jefferson had entered his mid-thirties having lost a bit of the dreamy wonder he had once reserved for the American West.

He resolved that he would never lose it again. He would never forget the vivid description of a land of untapped opportunity. And he would always believe that the enduring liberty of Americans' newborn republic depended on access to the continent profiled by Carver and the magnificent river that ran through it.

Twenty-two Years Later, June 14, 1800—Marengo, Italy

Eleven hours after the morning's first shots had been fired outside the tiny Italian village of Marengo, the diminutive, stocky man with a ruddy complexion surveyed the bloody battlefield with well-deserved pride. He had been outnumbered and outgunned. He had been fooled by false intelligence from a double agent. And he had been surprised by a sneak attack that nearly turned his right flank.

Yet, against all odds, Napoleon Bonaparte had won. The Second Alliance—Austria, Russia, Naples, and Great Britain—was in shambles. The battlefield was his, and due to his military prowess, so was continental Europe.

In four short years, Napoleon had risen from anonymity to a wealth, power, and fame unseen in Europe since the days of Charlemagne. As first consul of France, the thirty-year-old dictator had the power to impose his will on a nation that had rejected unrepresentative government only eleven years ago. And as the victor of Marengo, he was in a position to impose his will on Europe as well.

The question now was: What next? What does a dictator do after he has mastered a continent?

Napoleon's answer was to set his sights on another continent. In 1763, France had surrendered to Britain a North American empire. Now Napoleon Bonaparte wanted it back.[5]

A Year and a Half Later, February 23, 1802— Gonaives, Santo Domingo

When the battle of Gonaives began, it appeared to have little in common with the battle of Marengo. Gonaives was five thousand miles away. Napoleon was not in command of the French army there. And his enemies were not led by powerful princes, but by a former slave named Toussaint L'Ouverture.

As the French army was running in retreat, General Donatien de Rochambeau rode close enough to the oncoming Haitians that he was able to toss his hat into the lines of charging enemy soldiers.

"My comrades!" he shouted to his men, "you will not leave your general's hat behind!"[6]

Seeing their commander's courage and resolve, the French soldiers halted, then turned, faced the enemy, and charged. They were, after all, among the best-trained and -equipped soldiers on earth. And it was not long before L'Ouverture's Haitians were retreating as fast as they had been advancing only moments before.

When Rochambeau's army took Gonaives, it burned the town to the ground. In that way, it continued a war of attrition it had been waging with tremendous brutality against the colony of Santo Domingo's black men and women. The colonists had been winning a war of independence that began with a slave uprising eleven years earlier.

It was for this counterinsurgency that Napoleon had recently dispatched his best troops to Santo Domingo, and it was on the success of this war that his hopes for a French empire in North America hinged. First, he would subdue the Caribbean island. Second, he would send those troops—and tens of thousands more—to New Orleans and the 828,000-square-mile territory of Louisiana, which Spain had recently ceded to France in exchange for Tuscany, as part of a secret agreement. Louisiana was France's destiny—indeed, the very name of the territory was given to it by a French explorer as a homage to Louis XIV.

Once Napoleon's troops controlled New Orleans, they would be able to cut off Americans' access to the mouth of the Mississippi River, cripple its westerners' commerce, and pave the way for "La Nouvelle France," whose limits would stretch as far as the little dictator's armies could march.[7]

He was already preparing to assemble an expedition of twenty thousand men under the command of General Claude P. Victor, who was to begin expanding French influence into American territory by allying with Indian tribes east of the Mississippi River.[8] Napoleon gave Victor the title "Captain General of Louisiana."[9]

But first things first. Without control of Santo Domingo, nothing in North America was possible. Napoleon knew that it wouldn't be long before France and its nemesis Britain were at war again, and because Britain's superior navy could threaten or even blockade New Orleans, he needed a strategic stopover between France and New Orleans.

Santo Domingo was the only stopover available.[10]

Thus, Napoleon's dreams of a North American empire of nearly a million square miles depended on the success of his expeditionary army on an island a mere one-thirtieth the size of Louisiana.

Five Days Later, February 28, 1802—Washington, D.C.

The French chargé d'affaires, Louis-Andre Pichon, came to Thomas Jefferson's White House in a state of desperation. It was only one month into France's counterinsurgency campaign in Santo Domingo, and already supplies were running short. The French needed food, guns, and ammunition. They had expected to receive them from American merchants in the Caribbean. The matériel had not arrived.

Why, Pichon wanted to know, was the United States not being more accommodating to their loyal and steadfast ally? It was France after all that made the American Revolution possible. Why it was France, he believed, that had put Thomas Jefferson in his very seat.

Jefferson was at first inclined to support the French expedition to Santo Domingo. He liked the French, and came to know them well during his five years as the U.S. ambassador in Paris. Moreover, there were many Americans—particularly southern Americans—who didn't want Santo Domingo's slave insurrection to inspire any sort of example for the black men and women they called their property.

But, as Jefferson confronted his visitor, it was clear he had changed his mind.

Why, the president asked Pichon, was the expeditionary army so large? Why was its size kept secret from us?

What, Jefferson pressed, of the intelligence he'd received from the British that the force's final destination was not Santo Domingo, but the coast of Louisiana?[11] As with many diplomatic "secrets," word that France had obtained the Louisiana territory from the Spanish had spread quickly.

Pichon was startled. Either too honest or too ill-informed to lie, the Frenchman offered no direct responses. But to Jefferson, the nonanswers spoke volumes.[12]

Seven Weeks Later, April 18, 1802—Washington, D.C.

America's third president did not relish the prospect of fighting Napoleon in Louisiana. At worst, the United States would lose the war. At best, it would win at a cost far beyond the budget of the country's anemic federal government. The U.S. government was so small that it contained in its entirety only 293 civilian employees, including the 143 members of Congress and six Supreme Court Justices.[13]

Despite his affection for the French, he was as suspicious of dictators like Napoleon as he had been of the monarch he defied in 1776. He certainly wasn't going to let a European tyrant block his beloved small farmers in the wilderness west of the Blue Ridge from supporting themselves and their families by sending their flour, tobacco, and salt pork to markets through the mouth of the Mississippi River at New Orleans.

Jefferson decided he would do more than merely refuse to help Napoleon retake Santo Domingo. The United States would not support a French blockade of the insurrectionists. Nor would it supply the occupiers.[14] If the president did not use soft power to weaken Napoleon in Santo Domingo, he knew, he would be forced to either fight Napoleon in Louisiana or surrender the most important of national interests—the access of western farmers to the Gulf of Mexico to export their crops to the world.

For Jefferson, that last alternative was utterly unacceptable.

Nevertheless, Jefferson understood that strength leads to peace, whereas weakness provokes aggression. Short of surrendering a national interest as important as the Mississippi River trade's access to the Gulf of Mexico and markets beyond, the best way to avoid a fight over New Orleans was to show Napoleon that the United States was *ready* to fight for New Orleans. If ever there was a time for the young republic to lean forward and lead on the global stage, it was now.

On the third Sunday in April, he wrote a letter to Robert Livingston, the American minister in France, startling in its frankness. "There is on the globe," Jefferson wrote, "one single spot, the possessor of which is our natural and habitual enemy. It is New Orleans, through which the produce of three-eighths of our territory must pass to market."[15] As a lover of the West who had imagined its potential at an early age, Jefferson told Livingston that the American territories dependent on access to New Orleans "will ere long yield more than half of our produce and contain more than half of our inhabitants."[16] To surrender access to the mouth of the Mississippi was to surrender America's future.

Jefferson explained to Livingston why France was a much more dangerous neighbor than Spain, because "Spain might have retained it quietly for years."[17] France, however, had dreams of expansion. To be precise, *Napoleon* had dreams of expansion. "The day that France takes possession of New Orleans, fixes the sentence which is to restrain her forever within her low-water mark."[18]

Jefferson went on to declare what was unthinkable only a few years earlier. If Napoleon sent an army to Louisiana, the United States would ally with Great Britain and defend Americans' right to navigate the Mississippi by driving Napoleon's army of occupation from Louisiana. At the moment the French dictator's troops land in New Orleans, he wrote, "We must marry ourselves to the British fleet and nation" and "make the first cannon which shall be fired in Europe the signal for the tearing up any settlement she may have made."[19]

These were stunning words. The same king Jefferson had defied in 1776 still reigned over Great Britain, which retained Canadian colonies and had shown signs of hoping to one day recover the American colonies it lost at Yorktown. To ally with King George III required forgiveness of recent wrongs and risked trouble in future affairs. But it was a wager Thomas Jefferson was willing to make.

A product of the Enlightenment, Jefferson was not a bellicose man by nature. He preferred reason over bloodshed. But the patriot who had once pledged for himself and his comrades their "lives . . . fortunes and . . . sacred honor" had shown long ago that he was willing, if all other means failed, to fight and even die for what was right. The soft-spoken Virginian must have felt today, almost as much as he had felt on July 4 nearly twenty-four years earlier, that the die was now cast. A line in the sand had been drawn. Whether Napoleon would fight over it was, like George III's decision to reject independence, out of Jefferson's hands.

"Every eye in the U.S. is now fixed on this affair of Louisiana," he wrote. "Perhaps nothing since the revolutionary war has produced more uneasy sensations through the body of the nation."[20]

Also out of his hands was whether the recipient of his letter, Robert Livingston, was prepared to deliver to Napoleon the president's clear warning that the United States was prepared to assert its power to protect its interests. In fact, Livingston was not. He believed the letter was too belligerent. But in a town with a penchant for leaks even in the early nineteenth century, it didn't take long for the substance of Jefferson's words to travel across Washington, D.C., and from there to Napoleon's palace in Paris.[21]

A Year Later, April 1803—
Mississippi Territory; Washington, D.C.

To secure New Orleans, three companies of American artillery and four companies of infantry were making camp at Fort Adams, not far from the border of the Louisiana territory.[22] They were prepared to march to New Orleans, in the company of an additional two thousand Mississippi militiamen.

With the threat of war with Napoleon the growing talk of Washington, U.S. senators already had voted to construct fifteen gunboats bound for the Mississippi River. A resolution had been introduced to raise $5 million and fifty thousand men for the sole purpose of seizing all-but-undefended New Orleans from the French.[23] Word of such plans already had made its way to the European newspapers.

If Thomas Jefferson was bluffing, he was very good at it.

That Same Month, April 10–11, 1803—Paris, France

In many ways, Napoleon Bonaparte was his American counterpart's opposite. He loved war and wealth. And he cared little for the "inalienable rights" of man. Whereas Jefferson had written the Kentucky Resolutions of 1798 in defense of Americans' freedom of speech against the government, Napoleon was silencing France's once-free press. Whereas Jefferson believed governments should be selected by the governed, Napoleon was making plans for a hereditary succession to the dictatorship he had seized at the point of the bayonet.

For the year between Jefferson's letter of April 1802 and Easter Sunday of 1803, these two opposites played a delicate and dangerous game of chicken, on which hinged the fate of much of the Western Hemisphere. Jefferson was gambling that he could deter Napoleon's imperialist vision.

For the past year, the French dictator had received one disconcerting message after another from chargé d'affaires Louis-André Pichon. Some were rumors Pichon had picked up through gossip around the capital. Others were messages delivered straight from the mouth of the American president. And before long, Napoleon knew that if he sent troops to Louisiana, they would face a British navy and an American army, both of which were prepared to fight, with immense resources and a proven resolve, to defend against Napoleon's dreams of empire and expansion.

Meanwhile, Napoleon was waiting—to see what happened in Santo Domingo, to see whether it was really possible that Jefferson would ally with his old enemy King George III, and to see whether the United States was really ready to go to war with the great commander and conqueror Napoleon Bonaparte.

A year later, the waiting stopped. Shortly after Easter Sunday services, Napoleon called two of his closest advisors to a meeting in his palace of Saint-Cloud. He knew that in two days, an envoy from the United States named James Monroe was expected to arrive in Paris to seek a peaceful settlement of the New Orleans question through the purchase of the city from France. As Napoleon surely suspected, Monroe had also been given a second set of instructions: to sail for London if negotiations with Napoleon collapsed and the now-ready-to-depart General Victor-Perrin set sail with his twenty thousand men for New Orleans. If Napoleon wanted to prevent a war against Britain and the United States in North America, it was now or never.

Napoleon began the meeting at Saint-Cloud with a stunning declaration. "I think of ceding Louisiana to the United States," Napoleon told his finance and naval secretaries. "They only ask of me one town in Louisiana. But I already consider the colony as entirely lost."

Napoleon was not announcing a final decision. He still wanted to hear his advisors' counsel. But in one of the most profound about-faces in the history of Western diplomacy, he had just put on the table the abandonment of his quest for a North American empire, the relinquishment of New Orleans, and the sale of nearly all of France's land from the source of the Mississippi in the north to the Red River in the south, and from the banks of the Mississippi in the east to the Continental Divide in the west.

Even more startling, Napoleon was weighing this sale because he already considered the colony as entirely "lost"—before a single shot north of Santo Domingo had ever been fired!

There was much evidence to support Napoleon's analysis. One by one, Napoleon had received the answers he had been awaiting for the past year, beginning with the answer to the question of his army's fate in Santo Domingo. Three months ago, he had learned that Rochambeau's superior officer, Napoleon's brother-in-law Charles Leclerc, had died on the island of yellow fever. He was far from alone. In a little over a year, most of Napoleon's men had perished either at the hands of the Haitians or from the sting of mosquitoes.

"Damn sugar, damn coffee, damn colonies!" an exasperated Napoleon had sworn.

Napoleon had also received an answer to questions about the likelihood of an Anglo-American alliance. It was not only possible;

it was probable—a threat as ominous for his imagined empire as the deaths of twenty thousand French soldiers in Santo Domingo. Pichon had repeatedly warned Paris that Napoleon's plans for expansion into North America were well known and were "making a union with Great Britain universally popular" in the American capital.[24]

Finally, after the outgoing Spanish intendant of New Orleans had rescinded American shippers' right of deposit in local warehouses at the mouth of the Mississippi, Napoleon had learned that the Americans were serious about going to war over New Orleans.

The right of deposit mattered to American merchants because without it, their produce would rot on flatboats while waiting for sea vessels to carry it into the Gulf of Mexico and to markets beyond.[25] Moreover, they believed a treaty between Spain and the United States in 1795 had guaranteed them the right.[26] The Spaniards' actions were thus considered by many irate Americans to be an act of war, and while Napoleon at first celebrated the action—he had instructed the not-yet-departed General Victor-Perrin to take the same action when he and his army landed in New Orleans[27]— the Corsican was soon surprised by reports of the speed with which Jefferson's government was mobilizing for combat.

In short, the normally confident—and at times overconfident— Napoleon believed his prospects for a North American empire were, as he told his ministers, "entirely lost." Santo Domingo was a quagmire, and Louisiana was sure to be one as well.

The French naval minister, Denis Decrès, was unconvinced. "We should keep Louisiana," he argued. "There does not exist on the globe a single port susceptible of becoming as important as New Orleans."

That fact was obvious to anyone with a map—like the map drawn by Jonathan Carver that Jefferson had first seen twenty-five years ago. As Decrès pointed out, "The Mississippi does not reach there till it has received twenty other rivers, most of which surpass in size the finest rivers in Europe." Napoleon's naval minister could not believe France was going to give up a city of such magnitude without a fight.[28]

But the other advisor at the meeting at Saint-Cloud enthusiastically agreed with Napoleon's proposal. The fifty-five-year-old Marquis François de Barbé-Marbois, France's finance minister, loved the United States. A decade and a half earlier, he had visited the states, had made many American friends, and had even married a pretty young lady from Philadelphia. He considered America to be the forefather of revolutionary France, and while abroad, he wrote that "the progress of civilization" had "made more advance here in a hundred years than Europe has made in ten centuries."[29] Like Jefferson, he believed America was an exceptional nation, with an exceptional role to play in world affairs.

"We should not hesitate to give up Louisiana, which is about to slip from us anyhow," Marbois told Napoleon, without hesitation or reservation. Because France was refusing to abide by the terms of the previous year's treaty with Britain—and because Britain was in turn refusing to keep its side of the bargain—Marbois believed that war against King George III was inevitable. "Shall we be able with very inferior naval forces to defend the province against that power?" Marbois asked.[30] Not without Santo Domingo. If France lacked a secure way station in the Caribbean, Britain could seize Louisiana as soon as war in Europe broke out.[31] "This conquest," Marbois added, "would be still easier for the Americans."[32]

The debate between Napoleon's two ministers went on for the rest of the day and into the night. When the three Frenchmen finally went to sleep, none of them, perhaps not even Napoleon, knew what the dictator would decide.

The Next Morning, April 11, 1803—Paris, France

Summoned to the emperor's bedchamber, shortly after the sun rose on Easter Monday, a sleepy Marbois was not sure what to expect. Was Napoleon ready to send General Victor-Perrin to Louisiana and risk war with not just one but two English-speaking adversaries? Or was Napoleon ready to give up his dreams of an empire in North America and sell New Orleans when James Monroe arrived in Paris?

There was, of course, another option. The choice Napoleon had made for the past year. The choice *not* to decide. The choice to delay, for another day, another week, or even another month, a decision on North America.

This last choice, it quickly became apparent, was not Napoleon's. Not today. The general abruptly announced to Marbois, "Irresolution and deliberation are no longer in season."[33]

That left the strong possibility of a collision course with the Americans. After all, Napoleon had fought on battlefields from Italy to Egypt. His forces would later fight from the seas south of Spain to the frozen plains of Russia. With Napoleon Bonaparte, war was often a first resort. But on Monday morning, with the spring flowers of the Champs-Élysées in full bloom[34] and France at peace, if only temporarily, for the first time in a decade, Napoleon decided that there would be peace in Louisiana, a peace produced by his American adversary's resolute show of strength.

"I renounce Louisiana," Napoleon exclaimed to Marbois. "I renounce it with the greatest regret."

He handed his finance minister a draft treaty requiring 100 million francs in exchange for Louisiana, which amounted to more than twenty million American dollars.

Marbois said the price might be higher than the Americans could afford.

"Make it fifty million, then," Napoleon shot back.

As his foreign minister, Charles Maurice de Talleyrand, later quipped, "That was the fastest decline in property values in the history of the world."

The Next Day, April 12, 1803—Paris, France

The Marquis de Marbois was honest, thoughtful, and pro-American. But he was not without his quirks. Whereas it would have been normal to inaugurate negotiations on the sale of Louisiana by sending an official request to Robert Livingston at the U.S. embassy or to the lodgings of the newly arrived envoy James Monroe, Marbois found himself strolling through Robert Livingston's gardens while the American threw a small dinner. He walked among the flowers. He peered into the windows. And then, suddenly, he locked eyes with an incredulous-looking Livingston, shocked to look up from his dinner table and glimpse outside his window the French finance minister!

"Doesn't that look like Barbé-Marbois out there?" asked one of Livingston's guests.[35]

When the American ambassador's son-in-law invited Marbois inside for coffee and an unofficial introduction to the newly arrived James Monroe, Marbois had little choice but to accept. Although there was no way to justify trespassing through the grounds of a foreign embassy—perhaps he himself did not even know why he had chosen this time and this manner of approaching Livingston about the most important real estate sale in either republic's history—Barbois meekly offered that he "just happened" to be in the neighborhood and "just happened" to feel like walking through the embassy's gardens.[36]

Marbois and the Americans made small talk for the shortest

time consistent with whatever etiquette required of such an unusual incident, and when the opportunity arose, Marbois whis-
pered a secret message to Livingston.

Napoleon had reached a decision on Louisiana.

It was for sale.

All of it.

If Livingston wanted to learn more about Napoleon's proposal,
said Marbois, he could stop by the Finance Department around
midnight. Marbois would be waiting for him. And it was there, in
the dead of night, after the most bizarre of beginnings, that two
men, serving two great nations and two of history's titanic leaders,
began the somewhat anticlimactic negotiation over the purchase of
Louisiana.

Marbois asked for 100 million francs—22.5 million American
dollars. Livingston called the price too high. Marbois countered
with 80 million francs.[37] And for the next three weeks, Livingston
and Monroe attempted to bargain the Frenchman down.

The finance minister had been given permission to go as low as
50 million francs, but he knew he didn't need to. The Americans
could afford 80 million. It was, in fact, a bargain. And by April 30,
it was a deal. At around four cents an acre, Louisiana was America's.

Twelve Weeks Later, July 4, 1803—Washington, D.C.

At noon, on the day celebrating Jefferson's Declaration of Independence, the skinny, redheaded Virginian strolled onto the steps
of the Executive Mansion. He was, undoubtedly, smiling. He had
every reason to be.

His envoy's mission to France had succeeded beyond even the
wildest dreams of this most visionary of presidents. James Monroe, with Robert Livingston, had bought a territory four times
the size of America's original colonies, an area larger than Spain,

Portugal, Italy, France, Germany, Holland, Belgium, Switzerland, England, Scotland, Wales, Northern Ireland, and Ireland, combined.[38]

There was more to celebrate than Louisiana's size. There was the peaceful preservation of America's most vital of interests—free navigation of the Mississippi River, which the *National Intelligencer* celebrated by announcing, "We have secured our rights by peaceful means."[39] And there was, perhaps most of the all, the potential that the territory's 880,000 square miles held. After all, as Jefferson knew, this was the land that for centuries had promised explorers and pioneers a better, richer, freer world. It was the land he had imagined as a boy after hearing tales of his pioneering godfather. It was the land he had rediscovered as a young man after reading the exploits of explorers like Jonathan Carver.

Now, on this most unforgettable of July 4ths, as Jefferson basked in the adulation of the crowd before him—and of unseen crowds in places like Kentucky, Tennessee, and Ohio, where the flag-waving celebrations exceeded in intensity even the news of victory in the Revolution—the United States had redeclared its independence.[40] Not just independence from one foreign ruler. Independence from *all* foreign rulers. The heart of the continent now belonged not to Europe's despots, but to any Americans with the fortitude and faith in themselves to settle it.

There was a mystery to this wilderness—a place so vast and unexplored that almost everything about it, from the course of its rivers to the limits of its borders, remained unknown. But its mysteries were not unsolvable. The questions it raised were not without answers. And Jefferson couldn't wait to discover them.

That very day, little noticed among the cheering crowds and the banner headlines, President Jefferson's secretary exited his office in the Executive Mansion and set off for a meeting with a retired army lieutenant named William Clark.

The secretary's name was Meriwether Lewis.

★   ★   ★

Napoleon Bonaparte was neither the first nor the last dictator to view violence as a means of expanding his wealth, territory, and power. Nor was he the only tyrant to believe he could threaten the United States with impunity. But he was among the most dangerous an American president has ever faced, and Thomas Jefferson's masterful diplomacy in defiance of Napoleon and in defense of his infant republic's vital interests provides a clear lesson that is forgotten at our peril: Disengagement does not serve the security of our nation. Whereas weakness is provocative, an engaged foreign policy based on the unapologetic projection of American strength is a prescription for deterring aggression and protecting our citizens.[41]

Jefferson wielded American strength in a manner that secured the free navigation of the Mississippi for frontier farmers who depended on it, prevented a ruthless dictator from building a sphere of influence in America's backyard, made the United States a world power, and, probably most dear to the President's heart, purchased a wilderness of unbounded opportunity for the millions of future farmers and settlers whom Jefferson believed were the foundation of a free republic. As even John Quincy Adams, the son of Jefferson's political rival and presidential opponent, later said, the Louisiana Purchase was "unparalleled in diplomacy because it cost almost nothing" and was "next in importance to the Declaration of Independence and the adoption of the Constitution."[42]

Among the lives that Jefferson's purchase of Louisiana has profoundly affected is my own. I was born in Baton Rouge. I grew up in the shadow of the state capitol building and LSU's beautiful campus. My boys and I hunt in the marshes of Pecan Island and Kretz Springs. I fish around Port Fourchon and Lake Pontchartrain. I am blessed to live in and help lead a bountiful state with incredible people from a rich collection of heritages, with, in New

Orleans, a city whose music and cultures have helped define our nation, and with an unparalleled collection of natural resources, including five of the nation's twelve largest ports, one of which is alone responsible for handling much of the nation's oil and gas. All of this amazing state—and all or part of fourteen other states—was purchased by Thomas Jefferson for pennies on the dollar.

How did Jefferson do it? First, he helped starve the French forces fighting to re-enslave Santo Domingo. Second, he frightened Napoleon into believing—with good reason—that an Anglo-American alliance was imminent. And third, he made clear to the French dictator that the occupation of Louisiana and abrogation of our citizens' right to navigate the Mississippi River would be met by American bullets and steel. In short, as stated by a modern historian echoing many before him, the Louisiana Purchase "would have been inconceivable" without "Jefferson's dogged opposition to any incursion into America's neighborhood by French troops."[43] All of this was done without firing a shot or putting one American soldier in harm's way.

Unfortunately, our current president has offered "dogged opposition" to none of America's enemies and adversaries. Rarely if ever has he anticipated and deterred the risk of aggression before it directly threatened America's vital interests.[44] Instead, he has pretended that the world will get safer and risks will go away if only the United States responds to threats with rhetoric or ignores them entirely.[45] In crisis after crisis since his inauguration in 2009, President Barack Obama has demonstrated the failure of his attempts to lead from behind. The result has been the polar opposite of the product of Jefferson's diplomacy: a more vulnerable homeland; reduced access to the "common" areas of the world; instability in key areas of the world; and the empowerment of tyrants and terrorists who reject our values and harbor ambitions of carnage and conquest.[46]

President Obama has, for example, presided over a strategic re-treat in Eastern Europe. Like Napoleon, Russia's Vladimir Putin has attempted to create a new sphere of influence where he would exercise hegemonic power. He invaded Georgia in 2008 and never left. He has assimilated much of Crimea. And as with Napoleon's plan to stir up Native American insurrections in the United States, he has supported the Ukrainian insurrection, going so far as to send armored columns directly into Ukraine.[47]

It may be possible to deter future Russian adventurism with a strong sanctions regime backed up by NATO ground and air forces based in Eastern Europe. But at present the United States Army is so small that those brigades will not be available. If this weakness, coupled with President Obama's tepid use of economic sanctions against Russia, leads to further Russian aggression, it will continue a pattern where failing to take moderate, low-risk deter-rence measures—like those Jefferson took toward Santo Domingo and New Orleans—resulted in greater risk and few good options later for the United States and its allies.[48]

President Obama has also presided over a strategic retreat in Iran. The Islamic theocracy's nuclear program has progressed to the point where it is only a few months short of a nuclear breakout—when it would possess sufficient weapons-grade uranium to build one or more nuclear bombs. In addition, Iran has built missiles that can reach Eastern Europe, and within a few years, their long-range ballistic missiles will be able to reach the East Coast of the United States.[49]

The implications of Iran's nuclear program for American and allied security are profound. Just as Napoleon's occupation of New Orleans would have destabilized a key area for American commerce and security, a nuclear Iran will likely provoke a nuclear cascade in a crucial region as other nations, no longer trusting America's leadership to deter Iranian aggression, will seek nuclear weapons themselves. If there is a nuclear cascade in a destabilized Middle East, the likelihood of a launch, perhaps accidental or impulsive, will substantially increase.[50]

The rising threats in Eastern Europe and Iran are part of a pattern. There is hardly a key area of the world in which President Obama has not presided over a strategic retreat. Access to common areas of the world has never been more endangered, including threats to close waterways like the Strait of Hormuz, to restrict air travel over the East China Sea, and to militarize space. From China to North Africa, from Afghanistan to North Korea, Barack Obama has weakened allies, emboldened adversaries, and left each region a less stable and more troubled place.[51]

However, none of those failures match, in terms of this administration's shortsighted incompetence, the president's handling—or, rather, failure to handle—the rise of the Islamic State. ISIS insurgents gained control of much of eastern and northern Syria, routed Iraqi army divisions, and swept across much of western Iraq. Increasingly accomplished fighters—two thousand of whom hold Western passports that could allow them to export their bloody crusade—use mass executions, decapitations, burnings of captives, and even crucifixions, to establish what they call their Islamic caliphate. Just as Napoleon attempted to use Santo Domingo as a base of expansion across North America, ISIS is hoping to use its caliphate as a base for expansion across the region and well beyond the Middle East.[52]

Had the United States simply maintained a base in Iraq after 2011—in other words, had President Obama actually listened to his military commanders, and his then–secretary of defense—our presence likely would have short-circuited the whole chain of events leading to the current disaster. But now the United States must attempt to defeat ISIS under circumstances that are highly unfavorable, both politically and militarily. It's a classic example—

and one that ought to be burned into the consciousness of America's leaders—of how ignoring risk in the name of nonintervention can lead to a metastasized threat that cannot be ignored and that must be addressed at much higher cost and with much greater risk of failure.[53]

There are no easy solutions to the problems President Obama has allowed to fester, consume entire regions, and increasingly threaten the United States. The answer is certainly not to deploy troops to every country where tyrants and terrorists have gained ground since Obama's inauguration. But the next president can begin to roll back the record of the recent years by reversing the $1 trillion in cuts Obama made to our military; making clear our nation's determination to defend vital interests and loyal allies from adversaries seeking to expand spheres of influence; and recognizing that few good things happen in the world today unless America helps shape them.[54]

The story of the Louisiana Purchase illustrates the paradox of American military power: There will always be adversaries like Napoleon whose interests are inconsistent with ours and who do not share our respect for peace and human rights, but there is less need to use American military force against them when they fear and respect the strength and resolve of the United States. Peace through strength costs infinitely less in American blood and treasure than does war precipitated by weakness. When the United States engages in a global leadership role, it can prevail in the only kinds of wars that don't bring irreplaceable loss and incalculable tragedy— the ones in which the first shot is never fired.

3

BOOM

The First Energy Revolution and the
Rise of the American Entrepreneur

Because of a chance discovery in the hills of western Pennsylvania in August 1859, oil became one of the most prized commodities in the world almost overnight. America's first energy revolution would fuel the rise of a global economic power. And it would transform the entire world economy by offering light, power, and mobility to hundreds of millions of people who had never before known it.

Energy is personal to me. I was born and raised in Baton Rouge, a city that has grown and benefited from hundreds of jobs created by the Exxon refinery. My father is a civil engineer. My wife is a chemical engineer, like her father. My first job out of college was at a chemical plant. The energy industry has put food on my table. In Louisiana, where one out of every seven jobs is related to energy, everybody knows somebody who works in the energy industry.

Today, America is on the verge of a second energy revolution— and, if only Washington, D.C., can get out of the way, it will move forward, reducing energy costs, driving economic growth, creating millions of new jobs. The oil and gas industry already supports more than 10 million jobs across the U.S. economy. With new techniques in unconventional oil and gas, such as hydraulic fracturing and horizontal drilling, entrepreneurs are poised to create millions of new jobs and push energy prices lower and lower, igniting a manufacturing renaissance across America.

All of this can make our country an energy superpower and the envy of the world. For a glimpse of what we can accomplish, we need look no further than America's first oil revolution, which established this country as a haven for entrepreneurship, risk taking, and ingenuity. It was a true turning point in American history.

It all started with an oil well outside Titusville, Pennsylvania. This is its story.

Summer 1857—Tontine Hotel, New Haven, Connecticut

Not yet forty, Edwin Drake looked like a man twenty years his elder as he eased into one of the hotel lobby's soft leather chairs. Perpetually gaunt, Drake wore in his expressions the sadness that had dogged him his entire life. Even when he smiled, which wasn't often, it conveyed tragedy. Losing four children and a wife (his children died at or soon after childbirth, and his wife died while attempting to give birth) could do that to a person.[1] But Drake wasn't one for wallowing in sadness. He was enterprising and driven, and had an uncanny way of striking up a conversation and gaining people's trust.

The man with a bushy beard and a head of curls that turned upward at the ears grimaced as he leaned back in the lobby chair. For years he had suffered from debilitating pains and aches from his muscular neuralgia. The pain had become so bad that he had been forced into retirement from his job as a conductor on the New

York–New Haven Railroad line. Drake had taken a room upstairs. Jobless and in pain, Drake figured that the Tontine Hotel would be as good a place as any to rest up and search for work. The hotel on the New Haven green was a hub of social and business activity for the city's bankers and entrepreneurs.

The hotel lobby was quiet this afternoon. The manager moved about behind his desk, and in the adjoining saloon some men were talking business. The walls were thin, and Drake found himself eavesdropping. He closed his eyes to concentrate and listen to the muffled voices.

The talk was of vast riches to be made. Thousands and thousands of dollars. Some scheme involving oil. Drake's ears perked up.

"Oh, Townsend, oil coming out of the ground, pumping oil out of the earth as you pump water? Nonsense! You're crazy," bellowed a voice, clear as day through the walls.[2] It was the friendly needling of longtime friends, perhaps even business partners.

Drake stood up and walked through the wooden door of the saloon. He saw three men sitting at a round table, deep in conversation—and deep into a bottle of whisky. Their suits were well tailored; their shoes immaculately shined. Drake looked on intently from the doorway, the men too absorbed in conversation to notice that they had an observer. Drake could see one man vigorously waving a pamphlet with big block letters on the cover: "Report on the Rock Oil, or Petroleum from Venango Co., Pennsylvania, with Special Reference to its Use for Illumination and Other Purposes."[3]

"This chemist's report says it all, gentlemen. Need I remind you? It's right here on page one: 'We have in our possession a very valuable idea,' " said the man with the pamphlet.[4]

All they needed, he sighed, was an enterprising individual to implement it.

Drake approached. The cedar floors creaked under his uneasy

gait. The men looked up from their whisky. Drake stretched out his hand and introduced himself.

Later That Year, December 1857—Titusville, Pennsylvania

"I believe this here is what you're looking for," the general store clerk said, as he reached for a jar on a shelf behind the register.[5]

His customer looked haggard from his journey, not to mention his being covered in mud. The journey had taken the man over hundreds of miles by railway, and the final leg on the twice-weekly mail coach down winding and muddy backcountry road had been especially grueling.

But Edwin Drake had arrived at his destination: Titusville, Pennsylvania, population 125.[6]

Rock oil—100 percent pure rock oil, the clerk said, bemused. He didn't sell much of the stuff, he complained. Folks just didn't have much of a need. And there was plenty of it to be had a few miles down the road, down on the Oil Creek, the clerk offered, pointing outside.

He handed the jar to Edwin Drake, who held it in his hands. Drake's eyes were transfixed by the dark, viscous, tarlike substance with green and blue hues. He unscrewed the lid of the jar and held it up to his nose. It smelled wretched—of sulfur and other substances he couldn't place. This liquid, no matter how foul smelling, was Drake's quarry. He was determined to discover its source deep within the earth and make the men back in New Haven proud.

Drake handed the jar back to the clerk.

The good Lord willing, he'd be bringing barrels of this rock oil out of the ground, Drake said with a burst of enthusiasm. Agreeable and amiable, Drake made friends quickly.

A wry smile crossed the clerk's lips. He hadn't in his life encountered a man so determined to obtain something all but worthless. But the clerk, like most of the men and women of Titusville, would happily entertain Drake's delusion—at least as long as he paid his bills.

"All of us here in town wish you good luck in your endeavor, Colonel."

Edwin Drake, the man who had spent most of his professional life on the railroad, was now a colonel. Not that he had earned that rank through any advancement through the military. The investors back in New Haven—one in particular, James Townsend, a local banker—had decided that calling Drake "Colonel" might give him an air of authority and prestige when he went west—for moments precisely like this. Ahead of Drake's arrival, Townsend had sent letters addressed to "Colonel" Drake to Titusville so that the "backwoodsmen" would be impressed by their new visitor.[7] And as "Colonel" Drake was discovering in the Titusville general store, the ploy was working brilliantly.

The New Haven investors—lawyers and bankers—were savvy men, and not just because they had figured out a way for a city slicker like Edwin Drake to fit in among the trappers, farmers, and country bumpkins of rural Pennsylvania. Some thought their idea ludicrous, but they had a vision: that oil, or "rock oil," as it was dubbed at the time, could be useful and lucrative, especially if they could tap the original source deep underneath the earth's surface.

It wasn't as if oil was a new discovery for mankind. Across the ancient Middle East, the tarlike substance has oozed through the sand and burned indefinitely, giving rise to ancient religions of fire worship. Around the time of Christ, the Romans recorded that oil healed wounds and relieved fevers.[8] Native Americans in Pennsylvania had used the oil—or "Seneca Oil" as they called it, in honor of one of their chiefs—as a salve. Yankee salesmen tried to market

Seneca Oil's "wonderful curative powers." A poem was even written to help with advertising:

> *The Healthful balm, from Nature's secret spring,*
> *The bloom of health, and life, to man will bring;*
> *As from her depths, the magic liquid flows,*
> *To calm our sufferings and assuage our woes.*[9]

Local farmers mostly regarded the oil springs that dotted the creeks and fields of western Pennsylvania as a nuisance that tainted water and crops.

But James Townsend and his fellow investors suspected that rock oil might be valuable—extremely valuable. They knew that it was flammable. Perhaps its volatile properties could yield something, if only a commercial use could be found. So, for the astronomical sum of $526.08, Townsend had commissioned a Yale chemist named Benjamin Silliman to determine what the practical uses of rock oil might be. He sensed that if it was distilled, much like whisky, it could yield a substance that could emit light if burned. After researching the bluish-green rock oil in his laboratory, Silliman had told Townsend, "I can promise you that the result will meet your expectations of the value of this material."[10]

Besides producing some common lubricants for machinery, Silliman had determined, the oil could be refined into kerosene, which burned cleanly and efficiently with a bright glow. Millions of Americans could use the light of kerosene to illuminate their homes and businesses. At $2.50 a gallon, whale oil had been getting more and more expensive, making it a luxury even for America's wealthy. Herman Melville, who had published *Moby-Dick* a few years earlier, wrote that whale oil was used for "almost all the tapers, lamps and candles that burn around the world."[11]

Townsend and his fellow investors in the enterprise, called the

Seneca Oil Company, were convinced that kerosene was the future: a sustainable alternative to whale oil, as whaling ships had all but eliminated whales from the North Atlantic. With kerosene, they could illuminate all of America, and get rich doing so.

All Townsend needed was a general agent to help him out. It wasn't a job for any Yale-educated men in fine-tailored suits. What he needed was a go-getter. A doer. A man who could get his boots covered in mud.

And in the bar of the Tontine Hotel a few months earlier, Townsend had found his man. It had helped that Drake had a lifetime of free rides on the railroad from his days as a conductor, so the Seneca Oil Company could be spared the expense of Drake's travel. It didn't bother Townsend in the least that Drake had never drilled a well, much less seen even a drop of oil, in his life. What the man lacked in experience he made up in winning personality and grit, exactly what was needed to make his venture succeed.

That was what had brought Edwin Drake to the backcountry of Pennsylvania.

A Year and a Half Later, May 1859—Oil Creek, Pennsylvania

If only the clerk back in town had been right about the abundance of oil. After nearly a year and a half of his searching and digging, rock oil had proven elusive for Edwin Drake.

Drake had set up operations two miles outside of town on a farm near a small stream the locals called "Oil Creek." It was true, he had found a bucket here and a bucket there, but his quest for the ultimate source of the oil underneath the ground had ended in failure time and again. Holes he dug with picks and shovels with the help of local laborers flooded with underground water. Underground rocks continually broke his tools. Just when he thought he was making progress, a well would cave in, and he'd be back at square one.

Worse still, bills were piling up. Revenue was nonexistent. The western Pennsylvania winters—Drake had endured two already— with bitter cold and heavy snows that pushed south from the Great Lakes were especially punishing to a man accustomed to the civilization offered by New York and New Haven.

But spring had arrived, and Drake believed he had the summer to find oil. He penned a letter back to his investors in Connecticut. "I shall not try to dig by hand any more, as I am satisfied that boring is the cheapest," he wrote, referring to the method of drilling that had been used to search for salt nearby. He had concluded there was simply no way to reach deep into the earth without using a massive drill bit.

There was only one problem with his plan: He barely had a dime to his name. It was all gone. He couldn't purchase more equipment or the personnel to help him drill. He ended the note to James Townsend with a desperate plea: "Money we must have if we are to make anything. . . . Please let me know at once. Money is very scarce here."[12]

Though he wouldn't admit it to others, Drake was beginning to lose hope—maybe even his sanity. Still he remained convinced that below his feet was a giant basin of oil. What Drake needed was someone who could help him punch a hole hundreds of feet into the earth. He had interviewed and tried to enlist dozens of local men. Between their inexperience and their fondness for whisky, none had been able to last more than a couple of days alongside Drake. The man was as unforgiving and tough on others as he was on himself. His relentless drive was taking its toll on his reputation among the "backwoodsmen." Now an object of ridicule in Titusville, "Colonel Drake" was now "Crazy Drake." No one wanted to work for the absurd Yankee.

Three Months Later, August 25, 1859—
New Haven, Connecticut

If enthusiasm was waning in the backwoods of Pennsylvania, it was even bleaker in New Haven. The investors were pulling out. After nearly two years with their agent in the field and no results to show for it, the moneymen were ready to cut their losses. Two thousand dollars had already been wasted on the endeavor.

Townsend's stomach churned as he sat behind his desk and wrote to the man he had met in the Tontine Hotel almost two years before to the day. Townsend believed in the project more than any of his other partners. Indeed, the banker had poured almost all of his savings into it and was now funding it alone. But it wasn't the loss of money that galled Townsend most. He had developed a special fondness for Drake and his doggedness.

So it pained him as he wrote a final letter to Seneca Oil's general agent. Drake was to pay his outstanding debts, wrap up his business dealings, and return to New Haven. Seneca Oil was going bankrupt.

Same Day, August 25, 1859—Oil Creek, Pennsylvania

The hole was deeper than they had ever bored before. With the help of William "Uncle Billy" Smith, a local blacksmith, and his two young sons, Drake felt he was finally getting somewhere. The final note from Townsend declaring impending bankruptcy hadn't yet arrived, but Drake could see the plain writing on the wall. Seneca Oil was going belly up. Persistent Drake was undeterred. He had cobbled together his life's savings and even convinced a couple of local Titusville businessmen to back an additional five-hundred-dollar loan to keep his flailing operation on life support.

Several months earlier, Drake and Uncle Billy had made a modest technological breakthrough. They discovered that encasing the drill bit in an iron pipe meant that the drill bit could go deeper. It worked brilliantly. Their holes didn't collapse in on themselves, nor did they fill with water. With the help of a steam engine and a derrick, their drill bit bore deeper and deeper into the western Pennsylvania hills.

Two Days Later, August 27, 1859—Oil Creek, Pennsylvania

With minuscule fractions of an inch of progress with each turn of the steam engine, the drill had reached sixty-nine feet into the earth. It was late in the day and the sun was plunging in the west that Saturday afternoon. Mopping the sweat on his brow with his forearm, Drake was ready to call it quits for the weekend. A pious man, Drake gave his men Sundays off and spent the day in church. He gave Uncle Billy the signal to turn off the steam engine. As he heard it slowly grind to a halt, Drake peered down the pipe into the ground and he saw the drill bit give way and slip another six inches. It was somewhat curious, but nothing appeared out of the ordinary—there was nothing but water in the hole. Drake left the well for dinner at home.

Two Days Later, August 29, 1859—Oil Creek, Pennsylvania

Drake returned to the well Monday morning just after dawn. He found Uncle Billy and his sons standing around the drill pipe. Around them were tubs, basins, and barrels—every container they could get their hands on. They were filled with a dark substance. They had hit a deep pocket of oil.

Though he was not the most excitable of men, he embraced Uncle Billy and let out a sigh of relief.

By noon the news had spread like a prairie fire across western Pennsylvania. Neighbors had brought all the whisky barrels they could find to the well. They were filled up within minutes with a small hand pump. Farmers along Oil Creek had run into town yelling at the top of their lungs, "The Yankee has struck oil."[13] Telegrams were now issuing forth for investors and wildcatters to come and buy up property in the area. In the previous two years, kerosene had proven a valuable commodity. And now that oil could be found in vast quantities, not just by scraping it out of pools, the utility, and profitability, of Drake's discovery wasn't lost on anyone.

Maybe the Colonel wasn't so crazy after all.

Drake, too, had ventured into town at the end of the day. There was a great deal of work to be done in securing commercial deals—barrels, transportation, and ultimately consumers—for his newfound ample supply of rock oil. Bone-tired but running on adrenaline, Drake stopped by the general store, where mail from back East arrived from time to time.

There was the letter postmarked from New Haven, return address James Townsend.

If the note had arrived a few days earlier, he would have almost certainly complied with its demand to close up shop.

Now, Drake couldn't help but smile. The last line of the poem about rock oil echoed in his head: "To calm our sufferings and assuage our woes."

In the wake of Drake's discovery, the population of Titusville swelled literally overnight. The day after Drake had discovered oil, there were hundreds of people from the local countryside milling around the well in amazement.[14] Land prices along Oil Creek and in surrounding areas increased exponentially as speculators and investors poured into town.

Within months, an oil boom was under way in western Pennsylvania. By November 1860, seventy-five wells were already in full production.[15] Thousands of drillers sought the black gold. Production grew from 450,000 barrels in 1860 to 3 million barrels two years later.[16] The burgeoning supply of oil far outstripped demand, and oil prices, which had started at ten dollars per barrel in January 1860, dropped to ten cents per barrel by the end of the year.[17] Many of the overzealous investors went bankrupt within months.

But once kerosene hit the market, consumer demand ultimately couldn't be satisfied. Townsend's and Silliman's suspicions had been right. The first handbook on oil was published months after Drake's discovery: "As an illuminator the oil is without figure: It is the light of the age," it read. "Those that have not seen it burn, may rest assured its light is no moonshine; but something nearer the clear, strong, brilliant light of day, to which darkness is no party . . . rock oil emits a dainty light; the brightest and yet the cheapest in the world; a light fit for Kings and Royalists and not unsuitable for Republicans and Democrats."[18] Compared to whale oil, kerosene was an environmentally friendly alternative. In fact, you might call kerosene the first green energy source. In 1861 *Vanity Fair* ran a cartoon of whales toasting "the discovery of the Oil Wells in Pennsylvania."

The oil bonanza continued, but it was not without consequences. In April 1861, drillers near Oil Creek hit the world's first gusher, with oil and gas rocketing into the air. The gases were ignited and exploded. The inferno consumed nineteen people and could not be extinguished for three days. The news from northeastern Pennsylvania was eclipsed, however, by the start of the Civil War and the assault on Fort Sumter in South Carolina.

Throughout the oil boom of the 1860s, entrepreneurs and wildcatters descended on the region. Many came with empty pockets, looking to work their way up from the bottom; some risked their entire fortunes. As it happened, one such man was one of the most renowned actors in the country, a twenty-three-year-old named John Wilkes Booth. His epic swordfights and dramatic performances had earned him the titles of "youngest star in the world" and "most handsome man on the American stage."[19]

Booth no longer wanted to be an actor, and seeking an investment return on almost all of his life savings—a considerable six thousand dollars—he bought a 3.5 acre lease not far from Oil Creek in 1864.[20] He came up with a name for his new endeavor: "The Dramatic Oil Company." After modest initial success generating twenty-five barrels of oil per day, Booth's well ran dry. The aspiring oilman lost everything. He returned to his home city of Baltimore, where he would nurse his grievances and busy himself with a plot to assassinate the president of the United States.

But where some failed, others amassed great fortunes. Townsend and his fellow New Haven investors who had been on the brink of bankruptcy grew wealthy as they bought up more and more land. The son of a traveling salesman, John D. Rockefeller, would become the richest man in history after buying up Pennsylvania refineries and founding Standard Oil.

Edwin Drake was not so lucky. He moved to New York City to capitalize on his fame as the man who first struck oil. He became a partner at a Wall Street investment firm. After the Civil War, oil prices cratered again and Drake lost everything. His muscular neuralgia returned with a vengeance, leaving him all but paralyzed by the pain. Pennsylvania would eventually grant him a modest pension for his contributions to the state's economy. Drake died in poverty in 1880.

But history should record that Edwin Drake ushered in a worldwide energy revolution. From 1860 to 1900, Pennsylvania would be responsible for half of the world's production of oil. More than creating fortunes for those enterprising individuals willing to risk everything, what happened in the hills of western Pennsylvania sparked a wave of technological innovation and economic growth. It began with kerosene and the lighting of the homes of millions of Americans and continued with gasoline and the internal combustion engine.

★　　★　　★

There are still men and women like Edwin Drake in America. Go to North Dakota or Louisiana or Ohio or west Texas and you'll meet them. Or go to the hills of western Pennsylvania near Titusville. With new techniques such as hydraulic fracturing, entrepreneurs today are finding new ways to tap energy in the Marcellus Shale—the very same ancient deposits of oil and natural gas that Edwin Drake struck with the first oil well in the world. These men and women have dirt and oil under their nails. They have calluses on their hands. They wear hard hats. They drive trucks. They work in restaurants and bars and the small businesses that supply the men and women of the oil and natural gas industry. They aren't millionaires. They may not have college degrees. And they may not read the *New York Times* every morning. But they are the backbone of the American economy. And they are bringing back jobs to parts of the country that many had once written off as "the Rust Belt" where manufacturing jobs left and never came back.

It is no mere accident of history that this energy revolution happened in America. After all, dozens of other countries around the world have vast energy reserves and enterprising and resourceful people. But the discovery of oil and the subsequent rush to bring that energy to market in the 1860s happened because of a country that upheld the rule of law, protected the private property rights of its citizens, and incentivized them to develop and profit from their property.

Consider the remarkable thought that if you happen to discover oil, gas, diamonds, or gold on your property in the United States, it's considered a blessing. Not so in just about every other country in the world, where the government owns what is the below the surface, even if it's on your "private" property. Because of America's unique private property rights, the Pennsylvania oil boom could flourish. Even under British law, the rights to develop minerals under the ground belonged to the Crown, not usually to the owner of the property above them. In most of the world, the government gets to decide when, how, and where to drill resources. The individuals who own the land above those resources in those countries don't have a say, and very rarely do they have a financial stake in the outcome.

But in America in the 1860s—and in America still today— entrepreneurs can buy land and acquire leases, knowing that the government will not come in and confiscate their property or their profits. If those resources were in the hands of a government, production and innovation would have taken generations longer.

The truth is America has more oil, more natural gas, and more coal resources combined than any other country in the world. In the past decade, it's been discovered that America has vast amounts of domestic shale oil and natural gas—almost a century's worth of supply. The stunning increase in shale gas production has led to a much larger share of energy produced in America by clean-burning and low-cost natural gas, improving both our environment and our economy at the same time. The increased use of natural gas in power production has significantly reduced carbon emissions.[21] Despite a remarkably successful campaign by environmental radicals and a compliant media to scare Americans about the dangers of hydraulic fracturing—injecting fluid deep into the ground to break up shale rock and release natural gas—more natural gas production is one of the best ways of improving the environment.

America's blessings beneath its soil and coasts mean we can

make energy more affordable than it has been. The only thing that's holding us back is Washington. The ideologues in the Obama administration have bragged about shutting down entire sectors of the energy industry. They want oil prices to go higher and higher so that their quixotic dreams for green energy—not to mention the hundreds of millions of dollar in taxpayer-funded boondoggles like Solyndra—have a chance of success, even if that deprives every middle-class American of hundreds of dollars each year in gas savings. They oppose commonsense solutions like building the Keystone XL pipeline, which would bring America even closer to energy independence and create thousands of jobs.

It's true that gasoline is becoming cheaper than it's been in years, despite the best efforts of the Obama administration to keep prices higher by opposing and slowing production on federal lands and imposing punishing regulations on energy companies. President Obama has trumpeted America's oil production growth, ignoring the fact that it has happened entirely on state and private lands. His administration has hindered production on federal lands—a decline of more than one-third since he has been in office[22]—and opposed developing the vast oil reserves under the Arctic National Wildlife Reserve (ANWR) and on the outer continental shelf.

Energy can become cheaper still given the abundance of America's energy resources. Affordable energy is a prerequisite for a strong economy. Over the first six years of the Obama presidency, the average price of gas nearly doubled.[23] It's little wonder that in the years after the 2008 economic crisis America faced the most sluggish economic recovery in its history.

Even America's unique regime of private property rights that give subsurface rights to owners of land rather than the government is under assault by President Obama. New regulations and layers of red tape applied by the EPA and Department of Interior and other federal agencies make it harder and harder to get permits for exploration and drilling. From coal to natural gas to oil, Obama has tried to bury America's energy industry.

When common sense triumphs over left-wing ideology, remarkable things happen. Consider what we were able to do in my home state of Louisiana. Natural gas production has doubled since 2007, creating thousands of new jobs and driving down electricity prices to among the lowest in the nation. In 2013 alone, Louisianians saved $1.7 billion by paying less than the national average for electricity. That money has stayed in the state, allowing business to bring in more jobs and families to have an extra $350 per year in their pocketbooks. For the first time in its history, Louisiana boasts more than 2 million jobs. Economic growth is nearly double the national average.[24] I am incredibly proud of what Louisianians and energy companies have been able to do together.

With the vast resources under our land and the most innovative technologies in the world, such as hydraulic fracturing and horizontal drilling, America can be energy independent and no longer vulnerable to the whims of dictators and tyrants who have been propped up by international demand for their oil exports. I've seen what energy can do in the state of Louisiana, and it's high time Americans from Los Angeles to Miami to New York see the middle-class job growth and lower gas costs that come when we recognize our nation's vast natural resources are not the enemy but the answer to growing our economy.

There is a better way for America's energy policy than political posturing, picking winners and losers, and pushing for more and more federal control, as President Obama and his allies on the Left have advocated. We can promote responsible development of energy resources and the construction of infrastructure to support it. We can also encourage technological innovation in renewables such as solar, wind, and hydropower. We can unlock newfound economic potential with a manufacturing renaissance spurred by affordable natural gas and shale oil. We can unleash the power of the free market and the desire of individuals to innovate and prosper.

The truth is we are poised for another golden age of energy, just as America was in the days before Edwin Drake struck oil in Pennsylvania. The spirit and vision of Drake and the thousands of energy entrepreneurs who followed in his footsteps can unleash a second energy revolution, unshackled by Washington.

We live in a country with millions of Edwin Drakes, men and women of ingenuity, efficiency, and dynamism. Theirs is a special kind of genius: They not only see the world differently, they are willing to take risks to change it.

PART II

★ ★ ★

AMERICA OFF-COURSE

4

PREEMPTIVE SURRENDER

Joe Kennedy and the Perils of Appeasement

No conflict in human history caused more death and devastation than World War II. In the aftermath of a global conflagration that took more than 60 million lives, America's leaders vowed to do everything in their power to ensure war of that scale never happened again. A bipartisan consensus emerged that the United States needed to take a leadership role in the world. That the blissful isolationism that had allowed Fascism to amass the world's most formidable armies, air forces, and navies could never again be repeated. With Japanese aircraft descending on Hawaii and German U-boats patrolling Atlantic shores, America forever left behind an era when it could count on the safety afforded by two vast oceans.

The appeasement of one's enemies is a continual temptation among many leaders today—the notion that if you only talked with dictators and extremists, or tried to understand them, then we could all find common ground. With this very impulse in mind, the Obama administration initiated dialogues with Iran in order to halt their production of nuclear weapons, even as the Iranians called for death to the United States and our ally, Israel. I find this approach not only misguided, but also tragic. My parents did not cross an ocean and begin a new life in America in order to live in a nation whose president is willing to sell its security for a shot at another undeserved Nobel Peace Prize.

Unfortunately, making nice with maniacal leaders has deep roots in American politics. The most infamous example occurred in the days before World War II when leaders of many Western democracies worked overtime to placate Adolf Hitler—offering him various inducements in order to avoid confronting him with force. What is less known, perhaps because the media do not like to talk about it since it deals with one of the Democratic Party's most prominent families, is the outsized role Joseph P. Kennedy played in the appeasement of Hitler, often contradicting the views and intentions of his boss, President Franklin Roosevelt. The Kennedy family, of course, went on to dominate Democratic Party politics for decades.

The role of U.S. ambassador was a far more prominent one than it is generally considered to be—one that tended to capture people's imaginations. And Joe Kennedy, a self-made millionaire with grit and tenacity and a large and attractive family, was one of the best-known diplomats in the world. This gave him enormous influence and power—his freelancing in the Roosevelt administration may well have played a role in encouraging Hitler's view that Western democracies would pay almost any price for peace. Because Joe Kennedy would.

This is his story.

Fall 1937—The White House, Oval Office

Joe Kennedy knew that Franklin Roosevelt was eccentric, mercurial, and mischievous. But as they met in the White House that day, even he was struck momentarily dumb by the president's request.

Take his pants down? What on earth for?

But Kennedy complied. It was a humbling, slightly mortifying, experience to stand before the president in one's underwear. Which is probably what FDR intended. To put the forty-eight-year-old Kennedy in his place. He could be an arrogant man, which was not an uncommon affliction for a self-made millionaire.

Joseph Patrick Kennedy also had a talent for getting his name in the headlines, usually thanks to various journalists he counted among his friends. He indeed had to this point compiled an impressive resumé—a businessman who made a fortune in various enterprises, including the booming liquor trade (he long denied rumors he was involved in bootlegging during Prohibition); a bank president at twenty-five; a real estate mogul who increased his fortune during the Great Depression; a movie mogul who was said to have had a torrid affair with actress Gloria Swanson; and the first chairman of the Securities and Exchange Commission to crack down on corrupt practices on Wall Street. To FDR, the appointment was ingenious—Kennedy knew as much as anyone about questionable business dealings and manipulating the stock market. That was, after all, in large part how he made his money. "I set a thief to catch a thief," Roosevelt joked about the appointment.[1]

By the time he joined the Roosevelt administration, Kennedy was worth an estimated $200 million ($3 billion in 2014 dollars). He was a man of many ambitions, including occupying the office in which he was standing pantless.

Staring at Kennedy's bare legs, the president flashed his eager, indecipherable smile.

"Someone who saw you in a bathing suit once told me something I now know to be true," FDR said. "Joe, you are about the most bow-legged man I have ever seen."

In truth he was not the standard diplomat, especially to the aristocratic Court of St. James. Pale-skinned and red-haired, with owlish black glasses, Joe Kennedy looked like, and was, the quintessential Irish Catholic. Which was what made the prospect of being America's diplomat in England so tantalizing. Hobnobbing with the British upper classes, he finally would have made it.

FDR wasn't so sure Kennedy was right for the part, or at least he pretended not to be. No one knew what thoughts really motivated his legendary pranks.

"Don't you know that the ambassador to the Court of St. James has to go through an induction ceremony in which he wears knee britches and silk stockings?" Roosevelt asked. "When photos of our new ambassador appear all over the world, we'll be a laughingstock."[2]

Kennedy smiled at the president gamely. But their mutual contempt was thinly disguised. Whether FDR was serious or joking, the episode was not something that would have happened to someone the president really considered a friend.

Kennedy was being thrown into a Europe where the British empire was waning, just as the shadow of the Nazi war machine grew more pronounced. To outsiders, the appointment might have seemed a plum assignment, a gauge of Roosevelt's trust. Of course, that assumed that FDR had any intention of listening to his new ambassador.

The Next Year, March 11, 1938— U.S. Ambassador's Residence, London

Joe Kennedy was a practical man. This was how he made his fortune. He counted on consumers to be rational, for other businessmen to share his ambitions and want to cut deals. The world was run by reasonable men; this was how civilized societies worked.

Yes, Kennedy thought to himself, Adolf Hitler and Benito Mussolini were odd sorts. They played to their crowds, said ghastly things. But he was sure they were reasonable, too. They had to be. If only the British and Americans would call them out, they'd settle down. That, at any rate, was the thrust of Kennedy's note to the president from London. After all, nobody wanted another great war, devastating economies and making it that much harder to run a business.

He had full confidence in the British prime minister, who was the picture of the British aristocrat: handsome, lean, and tall. If the proud Irishman bore any resentment toward the English upper classes, he didn't reveal it much. In fact, he fit right in. Prime Minister Neville Chamberlain, Kennedy felt, was a "strong decisive man, evidently fully in charge of the situation here."[3] Chamberlain didn't want war any more than Kennedy did. No rational man would. And especially not a father. After all, as Kennedy would famously put it, he himself had "nine hostages to fortune"—his children, from the eldest Joe, Jr., to his youngest, six-year-old Teddy.[4]

Hitler surely must think the same way. He and his allies were threatening to annex Austria, but this had to be posturing. An effort to reach a deal with the other European powers.

"My own impression [of Hitler and Mussolini]," Kennedy wrote Roosevelt, is that they, "having done so very well for themselves by bluffing, are not going to stop bluffing until somebody very sharply calls their bluff."[5] If England and France simply said they'd back up the Austrian government, Hitler would buckle under. The Nazi leader was, Kennedy assumed confidently, a rational actor.

Hours later—Europe

Hitler accompanied Eighth Army troops and tanks across the Austrian border. The invasion had begun. Within hours, Hitler would establish a Nazi government in Vienna, and declare Austria a province of the Third Reich. No fighting had taken place.

The Anschluss, or annexation, of Austria had done nothing

to temper Kennedy's view of the European situation. Nor had it changed Prime Minister Chamberlain's determination to keep his nation out of war, a position overwhelmingly backed by British public opinion. There were, of course, a few malcontents, rabble-rousers like Winston Churchill, who claimed that if Hitler had really had a legitimate claim on Austria, he would have sought negotiation and diplomacy, rather than rule by tank.

But Kennedy believed Churchill was an irrelevancy; calmer heads would prevail.

Three Months Later, June 13, 1938—London, England

Herbert von Dirksen's natural expression was stern. Nearly bald, with cheerless eyes adorned by wireless glasses perched on his prominent nose, he carried himself through London as if he were the visible embodiment of Nazi intimidation.

But, as he cabled his superiors in Berlin, it would have been hard for a glimmer of pleasure not to find its way into his otherwise cold countenance.

He had just met with the American ambassador, von Dirksen noted, and he was every bit the man the Nazis had hoped.

Kennedy had informed him that President Roosevelt "desired friendly relations with Germany," von Dirksen reported. Kennedy had even touched favorably upon "the Jewish question"—in particular the growing rumors of Nazi brutality against the Jewish race—which Kennedy called "naturally of great importance to German-American relations."[6]

"In this connection it was not so much the fact that we wanted to get rid of the Jews that was so harmful to us," von Dirksen noted, "but rather the loud clamor with which we accompanied this purpose."

Kennedy himself "understood our Jewish policy completely," he wrote. "He was from Boston and there, in one golf club, and in other clubs, no Jews had been admitted for the past fifty years."[7]

The American was, von Dirksen would later go on to claim, "Germany's best friend in London."[8]

Nine Days Later, June 22, 1938—Washington, D.C.

As Kennedy returned for a visit to Washington, he was filled with satisfaction at his diplomatic performance. He had formed close relationships with the British government at its highest levels. He and his photogenic family were on the cover of newspapers and magazines, as he met with British royalty and worked assiduously to keep America out of war. And he was enjoying immensely the growing consensus that he was on the very short list of candidates to succeed Franklin Roosevelt, should FDR retire at the close of his second term.

"I suppose you know that you are being mentioned very frequently as a candidate to succeed Mr. Roosevelt," the publisher William Randolph Hearst wrote him a month earlier. "In fact, you are the most mentioned candidate."[9]

Arriving at New York harbor, he was greeted like a movie star, with photographers and reporters to chronicle his every step. But if he was expecting a similar reception at the White House, he was disappointed.

President Roosevelt was cordial, but not awestruck. And he seemed to take issue with some of Kennedy's advice. As aide Harold L. Ickes later recorded, Kennedy had urged FDR to avoid criticism of Fascism in his speeches.

The perplexed Roosevelt asked him why.

Because, Kennedy answered, "we would have to come to some

form of Fascism here."[10] Fascism could be appeased, but it could not be entirely defeated.

Two Months Later, August 30–September 2, 1938— London and Washington

President Roosevelt was in a fury. It was bad enough Joe Kennedy was pompously declaring himself an expert on European affairs—a not so subtle effort to bolster his presidential credentials—and lecturing the president of the United States on the tone of his speeches. Now he was insulting the American form of government, and Roosevelt in particular, in front of British audiences.

In an explicit rebuke of the administration, Kennedy had told assembled dinner guests in London that legislation in America was prepared after a "ten-minute" study by the Roosevelt brain trust, then passed by Congress, and "subsequently found to be imperfect or unconstitutional."

It was a contemptuous comment, designed to play to anti-American sentiments.

"I don't think there is much question but Kennedy is disloyal to his country," Roosevelt declared. He was so incensed by the report that he considered recalling him immediately.[11]

Ten Days Later, September 12, 1938—Nuremberg

A parade of Nazi soldiers held weapons and goose-stepped in formation. Tens of thousands of Germans in the frenzied crowd waved Nazi flags and cheered, especially when the Führer made his first appearance before the microphones to speak.

Dressed in military garb, Adolf Hitler called for Germans to

exercise their "natural right of unity," which had united them with
Austria and now called out to Germans living in Czechoslovakia.

Throughout his remarks, Hitler declared the Nazi Party an
organ of peace. "For the sake of peace in Europe, the National
Socialist State has made enormous sacrifices, enormous sacrifices
for the entire nation," he declared to cheers. "No European state
has done as much as Germany in the service of peace! No one has
made greater sacrifices!"

But Hitler made it clear that "one way or another" the voices of
Germans in Czechoslovakia would obtain "justice."

Of course, for Hitler, "justice" for Germans meant domination
of everyone else.

The crowd joined in calling out: "*Sieg Heil!*"

Hearing of the speech in London, Kennedy breathed a sigh of
relief. Hitler had not explicitly declared war on Czechoslovakia, as
some had predicted. Kennedy quickly made the rounds of the British government. There was still a chance that a diplomatic solution
would give Hitler what he wanted, while keeping England out of
armed conflict.

Nine Days Later, September 21, 1938—London

Now Kennedy was alarmed. Hitler's threats to move against
Czechoslovakia had unnerved the British public—where, they
wondered, would Hitler go next?—and given men like Churchill
some momentum. Even Chamberlain, in Kennedy's view the only
man in England still capable of maintaining the peace, was appearing to waver. There was only one course of action that might
salvage things. Or, more specifically, one person. Which was why
he'd sent such an urgent message to Paris.

It had been eleven years since *The Spirit of St. Louis* had made its historic voyage over the Atlantic Ocean, and in that time Charles Lindbergh had become one of the most acclaimed and best-known men in the world. When he was head of a movie studio, Kennedy had even offered the handsome Lindbergh a motion picture contract.[12] After the horrifying abduction of his son, which had garnered international headlines, Charles and his wife, Anne, left the United States for Europe.[13]

As ambassador, Kennedy had entertained the Lindberghs at a dinner. He knew the famed aviator shared his desire for peace.

After lunch, as he briefed his distinguished visitors on the sad state of affairs in England, he was in a sober mood.

It wasn't Chamberlain who was the real problem, the ambassador pointed out. He still realized "the disastrous effects" of war with Germany, "and is making every effort to avoid one." Hitler had made it quite clear to the British prime minister that he would risk a world war in order to obtain Czechoslovakia.

But the mood of the English public was changing; they needed something that would demonstrate how devastating a war with Hitler would be.

Lindbergh was horrified at the idea of war. He had affection for the German people and had been presented an award by Hitler's government. Indeed, on his own tours of Germany with Hermann Göring, Lindbergh had become persuaded that the Nazi war machine was all but unbeatable. It did not occur to him that he was shown exactly what the Germans wanted him to see.

Kennedy had a request of his guest. He knew that of all the men in the world few could command attention and respect as Charles Lindbergh could.

He urged him to write a report outlining the devastating effects to the British of war against Hitler. Kennedy said he would then be sure to circulate the report among key members of the cabinet.[14]

Lindbergh agreed, at once. He believed, as Kennedy seemed to, that "our only sound policy is to avoid war now at any cost."[15]

Nine Days Later, September 30, 1938—Heston Aerodrome

The dignified man with white hair and a graying mustache held aloft a piece of paper, one he believed would seal his fate as a man of historic importance. In that, he was right, but not for the reasons that he thought.

Neville Chamberlain had just returned to England from a meeting with German leaders, in which he had extracted a promise that the Nazi occupation of Czechoslovakia would mark the end to Germany's expansionism. To ensure that Hitler would keep his word, he had urged Hitler to sign a peace agreement with the British. And now Chamberlain displayed that paper, affixed with Hitler's signature, before the crowd that had come to greet his plane.

This settlement, Chamberlain said, "is, in my view, only the prelude to a larger settlement in which all Europe may find peace."

Returning to 10 Downing Street, he read again from the document and concluded with hope that Britain and Germany had found "peace with honor."

"I believe it is peace for our time," Chamberlain declared to the gathered crowds, all of whom were hopeful that London would be spared a second Great War. "We thank you from the bottom of our hearts. Go home and get a nice quiet sleep."

Just as he and Ambassador Kennedy had hoped, the Lindbergh report had strengthened Chamberlain's hands. And in a flurry of meetings with Lindbergh and members of the cabinet, arranged by Kennedy, Lindbergh shared his dire view that "German air strength is greater than that of all other European countries combined," "England and France are far too weak," and "I am convinced it is wiser to permit Germany's eastward expansion than to throw England and France, unprepared, into a war at this time."

Not everyone in England shared these sentiments—the most prominent being the cantankerous Churchill. But Chamberlain thought Churchill a crank and a false prophet. Besides, he had prominent and influential supporters on his side, particularly a very relieved American ambassador.

"Tonight," Kennedy wrote in his diary, "a feeling is spreading all over London" that peace was at hand. "It may be the beginning of a new world policy which may mean peace and prosperity once again."[16] And he believed—no, he knew—that he had played an indispensable role in bringing about that peace.

Forty Days Later, November 9–10, 1938— Europe; United States

A series of attacks on Jews in Germany and Austria provoked an international outcry. Synagogues were burned, Jewish-owned shops and homes were smashed and ransacked by mobs dressed in civilian clothes. These actions were clearly condoned by the Nazi government. The destruction was so great that the streets were lined with the broken glass of windows from Jewish stores and houses. It soon became known as the "Night of Broken Glass"—Kristallnacht.

The attacks were front-page news across the world, increasing a sense of rage and despair about the mentality and methods of the Nazi regime in Berlin. The specter of war, ostensibly dashed after the Munich agreement, was again looming across Europe. Opinion of the Chamberlain government was souring. Hitler would not be sated, or appeased, after all. That, however, was still not the view of the American ambassador in England.

"I am hopeful that something can be worked out," Kennedy wrote in a letter to Charles Lindbergh, "but this last drive on the Jews has really made the most ardent hopers [sic] for peace very sick at heart."[17]

Which led Kennedy to yet another plan to avoid war: move the Jews somewhere. He would urge the British Empire to find some room for a new homeland for German and Austrian Jews; once the Jews were out of the way, Kennedy reasoned, Hitler might be calmed. More to the point, Kennedy feared that if something wasn't done to satisfy the Jews he believed dominated the American media, they would lead the drumbeat to American involvement in war.

Asked about Kennedy's resettlement plans by reporters, Franklin Roosevelt made clear his view of his ambassador and their relationship.

"I cannot comment on the report," FDR replied coolly, "because I know nothing of what is happening in London."[18]

Seven Months Later, June 14, 1939—The White House

A confidential note from J. Edgar Hoover arrived at the mansion. Hoover had been director of the FBI for only four years, but he had no reluctance to share with the White House highly sensitive information about their most important personnel. The subject of this note in particular was one of the most prominent men, not only in the administration, but the entire country.

Hoover was of course well aware that the note he was sending to the White House, addressed to presidential secretary Stephen Early, had the potential to be explosive, especially in such delicate times. But he sent it nonetheless. In it, he had attached a copy of the June 1 edition of the *Observer*, which noted the alarming reaction of British officials to the views of the American ambassador.

British officials were said to be baffled that Roosevelt was keeping Kennedy in his post, "considering his record as an appeaser and an apologist for Chamberlain."[19] They were also alarmed by

Kennedy's obvious disdain for his boss and his penchant for indiscreet words.

Indeed, the publication quoted Kennedy as saying that Roosevelt's views were increasingly irrelevant and would no longer be a concern after 1940. The ambassador assumed that Roosevelt would bow to tradition and not seek an unprecedented third term in office. After the election, "it will be my friends that are in the White House," Kennedy had said. Roosevelt, Ambassador Kennedy went on, "is run by the Jews and all the anti-fascist sentiment in the United States is largely created by the Jews who run the press."[20] British cabinet officials wondered whether this was a true reflection of American opinion.

In short, Hoover's note was meant to put Roosevelt on notice that he had a big problem in London. It was a problem of which FDR was already quite aware.

Ten Weeks Later, August 25, 1939— Cabinet Room, 10 Downing Street

The situation was dire. Even Joe Kennedy could see that now. Invited to meet with the prime minister and his close aides, Kennedy knew that the proponents of war now had the advantage.

Hitler was threatening an invasion of Poland, and then—well, who knew? In the dispatches Kennedy read that day, Hitler made clear that he would get his way or there would be a war worse than the Great War that came before it.

Britain had pledged itself to Poland's defense. But still Kennedy felt that he might mount one last effort to avoid disaster and what he believed an inevitable British surrender.

Asked his view on Britain's next step, Kennedy was direct. "You cannot quit on Poland no matter what else happens," he said. But there might be another solution.

An answer to Hitler "might contain a suggestion that if he accepted a reasonable Polish settlement perhaps he could get the United States and other countries to get together on an economic plan that certainly would be more important to Germany."

"What do you mean by that?" Chamberlain asked.

Kennedy meant a bribe. "You have to make your solution more attractive to Germany than what she is trying now to get out of Poland," he said. Acting as if he were not a member of the American government—a complete betrayal of his responsibility to the president who selected him and the nation that he represented—he added that Chamberlain should "get the United States now to say what they would be willing to do in the cause of international peace and security. After all, the United States will be the largest beneficiary of such a move. To put in a billion or two now will be worth it, for if it works we will get it back and more."[21]

Chamberlain received the advice politely, but it was clear that he had finally faced reality. His appeasement policy was in tatters; he could not offer more of the same.

Kennedy walked over to the prime minister's chair and put his hand on his shoulder. "Don't worry, Neville," he said. "I still believe God is working with you."[22]

Nine Days Later, September 3, 1939—London

Neville Chamberlain appeared before the House of Commons with sad news. "Peace for our time" had not come after all.

For months, Hitler's declarations of peace had rung more hollow by the day. But after the Nazis invaded Poland, an English ally, even the most optimistic in the Chamberlain cabinet knew that the prime minister's efforts had failed.

So, in the first Sunday session of the House of Commons in

more than one hundred years, the prime minister entered the House with glum eyes, a darkened face, and a confession.

"Everything that I have worked for, everything that I have hoped for, everything that I have believed in during my public life has crashed into ruins," he told a quiet, sober Parliament. "There is only one thing left for me to do: that is, devote what strength and power I have to forwarding the victory of the cause for which we have sacrificed so much."[23]

Great Britain was now in a state of war.

Shortly after the speech, the prime minister received a call from his old ally, the U.S. ambassador.

"Neville, I have just listened to the broadcast," Kennedy said. "I feel deeply our failure to save a world war."[24]

One Week Later, September 10, 1939— The White House, Washington, D.C.

The "triple priority" telegram from Ambassador Kennedy to the president urged FDR to take direct action to stop the war that was now raging across the Continent.

Poland would be defeated in weeks, Kennedy reported, and Hitler would then offer France and England a new deal.

"If the war were stopped," Kennedy reasoned, "it would provide Herr Hitler with so much more prestige that it is a question of how far he would be carried by it.

"It appears to me that this situation may resolve itself to a point where the President may play savior of the world." Kennedy, it appeared, had learned nothing from Munich. His advice was that Roosevelt should make a peace pact with Hitler.[25]

If the president even read the note, he would have laughed. Nothing Kennedy was advising was of any use to him.

Secretary of State Cordell Hull responded bluntly to Kennedy's proposal: "The people of the United States would not support any move for peace initiative by this Government that would consolidate or make possible a survival of a regime of force and aggression."[26]

The Next Month, October 1939—London

It was over for England. The Nazis were too powerful. France would be swallowed, and then the Germans would make their way across the Channel. That was Joe Kennedy's assessment now—one he shared with anyone who'd listen. One he shared so often that the British government was now collecting files on him and worrying about his defeatist propaganda and its effect on the war effort.

The British sought the advice of a former Hearst correspondent to try to figure out what was happening in Kennedy's mind.

Kennedy had "made a pile of money" and feared for his family's future, the reporter explained.

"Bankruptcy and defeat were now obsessions in the ambassador's mind," he said. "He was not amenable to reason, his argument being that Hitler and the Nazis could not last forever and that there was bound to be a change in Germany one day if we had only let it alone."[27]

His popularity in Britain, especially among elite circles, had taken a sharp turn. Almost no one would defend him. Almost.

Five Months Later, March 1940—Cambridge, Massachusetts

The twenty-three-year-old Harvard student finished his 147-page thesis in the field of international government. The topic was a

provocative one, indeed what the writer called "the most controversial subject in modern diplomacy." It was entitled "Appeasement
at Munich."[28]

The author was not just any Harvard pupil, but the son of the
U.S. ambassador to the United Kingdom. To some, John Fitzger-
ald Kennedy's work was notable for its defense of appeasement and
Munich. To others, it was an apology, or at least an explanation,
for his father's all but universally unpopular views in support of the
now widely discredited Munich Pact.

"In this thesis," young Kennedy wrote, "it is proposed to show
that most of the critics have been firing at the wrong target."
"The Munich Pact itself," he asserted, "should not be the object of
criticism."[29]

The Munich Pact was necessary, Kennedy argued, to give the
English democracy another year of life. The author stopped just
short of saying democracy was imperiled, but he offered dire warn-
ings: "Democracy has got to stop and take stock in itself. . . . It
must stop patting itself on the back for its past performances."[30]

As for America, Kennedy struck a hesitant note. "We may be
able to stave off totalitarianism here," Kennedy wrote, "due to
our geographic position and great national wealth." But it did not
sound like a sure thing.

Many of these sentiments would soon be echoed and even em-
bellished, in a manner much more forceful and extreme, by his
father.

Two Months Later, May 14, 1940—
Office of the First Lord of the Admiralty

Large and ruddy, the incoming prime minister was not a pleas-
ant sight to the American ambassador. Kennedy had thought so
highly of the refined Neville Chamberlain; now after Chamber-

lain's resignation, the world's future was in the hands of a border-line alcoholic.

Though they had forged friendly ties at one point, the years had not been kind to the Kennedy-Churchill relationship. Kennedy noted how "ill-conditioned" Churchill looked. At his meeting with Churchill, Kennedy noted the tray with plenty of liquor beside him. Churchill was drinking a "scotch highball, which I felt was indeed not the first one he had drunk that night."

Churchill had summoned Kennedy to let him know the British were going to request a loan of thirty- or forty-year-old American destroyers and any airplanes the United States could spare.

Kennedy responded that the United States would do what it could to help "that would not leave the United States holding the bag for a war in which the Allies expected to be beaten."

Churchill's tone was far less pessimistic. Regardless of what Germany does to England and France, the new prime minister said, "England will never give up as long as I remain a power in public life even if England is burnt to the ground. Why, the government will move to Canada and take the fleet and fight on."[31]

The response left Kennedy horrified. Churchill would fight on pointlessly until he could pull the Americans into the conflict, he deduced. And then all of us would lose.

Almost Four Months Later, September 7, 1940— The Skies Over London

They first appeared as tiny blips in the air, metallic, even tinfoil-colored. Weather balloons, perhaps. Then the gray images grew clearer and multiplied. They were Nazi warplanes over the city of London. Sirens sounded. Antiaircraft guns crackled. Bombs fell. The Blitz of London had begun.

The first wave of bombers was followed by a second. The planes targeted bridges, docks, factories, warehouses. The English capital was ablaze by nightfall; the London fire department soon found itself overwhelmed.

Walking with a friend down Piccadilly, Ambassador Kennedy, as was his wont, foresaw the worst. "I'll bet you five to one any sum that Hitler will be in Buckingham Palace in two weeks," he said.[32]

A Month and a Half Later, October 22, 1940—London

Joe Kennedy left London for the last time as America's ambassador. That the British had managed to resist bombardment, that Churchill continued to express great defiance against the Nazis, left no impression. Britain was doomed. So was Europe. But if by some miracle the British managed to hold off at all, it would be because Neville Chamberlain had given them the time to build up their forces. The Munich agreement, for which he'd fought so hard, had to have meant something.

He left a very different country from the one he'd found; the public was firmly in the Churchill camp now. Kennedy and his appeasement policies were widely disparaged. His tendency to go to the countryside during the worst of London's bombing left him branded a coward. As one observer put it, "I thought my daffodils were yellow until I met Joe Kennedy."[33]

One of his final visits in England was with his old friend and confidant Neville Chamberlain, a man he had tirelessly defended, and who now was dying of cancer. "Your conception of what the world must do in order to be a fit place to live in," he wrote Chamberlain in a letter, "is the last sensible thing we shall see before the pall of anarchy falls on us all."[34]

Fifteen Days Later, November 6, 1940—
The Department of State, Washington, D.C.

Two days after Roosevelt's landslide re-election to a third term in office, dashing another of Joe Kennedy's dreams, the ambassador was meeting at the State Department on the latest events in the war. The news was good. The Royal Air Force had pushed back the Luftwaffe and cleared airspace over the English Channel. The Brits were showing steel. Hitler had canceled invasion plans.

But that was not encouraging news to one participant at the meeting.

Kennedy believed these were temporary setbacks to German forces. The Nazis had taken Poland, Belgium, the Netherlands, and France. It was only a matter of time.

The American people needed education in foreign affairs, he told a colleague.[35] He was determined to provide it.

Next Day, November 7, 1940—Boston, the Ritz-Carlton

He had been asked not to speak to the press by his colleagues at the State Department, but Joe Kennedy had shown he wasn't much for listening. Besides, they'd only stop him from saying what had to be said.

Snacking on apple pie and cheese at the Ritz-Carlton hotel, Kennedy was direct and expansive with the two reporters visiting with him. Sitting in a dress shirt, without a jacket, with his suspenders hanging by his hips, he declared that Hitler was on the path to victory. America was right to stay out of the war. "There's no sense of getting in," he declared. "We'd just be holding the bag."[36]

The multimillionaire vowed that he'd "spend all I've got left to keep us out."

He would make his case to members of Congress, to influential editors, and to opinion makers. "I know more about the European situation than anyone else," he declared, "and it's up to me to see that the country gets it."

They call me a pessimist, he said sadly. "What is there to be gay about?" he asked. "Democracy is all done."

The reporters pressed him. "All done? In England or in this country, too?"

"I don't know," Kennedy replied. "If we get into the war it will be in this country, too." National socialism is the future for Britain, he declared. Then he added, with extra assurance, "Democracy is finished in England. It may be here."[37]

But democracy was not finished; Joe Kennedy's diplomatic career certainly was.

★   ★   ★

Not since the 1930s have America and the free world been in as perilous a position as today. The gathering storm that was fascism was ignored by men like Joseph Kennedy. He believed that goodwill and well-meaning diplomatic efforts would keep evil at bay. He was not alone. Millions of Americans believed that war would not visit our shores and that anything that risked dragging us into conflicts in Europe or Asia would be a grievous mistake. Fortunately, the United States had a commander-in-chief in FDR who knew better. Isolationism and appeasement had yielded bitter fruits for Europe, which almost succumbed to Hitler as a result.

Fortunately for America, leaders from both parties saw things differently. Franklin Roosevelt responded squarely to the Nazi threat, just as such successors as Harry Truman, Dwight Eisenhower, John F. Kennedy, and Ronald Reagan would not back down to the Soviets. (Indeed, despite his college thesis mentioned above, as president, John F. Kennedy took a much stronger stand against threats to democracy than his father had.)

In 2015, America faces not just one gathering storm, but a multitude of them. Radical Islamists in the guise of the Islamic State (ISIS) now have a caliphate—a home base in Iraq and Syria from which to murder, plot terror, and sow their ideology of hate around their world. Iran is pursuing nuclear weapons to threaten Israel and our other allies in the region, while President Obama seeks an accord that will only buy the Iranians more time to develop nuclear weapons and the missile systems to deliver them. China is secretly building up a vast military and not so secretly declaring its designs for regional hegemony. Vladimir Putin is seizing new European territories on Russia's borders with an audacity that would make Stalin proud, all while the West stands idly by.

These are adversaries who make no secret of their contempt for America and our current leaders. One of the most extreme examples is ISIS. They behead Christians, enslave women and children, and are plotting to spread terrorist mayhem around the world in pursuit of a deranged dream to impose Sharia law and raise the Islamic flag over every capital between Washington and Baghdad. Hillary Clinton, our former secretary of state, said that we need to "show respect for our enemies" and "empathize with their perspective and point of view."[38] But the men of ISIS do not deserve our respect or our empathy. They deserve nothing but our commitment to their destruction.

We can pretend, as President Obama, Hillary Clinton, and John Kerry do, that what animates ISIS and Al Qaeda and their affiliated groups is a misunderstanding of the West or a lack of jobs and opportunity in the Middle East. We can pretend that these are reasonable men who seek nothing more than a solution to the Israeli-Palestinian conflict or an apology for a drone strike in Pakistan and Yemen. But these are excuses. They are lies we tell ourselves to avoid the politically incorrect and troubling truth that what animates these terrorists is radical Islam.

Americans are not at war with Islam itself. The vast majority of Muslims do not share the views of these terrorists and mass murderers. But Muslim leaders have a responsibility to condemn individuals committing such violence, making it clear they are not martyrs for Islam. Islam has a problem when many of its leaders and faithful either support, condone, excuse, or just as troubling, turn a blind eye to those who use the religion as an excuse to murder innocents and seek to impose a brutal version of law that discriminates, silences, and slaughters.

It is all well and good to suggest that we let the Egyptians, Israelis, and Jordanians deal with their neighbors. Or that this is only a problem Europeans will face when synagogues are attacked, cartoonists murdered, and Jewish cemeteries vandalized. But unless we begin a full-scale ideological offensive to delegitimize radical Islam by calling it what it is, much as Ronald Reagan declared communism "the focus of evil in the modern world," we can be sure that these problems will come to America. They already have in the form of the Boston marathon bombing, the Fort Hood massacre, 9/11, and numerous other potential attacks that were thwarted only by vigilance and robust intelligence operations.

Isolationism, whether from those on the left who consider foreign affairs a distraction and put their faith in such organizations as the United Nations to keep America secure or from those on the right who believe open borders, free trade, and dismantling every U.S. military base overseas will keep America secure, puts us at risk. The world will not get safer on its own. Our enemies will not pack it up, throw in the towel, and go home. We have seen the fruits of two terms of an American president "leading from behind," and the world is more dangerous than it's been in decades. Appeasement, whether in the form of prisoner exchanges of hardened Guantánamo Bay terrorists to the Taliban or a lifting of U.S. sanctions on Iran in exchange for empty promises of delaying its nuclear ambitions, only emboldens. As Churchill put it, "An appeaser is one who feeds a crocodile, hoping it will eat him last."[39]

The solution is an American president who has a sober understanding of today's threats and a willingness to invest in building up U.S. military power. The paradox at the heart of U.S. foreign policy is that the greater the capability of our armed forces, the less likely they will have to be used.[40] In the months and years after World War II, this was understood by Democrats like Harry Truman and Scoop Jackson and Republicans like Arthur Vandenberg and Ronald Reagan. True, there were outliers, like Joe Kennedy, who was unchastened by World War II and went on to declare that America should "permit communism outside the Soviet Union to have its trial," shortly after President Truman announced the Marshall Plan in 1947.[41] Fortunately, Joe Kennedy was in the minority, and two generations of leaders, both Democrats and Republicans, crafted and executed a strategy to contain and ultimately defeat communism. The United States and the free world prevailed over the ideology "without firing a shot," as Margaret Thatcher said.

Today Barack Obama, Hillary Clinton, and the current crop of Democratic leaders have led us down the road of Joe Kennedy and shunned the legacy of Harry Truman. The same foolish plans to disarm in the 1930s that gave rise to Hitler's armies, Mussolini's air forces, and Hirohito's navies have been put in place again with more than $1 trillion in defense cuts. This was dangerous enough in an era of battleships and bombers. Today, when threats are more disparate and more lethal than ever with the proliferation of asymmetric weapons and nonstate actors who can kill thousands of innocents in a single act of terror, it is suicidal.

5

IN DEFENSE OF FEDERALISM

Ronald Reagan and the Fight Against
Richard Nixon's Welfare State

Every four years we tend to hear a lot about Ronald Reagan. There isn't a Republican candidate running for president who won't invoke his name. They will compare their records to his. They will cite his accomplishments. They will praise him. And they should. Our nation's fortieth president was the only twentieth-century president who successfully stood athwart the march of progressivism. His is a model not only for how to restrain the growth of big government, but also for how to do so cheerfully.

When Ronald Reagan came to Washington in 1981, he ushered in a revolution to restore limited government that bore his name. What followed were eight years of policy victory after policy victory, from lowering taxes to restoring the military budget and sending the Soviet Union to the ash heap of history. These were historic accomplishments at a time when the bipartisan consensus favored more government power in Washington, D.C., and détente with communism. Combined with the leadership of other great Cold Warriors like Pope John Paul II and Prime Minister

Margaret Thatcher, it was an inspiring time for a young man like me whose political and spiritual beliefs were still being formed.

But one of Ronald Reagan's greatest conservative achievements on the national level happened more than a decade earlier.

In 1969, when Reagan was governor of California, progressivism was on the march, and Lyndon Johnson's so-called War on Poverty was at the height of its popularity. In at least some ways, it was similar to the years I have been a governor. Then as now, Washington thought it knew best, as shown today in the federal government's attempts to impose the Medicaid expansion on state governments and to stand in the way of education reforms such as school choice. And then as now, the problem was not always a clash of political parties, as evidenced today by the justified frustration I hear from governors on both sides of the political aisle about all the ways Washington gets in the way of states' innovation and experimentation.

In 1969, it was not yet clear to many D.C. experts that the War on Poverty would cost more than $20 trillion in taxes and would wreak havoc in America's inner cities by destroying marriages, spawning crime, crushing minority urban families, and giving rise to a permanent underclass and a dependency culture. Unaware of what the welfare state would produce, Johnson's Republican successor in the Oval Office, Richard Milhous Nixon, believed in some of its principles, especially when it came to taking away power from the states and centralizing it in Washington.

Reagan disagreed. He understood that the number of persons living below the poverty line in America had been declining from 30 percent of the population in 1950 to 17 percent in 1965, and that the expansion of welfare policies Nixon sought would help lead to a dramatic increase in poverty in the years that followed. He also understood that there are limits to what the federal government

can do—constitutional limits to what is legal and practical limits
to what is possible.

Beginning in 1969, Reagan's principles led him to oppose a
bipartisan plan championed by a president of his own party that
would amount to the biggest expansion of welfare in American history. Instead, Reagan carved a different path for welfare reform. It
would be modeled decades later at the national level by a Republican Congress and President Bill Clinton in 1996.

Reagan provided a textbook example of how to craft policies
that helped the poor, despite familiar rhetoric from the Left about
Republicans' indifference to "income inequality" and lack of compassion for the needy. His welfare reform encouraged hundreds
of thousands of able-bodied Californians to leave the welfare rolls
and become productive, working members of the economy. He
also showed remarkable courage in being the lone governor among
forty-nine others who opposed Richard Nixon's attempt to federalize welfare.

Governor Reagan's success was all the more unlikely given that
big-government liberalism seemed all but invincible. But something remarkable happened when a governor from California
had the temerity to stand up against a president of his own party.
Conservatives fought back with arguments. They persuaded. And
they began chipping away at the liberal consensus that Washington, D.C., was the solution to poverty, which even most Republicans
had come to agree with. Ronald Reagan's—and arguably modern
conservatism's—first national policy victory halted a misguided
Republican attempt to expand LBJ's Great Society redistribution-
ist polices and further consolidate power in Washington, D.C.

This is that story.

January 5, 1967—Sacramento, California

The formidable task at hand couldn't shake the smile from Ronald Reagan's face as he addressed his constituents for the first time as their governor. The former movie star, who still sported his matinee-idol good looks, spoke calmly, with equal assurance in his delivery and in his convictions, the product of decades behind a microphone as a sports broadcaster and later as a national spokesman for General Electric. As he looked upon the swarm of well-wishers before him, he smiled frequently, even though there was little to smile about.

In many ways it seemed as if everything was stacked against the conservative upstart as he assumed his new duties as governor of the nation's most populous state. The sexual revolution was in full swing. Elements of the anti–Vietnam War movement had morphed into a full-fledged anti-American movement with powerful engines of support in the media and on university campuses. Only two years earlier, conservatism had suffered an electoral rout with the great Barry Goldwater at the top of the presidential ticket. Conservatism, it was thought, was a fringe movement confined to the pages of William F. Buckley's *National Review* and the mutterings of a few overzealous politicians. The Republican Party of Dwight D. Eisenhower and Richard Nixon might occasionally appease these so-called conservatives for political purposes, but the party had no intention of ever elevating one to national office again.

As he began his inaugural address to the people of California, Ronald Reagan had a different idea.

Reagan had inherited a budgetary basket case. The state would be bankrupt within months with the debt and deficits his liberal predecessor, Pat Brown, had racked up over eight years.

As a candidate, Reagan had made one of the centerpieces of his campaign a promise to rein in spending and reform the welfare program that was bankrupting the state. One in thirteen Californians was on welfare, and the rolls were increasing by forty thousand each month.[1] His advisors had told him that his only option was to raise taxes. Reforming the system was impractical, impossible. It wasn't the first time Reagan would overrule his advisors.

"We are a humane and generous people and we accept without reservation our obligation to help the aged, disabled, and those unfortunates who, through no fault of their own, must depend on their fellow man," Reagan declared. "But we are not going to perpetuate poverty by substituting a permanent dole for a paycheck. There is no humanity or charity in destroying self-reliance, dignity, and self-respect—the very substance of moral fiber."

His remarks provided a stark contrast to the national consensus. Lyndon Baines Johnson was at the zenith of his power in the White House, expanding government programs across the board. There were few problems in America, he believed, that couldn't be solved by more money and more manpower. It was how he approached the war in Vietnam and the so-called "War on Poverty" he had declared at home. LBJ's "Great Society" was a set of top-down government programs based on the assumption that states lacked the political will and ability to tackle poverty.

A generation earlier, Franklin Roosevelt had signed into law the first "welfare" program to provide relief to single, jobless mothers in the throes of the Great Depression. Even FDR saw it as a temporary emergency salve. He called government relief "a narcotic, a subtle destroyer of the human spirit."[2]

The program began the steady erosion of the family, with only single women eligible for the benefit, thus discouraging marriage and encouraging unwed motherhood. It also discriminated against African-American women, many of whom had jobs that therefore made them ineligible for the benefit. But the most perverse result of welfare was that it disincentivized work. It amounted to a

100 percent tax on earned income. Getting a job meant losing your welfare benefit.

Bearing the burden of the costs of the government program fell on the states. The welfare rolls swelled into the millions, creating a permanent class of Americans dependent on the government and with little motivation to seek work. Making problems worse, throughout the 1960s, liberal-leaning federal courts expanded the benefit. A 1968 Supreme Court decision struck down a requirement in forty states that required welfare recipients to live in a state for one year before receiving funds.

The new governor of the Golden State was incensed that the Supreme Court had created "instant welfare." The federal mandate, Reagan maintained, "creates nothing less than a bonus for migrating to California merely to get on our relief rolls."[3]

Though it was no secret that Ronald Reagan had ambitions for national office, he would not wait to begin chipping away at LBJ's failing welfare programs and changing the direction of the national debate about poverty from California. He ended his remarks by reminding those sitting before him of the curiously small flag atop the flagpole on the state capitol behind him.

"If, in glancing aloft, some of you were puzzled by the small size of our state flag . . . there is an explanation. That flag was carried into battle in Vietnam by young men of California. Many will not be coming home. One did—Sergeant Robert Howell, grievously wounded. He brought that flag back. I thought we would be proud to have it fly over the Capitol today. It might serve to put our problems in better perspective. It might remind us of the need to give our sons and daughters a cause to believe in and banners to follow.

"If this is a dream, it is a good dream, worthy of our generation and worth passing on to the next," he concluded. "Let this day mark the beginning."

A Year and a Half Later, August 8, 1968—Miami Beach

As the hour drifted past one o'clock in the morning, Richard M. Nixon was tired as hell.[4] It was pure adrenaline that kept him wide awake as he stared blankly at the television in his hotel suite.

The screen beamed the goings-on of the Republican National Convention across the street, which was on the verge of descending into total madness.

Hours earlier, Nixon had been convinced he was about to earn the party's nomination for president for the second time in his career.

Now he had serious doubts.

Eight years ago, he had come within a whisper—or, he felt, a few fraudulent votes in Chicago and LBJ's Texas—of the presidency against the charismatic John F. Kennedy.

And he was damned if he was going to let the presidency slip from his grasp yet again. And certainly not because an upstart Hollywood actor fancied playing the role of president of the United States.

The irony was that Ronald Reagan hadn't even wanted to be president. He had been dragooned into the race by a handful of overzealous aides. He also had no designs on the vice presidency. "There is absolutely no circumstance whatever under which I would accept that spot. Even if they tied and gagged me, I would find a way to signal by wiggling my ears," he had remarked. From the start, the convention had been a study in total chaos, thanks in Nixon's view to Reagan forces. Reagan demonstrators marched around the Miami Beach Convention Center to the tunes of "California" and "Dixie," with placards bearing slogans such as "I'm Gone on Ron."[5]

But Reagan wasn't the only problem. There was Rockefeller. There was always Nelson Rockefeller, the perennial liberal Republican spoiler, who was threatening Nixon's candidacy from the political left. A whisper campaign was making the rounds that Reagan and Rockefeller had united to deny Nixon the nomination, or at least to force a second ballot and a compromise candidate. As the chairman of the Republican National Convention, Congressman Gerald R. Ford, began the roll of the states to decide the party's nominee for president, the ever-paranoid Nixon was not entirely certain about how it would end.

As the roll call of states proceeded in the Miami Beach Convention Center, Nixon tallied more and more votes in his column. He needed 667 to forestall another round of balloting. And what was most disconcerting was that the two biggest states in the Union—Reagan's California and Rockefeller's New York—weren't going Nixon's way.

"California . . . eighty-six votes for Governor Ronald Reagan," Ford announced.

"New York, eighty-two votes for Governor Nelson Rockefeller."

And then there were the favorite sons in each state—not serious contenders, mere nuisances, but they, too, were eroding Nixon's lead.

Finally, it was Wisconsin, the state toward the end of the alphabetized roll call, that allowed Nixon's worries to fade. Its thirty votes put the former vice president over the top on the first ballot.[6] The pincer movement from the conservative and liberal wings of the party had failed.

If Reagan harbored any disappointment, he wasn't showing it. He appeared on the platform in front of thousands of cheering party faithful.

"This nation cannot survive four more years of the kind of policies that have been guiding us," he said into the microphone. He "proudly" endorsed the Nixon nomination for president and moved that the convention declare him the nominee unanimously. The audience before him roared.

Nixon sat back in his chair in his air-conditioned hotel room.

A smile crossed his face. He was on the verge of one of the most unlikely political comebacks in history. But the Ronald Reagan challenge would never quite go away.

One Year Later, August 8, 1969— White House, Washington, D.C.

"Mr. President," someone behind the camera told him, "we're live in five . . . four . . . three . . . two . . ."

On cue, Nixon looked up from his papers and flashed one of his strange smiles. "Good evening my fellow Americans," he said.

He had nervously shuffled his papers more than once before the red recording light on top of the camera in front of him came on. Since his razor-thin defeat of Democrat Hubert Humphrey in the general election, he had delivered a few addresses to the nation. But the natural introvert was never quite comfortable with the task. He couldn't shake the butterflies that accompanied the thought that he would momentarily be appearing in the living rooms of millions of Americans.

He had just returned from a trip around the world that had taken him to eight countries in nine days. On his way, he had met Neil Armstrong, Buzz Aldrin, and Mike Collins, who had just returned to Earth from the world's first moon landing. He had told the men that their endeavor had made it "the greatest week in the history of the world since the Creation." Now he was to address the nation on a totally different issue, but one that he felt would make some history of its own.

This evening's address was not on global, let alone celestial, matters. It was to turn to domestic affairs, to offer the nation his signature legislative initiative of his first term: a sweeping plan to reform, federalize, and expand welfare. Nixon had dubbed it the

"Family Assistance Plan." The name had come to him at the last minute. Not that he liked it very much. "It sounds kind of blah," Nixon confided to his aides.[7] But behind the bureaucratese was something deeply ambitious: a new federal entitlement program that even LBJ wouldn't have dared. In fact, some of the more progressive among LBJ's cabinet and economic advisors had considered a welfare program that would give every American a yearly minimum income, but they had considered proposing it political suicide.

Nixon was attempting a grand turnabout in domestic policy by taking welfare programs around the country and putting them in the hands of bureaucrats in Washington.

"After a third of a century of power flowing from the people and the states to Washington it is time for a New Federalism in which power, funds, and responsibility will flow from Washington to the states and to the people," Nixon announced that evening to millions of Americans who had turned on their televisions to see the president's address rather than their usual favorite programs, such as *Hogan's Heroes* and *Name of the Game*.

The "New Federalism" would give the federal government some powers, and delegate some powers to state and local governments. Welfare was firmly in the former camp. Welfare was a program that the federal government could handle more efficiently and fairly than the states. It demanded a national standard. The Social Security Administration would issue the checks. With a few more federal bureaucrats, Nixon thought, there would be efficiencies, maybe even cost savings.

With this proposal, Nixon was convinced, he had struck political gold. Which was one of the reasons press aides had requested time from the networks for a prime-time address. He believed he had found a policy solution that would satisfy everyone. If he took welfare programs from the states and gave the power to administer them to Washington, D.C., at a cost to the taxpayers of $6 billion, liberals would applaud the massive redistribution of wealth. Conservatives and many working-class Democrats, Nixon felt, would like the idea of a work requirement to penalize freeloaders taking taxpayer dollars.

"Nowhere has the failure of government been more tragically apparent than in its efforts to help the poor, especially in its system for people—wherever in America they live—to receive their fair share of opportunity," Nixon offered. He continued for another twenty minutes, occasionally glancing at the remarks in front of him.

"Abolishing poverty, putting an end to dependency—like reaching the moon a generation ago—may seem to be impossible. But in the spirit of Apollo, we can lift our sights and marshal our best efforts," Nixon said. He was convinced he would be the president who finally ended poverty. Providing an income floor for every American—$1,600 for a family of four with an additional $800 in food stamps—would ensure that no man, woman, or child would go hungry in America.[8] Nixon also wanted to provide an incentive for work, and therefore the first $720 of earned income was excluded from the benefit calculation.

Nixon concluded his address: "We can resolve to make this the year not that we reached the goal, but that we turned the corner—turned the corner from a dismal cycle of dependency toward a new birth of independence; from despair toward hope; from an ominously mounting impotence of government toward a new effectiveness of government, and toward a full opportunity for every American to share the bounty of this rich land. Thank you and goodnight."

He waited at his desk until the red camera light went dim.

Five Days Later, August 13, 1969—
Western White House, San Clemente, California

Back home in California, Nixon was feeling jubilant. His prime-
time address had drawn rave reviews. True, there was some belly-
aching from a few malcontents in the liberal wing of the Democratic
Party who were insisting Nixon hadn't gone far enough in providing permanent benefits to the nation's poor. But that couldn't be
helped, Nixon thought to himself. You couldn't please everyone.

The media, as the president had predicted, had lined up almost
unanimously in support of the Family Assistance Plan. "It is no
exaggeration to say that President Nixon's television message on
welfare reform and revenue sharing may rank in importance with
President Roosevelt's first proposal for a social security system in
the mid-1930s," declared the *Economist*. But it was the praise of his
old enemies in the liberal media that he treasured most. *The New
York Times* offered warm praise: The administration was to be applauded, the paper said, for its "abandonment of outmoded conservative doctrine."[9]

Congressional Republicans were also enthusiastic; the party's
leaders were already drafting the legislation to implement the plan.
The *Republican* war on poverty was even winning support from
surprising quarters—staunch conservatives. Nixon's federal welfare expansion was effectively a negative income tax, which had
been championed by renowned free market economist Milton
Friedman. The negative income tax was Friedman's brainchild, so
when it appeared in Nixon's proposal, he offered his wholehearted
support.

There was, however, one exception. A notable one. Ronald
Reagan was skeptical of the Nixon plan, which he was convinced
would cost taxpayers billions of dollars more than Nixon and his
administration were admitting. Reagan had become a conservative

icon; his views held sway. Which is what convinced the president to invite the California governor to his home.

Nixon's mission was simple: to charm Reagan. Even if he could not win him over to supporting his welfare reform program, Nixon would at least convince him to keep his opposition silent. Nixon was a longtime dealmaker. And, surely, Reagan couldn't ignore the political genius of the once-reviled Nixon's winning praise from the Left. Surely, Nixon felt, the two Republicans from California could come to an accord.

As Reagan exited his motorcade, accompanied by an aide, a young lawyer named Ed Meese, the president hurried to greet him. The two most prominent men in Republican politics smiled warmly, but they eyed each other warily.

The president directed Reagan to a small couch in his living room. On the left of the couch sat the president, in dark jacket and tie and immaculately polished wingtip shoes, his demeanor awkward and uncomfortable. On the right was the governor, tanned and relaxed, wearing a light tan jacket that seemed more fitting for the California weather.[10] In the room were a handful of the president's aides. Most notable among them was Daniel Patrick Moynihan.

Moynihan was to domestic policy what Henry Kissinger, Nixon's chief consigliere, was to foreign policy. A brilliant, Harvard-educated mind, Moynihan came to Washington in the Kennedy administration. The Democratic intellectual had impressed Nixon. Indeed, the Family Assistance Plan was a Moynihan brainchild.

Nixon and Moynihan made their pitch, knowing Reagan and Meese were suspicious of any plan to boost the welfare rolls by giving more power to Washington. Moynihan could be persuasive and today he was at his best. A new work requirement would incentivize job growth; states would have the welfare burdens of their overstretched budgets lifted; and "the welfare mess" would be cleaned up for good—and by a Republican administration, no less.[11]

Nixon smiled to himself as he watched Moynihan's case unfold. He could tell that Reagan and Meese were being convinced. And indeed they were—almost.

Two Years Later, June 1971—Sacramento, California

Reagan had found the Nixon presentation interesting, the arguments logical. But the plan didn't sit right. It rankled his conservative instincts. Even though the 1960s and 1970s were a time of broad social action on the national level by both parties, this didn't seem the right direction for the nation.

Since the San Clemente meeting, Reagan had appointed a task force, headed by his aide Robert Carleson, to study the issue. Fresh off a decisive re-election campaign as governor, Reagan intended to invest his political capital in a total overhaul of the state's welfare program.

He and his aides had dug deeply into research about welfare reform—both President Nixon's federal proposal and alternatives. What they discovered was troubling.

Nixon and Moynihan hadn't told the truth about how much their plan would cost. It would be billions more than they had estimated—as much as three times the $5 billion they have been telling the American public. Worse, the plan likely would increase the total number of welfare recipients, not reduce them.

Much to Nixon's chagrin, Reagan could not stay quiet about his concerns. Instead, he decided to come out, forcefully and publicly, against the Family Assistance Plan.

"I believe that the government is supposed to *promote* the general welfare," Reagan said in a televised debate on the Nixon plan. "I don't think it is supposed to *provide* it."[12]

Reagan had concluded that centralizing welfare in Washington and giving more power to the federal government over the lives of

Americans was the exact wrong thing to do. It wouldn't do any-thing to reduce the welfare burden to the taxpayer or encourage those who were down-and-out to find new work opportunities. It would make future welfare reform all but impossible: With Wash-ington in charge, it biased the program to provide *even more federal funding* in the future.

"Raising the annual family grant would become an election-year must," Reagan declared. "If there is one area of social policy that should be at the most local level of government possible it is welfare. It should not be nationalized—it should be *localized*," a mantra Reagan would repeat in speeches across the country.[13]

Reagan knew the logic of his case. And more important, he knew that if he explained it to Californians, they would understand it, too.

He proposed an alternative plan that would put states—not the federal government—in charge of the future of welfare. As governor of the most populous state in the country, he was well-positioned to do so. He could tinker and try reforms. This is what is meant by the states' being "laboratories of democracy," after all. He could try work requirements, making welfare "workfare." He could try increasing benefits to those who needed them most. He could limit the program by barring those fathers who left their children.

The only thing standing in his way was the Democrat-controlled state legislature. If they wouldn't budge, Reagan concluded, he would go over their heads with a ballot initiative that put the issue in the hands of voters. But the governor believed in the powers of persuasion. His staff organized 120 local groups around the state to deluge legislators with thousands upon thousands of letters sup-porting reform.

By the middle of that summer, the Democratic General Assem-bly Speaker, Robert Moretti, had had enough.

"Stop your cards and letters," he pleaded. "Governor, I don't like you, and I know you don't like me, but we don't have to be in love to get something worked out around here."[14]

Eight Months Later, February 1, 1972— Senate Finance Committee, Washington, D.C.

Nixon had so prioritized his welfare plan as his signature first-term achievement that he had it dubbed "H.R. 1" in the House of Representatives. It was supposed to be on a fast track to passage. But supporters of the bill hadn't counted on the opposition of Ronald Reagan, who had proved much more nettlesome than anyone expected. The California governor almost singlehandedly had kept the bill from passing.

He had successfully championed his own kind of welfare reform in California. To enact it, he had undertaken dawn-to-dusk, face-to-face meetings with the Democratic leadership in Sacramento.

They had gone into the negotiations thinking the governor a lazy, uninformed actor. They came out recognizing that he was a pro negotiator, a skill no doubt honed from his brass-knuckled negotiations with Hollywood studio executives as head of the Screen Actors' Guild. Reagan emerged with 80 percent of what he wanted out of a welfare reform bill, the California Welfare Reform Act.

Most important, the bill included a robust work requirement that every able-bodied welfare recipient accept regular employment, find a job, or participate in job training. Welfare recipients had to work off their welfare checks in community programs if they couldn't find jobs in the private or public sectors.

Once it was passed and signed into law, state welfare rolls began dropping almost immediately. Until the Reagan reform plan, the numbers had been growing at more than forty thousand individuals per month. Now they were declining by eight thousand per month.

The law saved California taxpayers $2 billion—not bad for a state whose overall annual budget was $9 billion.[15] Because able-bodied adults were working, and paying back their welfare checks, the state of California was able to increase the assistance it offered the truly needy by 43 percent.

Reagan's success in California hadn't deterred Nixon, who was still hell-bent on passing his signature domestic legislative proposal. He felt the momentum was with him. The bill had come out of the Ways and Means Committee on a vote of 21–3. Nixon had found an especially eager congressional ally in a young House member named George H. W. Bush, who had pushed the legislation forward. It subsequently went to the floor of the U.S. House of Representatives, where it passed 243 to 155.

Bush, Reagan's future running mate, had engaged in a spirited exchange of letters with the California governor—one of hundreds sparked by Reagan's missives to every federal legislator and governor in the country. Siding with Nixon, Bush challenged Reagan's estimates of the cost of the program. But Bush's support on the Nixon federal welfare plan had doomed his 1970 run for U.S. senator from Texas; his opponent, Lloyd Bentsen, repeatedly attacked Bush's support of "big welfare" and "higher taxes."[16]

Reagan had become an evangelist on behalf of welfare reform, not to mention a constant thorn in the side of the Nixon administration. Many in the White House called it "The Reagan Problem," and dealing with it had been one of Richard Nixon's preoccupations during his first term in office. Still, Reagan bore no ill will toward the president. The California governor had enthusiastically supported the commander-in-chief's Vietnam policies and the historic opening of China.

But his opposition to Nixon's Family Assistance Plan was unrelenting. He wrote letters to every governor and every member of the House and Senate with his analysis of why the FAP was a disaster.[17] He stood alone as the only one of the fifty governors at the National Governors Association to vote against the measure. It was a lonely road, but Reagan was determined to do right by the American taxpayer.

"The big villain . . . that has kept virtually all of our savings from being returned to the people in reduced cost of government," Reagan said in one interview, "is the thirty-five-year heritage of welfare programs that are out of control. And we find ourselves in a position of cutting back on the type of things people should ask of government—parks and everything else—actually cutting those to feed this welfare monster."[18]

As the bill was making its way through Congress, Reagan had flown to Washington to testify against the legislation. His genial, fact-based, and persuasive efforts put a final nail in the coffin of the Family Assistance Plan, and ground any momentum Nixon felt to a halt.

"We should measure welfare's success by how many people leave welfare, not by how many more are added," Reagan stated in front of the members of Congress. He proceeded to tell them that in California one of every twelve persons was on welfare; if Nixon's plan passed, that would increase to one out of every seven.

"It doesn't seem right to reduce a man's take-home pay with taxes and then send him a government dole which robs him of the feeling of accomplishment and dignity which comes from providing for his family by his own efforts," he testified. "By the same token, we feel that the able-bodied recipient should be given the maximum opportunity to support his family by doing work in his community which will benefit the community."

There was something remarkable about Reagan's testimony: his belief in decentralization, that programs could be better handled at the state and local levels than in Washington. Far ahead of his time and certainly out of step with Richard Nixon, Reagan insisted on autonomy from Washington bureaucrats. "It is almost impossible to hold a state accountable for effective administrative practices and policies under the present straight jacket of federal statutes, court interpretations, regulations, and abuses of administrative discretion. Give the states the broadest authority to administer the system with proper goals and objectives and then hold us accountable for our effectiveness in meeting these goals and objectives."[19]

Reagan's persuasive testimony—and his example of conservative principles to reform welfare put into practice in his home state—killed Nixon's plan once and for all. Amid growing opposition across the country, especially from conservatives, Nixon abandoned the plan amid his re-election campaign in 1972.

Even its most ardent supporters, such as Pat Moynihan, came to recognize the mistake that was federalizing welfare and providing a national minimum income. In a letter to William F. Buckley, Jr., in 1978, Moynihan wrote, "We were wrong about the guaranteed annual income! Seemingly it is calamitous. It increases family dissolution by some 70 percent, decreases work, etc. Such is now the state of the science, and it seems to me we are honor bound to abide by it for the moment."[20]

★   ★   ★

For Ronald Reagan, rejecting the welfare state wasn't just about the numbers and monetary cost of a broken system. It was about the moral cost. He saw a permanent class of Americans dependent on government handouts as eroding the dignity and self-sufficiency of the individual. What disturbed the California governor most wasn't that it was impossible to balance his state's budget with an exploding welfare program, but that an out-of-control welfare program meant more children being abandoned by their fathers, more addiction, more hopelessness. He wanted California parents to teach their children, by their example, lessons about the dignity of work, not lessons about how to stay dependent on government bureaucrats.

Reagan had also persuaded a historically blue state, and a Democratic legislature, of the merits of his case. It was a philosophical sea change in the way Californians, and ultimately the nation, viewed welfare. It also marked a major moment in his political career when even his critics acknowledged that he could get things done, not just talk eloquently about them.

In 2010, President Obama signed into law the Patient Protection and Affordable Care Act, better known as ObamaCare. Without a single Republican supporter, this was arguably the most partisan vote of a major legislative program in U.S. history. From a policy perspective, the horrors of ObamaCare are documented at length in the next chapter. From a constitutional perspective, the tip of the iceberg of its horrors is perhaps best captured by a question for which the Obama administration has never provided an adequate answer: If the federal government can make you buy something—such as an insurance policy—what can it *not* make you do?

Most of the opposition to ObamaCare centers on its mandate on employers and individuals to purchase health care, but its vast expansion of Medicaid, a health care safety net for those Americans who can't afford it, was in many ways more troubling. Ignoring the Tenth Amendment and the powers given to the states in our Constitution, the legislation required every state to expand Medicaid to nondisabled adults living at up to 138 percent of the poverty level. If the governors complied, the federal government would pick up the tab for the first few years. If governors didn't comply, they would lose all federal support for Medicaid in their states.

The U.S. Supreme Court agreed that the Medicaid expansion

was unconstitutional. The federal government could not compel states into submission. While the better-known part of that decision was that the ObamaCare mandate was constitutional under Chief Justice John Roberts's bizarre rationale that its penalties amounted to a "tax," the Court's conservative-leaning justices, along with liberals Elena Kagan and Stephen Breyer, rejected the legislation's sweeping assertions of federal power over the states. Chief Justice Roberts concluded that the Medicaid expansion was "a gun to the head"—an unconstitutional coercion of the states by Washington, D.C., and a violation of the Constitution's principle of federalism. ObamaCare could give states the option of expanding Medicaid, Roberts wrote, but if states decline to expand it, the Constitution does not allow the federal government to take away all of a state's pre-ObamaCare Medicaid funding.

Before ObamaCare, we didn't talk much about federalism—about the role of state and local governments in crafting policy. That's because it had been assumed and championed by both parties, at least for most of the twentieth century, that Washington, D.C., is where decision-making belongs. But that's not what our founding fathers had in mind when they crafted the Constitution. James Madison wrote in *Federalist* 45 that the powers of the federal government were to be "few and defined . . . most extensive and important in times of war and danger; those of the State governments, in times of peace and security."[21]

The manner in which our founders divided power between the federal and state governments was unique in the annals of political history. Never before had a nation "split the atom of sovereignty" by providing its citizens with "two political capacities, one state and one federal, each protected from incursion by the other."[22]

For the framers, this invention of federalism was no academic exercise. Every single one of them had lived under the tyranny of King George III *and Parliament*. Although the oppression they rebelled against was exacerbated by their exclusion from elections to choose members of Parliament, the founders understood that elections alone are no guarantee of liberty. History is rife with elected tyrants—and tyrannies of the majority.

In addition to elections, free societies require structural protections of freedom. One example is the separation of powers, on which political philosophers like Montesquieu placed a heavy emphasis, and in which the founders held great faith. But another example of a structural protection is federalism. The founding generations worried that politicians in a distant national capital would lose touch with the people of their states, a recipe for aristocratic rule and the abuse of power. As a result, the founders denied the federal government most governing powers. They gave those powers to the states, believing that national politicians wouldn't be able to abuse powers that the Constitution completely denied them.

As governor of Louisiana, I understood that the Medicaid expansion, as conceived by ObamaCare's original (coercive) language, was inconsistent with the balance of powers federalism strikes between state and federal governments. That alone was reason enough to oppose it. Like the dissenting opinion in the Supreme Court's ObamaCare decision, I believed that the "fragmentation of power produced by the structure of our Government is central to liberty, and when we destroy it, we place liberty at peril."[23]

In addition, at a more concrete level, I also believed the Medicaid expansion was, and remains, a raw deal for Louisianans, our state budget, and the quality of our health care. It would have moved as many as 171,000 Louisianans off private insurance and kept another 77,000 from obtaining private insurance. It would also have dramatically increased Medicaid's share of our state budget over the years, consuming resources that could have been spent on roads, education, or tax cuts.

The Left attacked me because I had turned down billions in federal money. That was "free money," I was told. Here's the rub: It wasn't free money. It was money that was hard earned by a taxpayer or money that we borrowed from China, placing a burden on our children and grandchildren.

Had we accepted that money, we would have bought into a system that is the exact wrong solution to rising health care costs. Medicaid is one of the most inefficiently run government programs in America. It not only costs billions of dollars per year, it delivers health care that in some cases is no better than if those on Medicaid had no insurance at all. In fact, one study in Oregon found that Medicaid "generated no significant improvement in measured physical health outcomes."[24] In other words, those who were completely uninsured were just as well off as those on Medicaid.

The American taxpayers spend $450 billion per year on this broken program, and President Obama wants to add 11 million more Americans into it, instead of privatizing health care and allowing states to chart their own path, as Reagan advocated on welfare reform. Like Hillary Clinton in the early 1990s, Obama has complete faith in a top-down approach that allows government to run—and ruin—your health care.

With exploding deficits, snowballing bureaucracies, and continuing layoffs from employers burdened by ObamaCare's mandates, the United States cannot afford many more years of the Obama-Clinton brand of government-run health care. It cannot afford many more years of a philosophy that has failed in every country and in every era that has tried central planning by national bureaucrats who turn citizens into subjects. And it cannot afford four more years of that philosophy's champions in the White House.

6

★ ★ ★

FROM HILLARYCARE TO OBAMACARE

The Left's Quest for Socialized Medicine

Health care represents an almost—but not quite—impossibly complex arena of public policy. It was an animating interest for me from a young age, in part because it is an area that touches all Americans during the course of their lives in profound ways. Before I became a governor, I worked at the U.S. Department of Health and Human Services, the National Bipartisan Commission on the Future of Medicare, and the Louisiana Department of Health and Hospitals.

During my lifetime, many attempts have been made to fix the broken aspects of our system, some more successful than others. President Barack Obama's Affordable Care Act is just the latest in a long line of wrongheaded steps. It is also, by far, the worst yet.

The political Left has been on a relentless march to socialize the U.S. health care system for a century now. Woodrow Wilson and his associates had pushed for national "sickness insurance" that would forever do away with poverty.[1] FDR had flirted with the idea as part of the New Deal, but ultimately decided against it. Bill and Hillary Clinton reintroduced the idea again in 1993. As this chapter details, their effort foundered on the rocks of a small but determined opposition. But the Left did not rest. They waited for the right time and the right president, and after sixteen years, they succeeded by passing ObamaCare in one of the most partisan votes in the history of the U.S. Congress. And as many of the most passionate advocates on the left openly admit, they are not satisfied. They seek nothing less than what they call a "single-payer" health care system, abolishing even the pretense that Americans have any choice in deciding which doctors to go to and which treatments to seek. It's what the rest of us call "socialism."

As someone who believes in empowering patients and using market forces to improve American health care, I oppose President Obama's law and believe we must repeal all of it—no matter what the conventional wisdom in Washington says. But we must also enact positive reforms to move our health care system in the right direction, because the status quo of American health care and insurance is simply not defensible.

The most fundamental question in health care policy is: Do you want the patient to be in control, working with his or her own doctor, or do you want a bureaucrat—whether from the government or your insurer—to be in control? The Left has its answer to this question: all-encompassing government. But as this chapter's story demonstrates, that is not an answer that the American people wanted when Hillary Clinton proposed it in 1993.

It is not an answer we want now.

And it is not an answer I will ever accept.

To paraphrase the leading protagonist of this chapter's story, government-run health care—be it HillaryCare, ObamaCare, or any variation—will remain the law over my cold, dead political body.[2]

This is HillaryCare's story.

September 24, 1992—Rahway, New Jersey

New Jersey had not voted for a Democratic presidential candidate since 1964.[3] But 1992 was going to be different. Bill Clinton was sure of it. The young and (relatively) handsome governor from Arkansas with the smooth tongue and upbeat attitude appeared unlike anything presidential politics had seen before. A baby boomer. A moderate who promised to marry the best of free enterprise with the empathy of an I-feel-your-pain attitude. A New Democrat.

All his life, Clinton's ambitions had been limitless. He had been told—by friends, family, teachers, and probably even a few nemeses—that he would one day be president. When he received cards from his girlfriend at Yale Law School, a head-turningly precocious liberal named Hillary Rodham, the cards usually had a picture of the White House on them. It was Clinton's lifelong dream, as he once said, to earn "a little asterisk by my name in the billion pages of the book of life."[4] Today's campaign stop in New Jersey, he believed, would put him one step closer.

The typical Clinton rally featured the campaign's theme song, Fleetwood Mac's "Don't Stop." Though it was originally written as a breakup song—"I know you don't believe that it's true," says a divorcée to her ex-husband, "I never meant any harm to you."—Clinton's cheering fans saw the song as an anthem of optimism. "Don't stop thinking about tomorrow," his supporters would sing. "Don't stop, it'll soon be here." The next four years would be "better than before," because "yesterday's gone, yesterday's gone."[5]

There was a sort of euphoria at events like this. A hope that after a painful recession, the future would be "better than before." That this young man—the Rhodes Scholar, the "first in his class," the political prodigy—would make their problems go away.[6] "Yesterday's gone, yesterday's gone."

At today's rally inside the headquarters of the pharmaceutical giant Merck & Company, there was the promise of changing America's health care system, which Clinton had blasted President Bush for ignoring. Bush, according to Clinton, had no solution to health care's rising costs. He had no help for the uninsured. He had no answers. He didn't care.

Clinton pledged to care. It was a premise at the center of his campaign. And to prove he cared, he was there today with a promise to unveil the details of his health care plan.

Health care, Clinton declared, "is a matter that is critical to the future of this country's survival." Its problems include rising costs, bureaucratic complexity, and millions of uninsured. "We cannot go on like this."[7]

There was much in Clinton's speech that everyone, of any ideological perspective, could embrace. When he vowed to "drastically simplify the administrative costs of the American health care system," he sounded like a wonky technocrat. When he pledged to find $700 billion in savings, without cutting Medicare benefits, he sounded like a magician. When he said we must "quit having the Federal Government try to micromanage health care," he sounded like a Republican.[8]

There were, however, some ominous elements—and omissions—in Clinton's plan, for anyone who cared to look for them. It appeared that Clinton was prepared to saddle small businesses with a burden many believed they couldn't afford. And despite Clinton's promise of details, the speech left most of the hard questions about health care unanswered, including the hardest, and most important, question of all: Who, other than small business owners, would pay for the universal coverage Clinton promised?[9]

No matter. Details were bait for critics. They could wait. Until after the election. Until after the White House was his. Until after he earned that "little asterisk by my name in the billion pages of the book of life."

For now, for today, the young governor on the cusp of victory could feel sure that the speech accomplished everything he wanted. The next day's newspapers would run headlines touting his "Plan to Curb Health Care Costs" and his speech's emphasis on "Free-Market Forces."[10] Audience members would tell reporters they were "glad to hear him say that private enterprise has to stay in the center of this issue."[11]

As Clinton worked the rope line after the speech, with perhaps the sound of applause and the lyrics of "Don't Stop" ringing in his ears, he eyed a mom holding a baby. Approaching the couple, like the natural politician he was, he got close enough to say hello; close enough to shake her hand; and even close enough for the baby to throw up on him.

"That's what babies do," Clinton said with the smile of the born politician.[12] Of the natural campaigner. Of the unflappable. Of the unstoppable.

Nine Months Later, June 15, 1993—Washington, D.C.

Sitting in an increasingly tense meeting across from Congressman Jim Cooper, the First Lady of the United States may have been reminded of her husband. Like the president, Cooper was a young (thirty-nine), southern (Tennessee) former Rhodes scholar who had graduated from a top law school (Harvard). True, there were differences. Cooper was thinner, more formal, and far more aloof.[13] But there was one similarity that mattered more today than any other. Both men claimed to be "New Democrats."

Hillary Clinton was not a New Democrat. Nor was she a self-proclaimed Old Democrat. In the summer of 1993, the only thing close observers were sure Hillary Clinton believed in was Hillary Clinton.

Profiled as a college senior by *Life* for an impromptu commencement address that blasted the supposed conservatism of Wellesley's invited guest (the first black senator elected in American history), Hillary Rodham had always stood out from most of the men and women around her. She seemed smarter, more ambitious, and much more confident in her own ability to ask the right question, find the right solution, and arrive at The Truth.[14] From college to law school to Arkansas, she couldn't help but often look around a room and assume that she, with the possible exception of her husband, was the smartest person in it.[15] And if she often seemed quick to judge, it was only because she was judging inferiors. If she often seemed uncompromising, it was only because she was so sure she was right.

For the past five months, ever since her husband had appointed her to direct the White House's Health Care Task Force, her virtues had been on full display—not to the public (the task force's proceedings were secret), nor to the six hundred members of the task force (who toiled away writing policy papers sent to the task force's high command), but to the small group of a half dozen cabinet secretaries and handful of White House advisors who were privy to her decision-making process.[16] She worked tirelessly, absorbed vast amounts of information, and directed a mind as impressive as her husband's, but with a discipline and focus he could never match.

But if the task force had brought out Hillary's virtues, it had also brought out her less appealing characteristics. Information was kept from economic advisors skeptical of a big, bureaucratic, expensive solution.[17] Skeptics were dismissed as "part of the system," and thus "part of the problem."[18] Republicans were excluded almost entirely. Secrecy was mandated. Control was essential. The Truth was out there, and once Hillary had discovered it, she would deliver it to the nation's mere mortals like Moses coming down from Mt. Sinai. Heretics beware.

In today's meeting with Congressman Jim Cooper, Hillary quickly realized that Cooper was among the heretics standing in her way. She had probably hoped to hear that he was ready to support her, or at least to reserve his judgment until the task force had completed its business and proposed a bill to Congress. But that's not what Hillary was hearing now from Cooper.

A New Democrat, Cooper was worried about the ideological direction of the task force.

He said he would not be able to support her plan.

He said he would be proposing his own.[19]

As Hillary listened to Cooper's message, outrage and shock built inside her. Who was *he* to defy *her*? How dare a junior congressman oppose a mission as right and righteous as hers![20]

If her husband had been in her place, he might have left Cooper with the impression that the dialogue should remain open, that they were still friends, and that he still wanted Cooper on his team. But Hillary was not her husband. And the meeting, though clarifying for both parties, was not a happy one.[21]

This was war. Cooper wasn't a principled public servant searching for a compromise. He was an enemy soldier, and in the face of the enemy, it was not in Hillary's nature to hold her fire or show any quarter. The Cooper plan must be destroyed.[22]

Three Months Later, September 22, 1993—Washington, D.C.

Senator Phil Gramm was a Civil War buff, and tonight he was thinking of a small hill in southern Pennsylvania called Little Round Top.[23] It was there, in the summer of 1863, that Colonel Joshua Lawrence Chamberlain had led his outnumbered regiment, the Twentieth Maine, against charge after charge of gray-clad attackers. "We've got to be stubborn today," the Maine professor-turned-soldier had said to himself.

One hundred and thirty years after Chamberlain's men saved the Union army's left flank, and perhaps the republic itself, Phil Gramm, another former professor, surveyed the scene at tonight's joint session of Congress. Before the Texan was a popular Democratic president, emboldened by the Left's euphoria over returning to the White House after a dozen years in the wilderness, about to unveil the signature legislative initiative of his eight-month-old administration. High above Gramm in the gallery was the First Lady, author of that initiative, peering down on a landscape largely of her making. And around him were members of the House of Representatives, where Democrats outnumbered Republicans 258 to 176, and his fellow members of the Senate, where there were 12 more Democrats than Republicans.

"We've got to be stubborn today," Gramm told himself.[24]

Gramm was nothing if not stubborn. "I didn't come to Washington to be loved," he often said, "and I haven't been disappointed."[25] Elected to the House as a conservative Democrat in 1978 (back when such things existed), he fought so hard for Ronald Reagan's budget that his party kicked him off the Budget Committee. Gramm promptly resigned his seat, switched his party, and campaigned for his old seat as a Republican. He won in a landslide. Two years later, in 1984, Texas sent to the Senate the former economics professor with the heavy drawl, balding head, squinty eyes, rimless glasses, and awkward-looking face, which some said looked a lot like E.T.'s grandfather—or Darth Vader, minus the helmet.[26]

Tonight, Gramm listened intently as President Clinton declared to Congress and a television audience of millions that his wife's task force was almost finished. Their efforts, and the future enactment of their plan, were akin to "settling the frontier" or "landing on the moon"—another chapter in a national history of "obstacles overcome" and "new horizons secured." They had found the perfect solution to the problems within America's health care system. "It is a magic moment," he proclaimed, "and we must seize it."[27]

Throughout Clinton's hour-long address, Gramm heard compelling stories of people the president and First Lady had met in their travels across America. Biting his lower lip and exhibiting the empathy that had helped him beat his predecessor, Clinton challenged legislators "to look into the eyes of a sick child who needs care; to think of the face of the woman who's been told not only that her condition is malignant but not covered by her insurance; to look at the bottom lines of the businesses driven to bankruptcy by health care costs," and "to look at the for-sale signs in front of the homes of families who've lost everything because of their health care costs."[28]

These stories were not news to Senator Gramm. He knew the system needed fixing, and he had a plan of his own, which could not have been more different from ClintonCare or HillaryCare, as many were already calling it due to the involvement of its principal architect. Gramm wanted to empower patients through tax-free savings accounts and tax credits for working families that needed them. He would use market forces to bring down costs and expand access to insurance. His proposal included no mandates on businesses, no mandates on individuals, and no big new government bureaucracies.

Gramm also knew that HillaryCare, far from fixing problems, would only exacerbate them. It would perform "life-threatening surgery on the world's greatest health care system"—a system that, despite serious flaws, still discovered 90 percent of the world's prescription drugs, developed 95 percent of its medical procedures, and attracted large numbers of sick Canadians and Europeans who traveled to the United States to escape waiting lists and receive the kind of high-quality medical care they could not find in their own countries.[29]

Gramm understood that HillaryCare would make the United States look a lot like socialist countries with government-run medicine. It was based on (1) government subsidies; (2) a government mandate on employers to purchase employees' insurance; (3) government standards for all insurance plans; (4) government-run cooperatives called alliances that would negotiate insurance contracts, collect premiums, and buy insurance for entire regions; and (5) a new government agency called the National Health Board, which would impose price controls on doctors and insurers.[30] The results would include layoffs, rationing, canceled plans, higher taxes, explosive spending, fifty-nine new programs or bureaucracies, and seventy-nine new federal mandates.[31]

To his dismay, Gramm watched President Clinton deny, hide, or gloss over all these realities in his speech. Americans were not told that they'd no longer be able to see the doctor of their choice. Or that many owners of small businesses would face bankruptcy because of the employer mandate. Or that their president, a supposedly New Democrat, was proposing an intrusion into one-seventh of the nation's economy unrivaled in its scope by the New Deal or the Great Society.[32] Instead, Americans heard lofty rhetoric about "new horizons" and a "magic moment."[33]

Even more dismaying to Gramm was that most Republican senators believed it was politically necessary to give the popular president most of what he wanted, lest they be accused of standing athwart the march of progress. Twenty-three of his fellow Republicans, including Senate Minority Leader Bob Dole, had already signed on to a plan that Gramm considered "socialism with a smile."[34] It included government subsidies, purchasing alliances similar to Clinton's, and even an individual mandate to purchase health insurance. "Effective January 1, 2005," the *Republican* bill said, "each individual who is a citizen or a lawful permanent resident of the United States shall be covered under a qualified health plan."[35]

Gramm knew that the attitude of most Republicans in Washington was, as Bob Dole said, "If we want to be players, we'd better participate. The train's going to leave the station." But sitting stone-faced at tonight's joint session of Congress, at the high-water mark of the Clinton presidency, Phil Gramm had a different strategy in mind.

"We," he said to himself, "have to blow this train up."[36]

Eleven Days Later, October 3, 1993—Aboard Air Force One

Hillary Clinton was flying high, literally and figuratively. As she boarded *Air Force One* for today's flight to California, a "chorus of applause" greeted her. And why not? In the ten days since her husband's speech, she had wowed audiences at town hall meetings, the United Nations, and five congressional committee hearings.

Speaking without notes—as, in her carefully chosen words, "a mother, a wife, a daughter, a sister, a woman"—Hillary had disarmed critics and won over skeptics left and right. True, she may not have had all of the president's natural charisma—maybe no one else did—but she made up for it with a tireless work ethic, including months of studying the plan she was presenting. Throw in a steady dose of sucking up to old congressmen—she even called in to Representative John Dingell's radio interview to note the anniversary of a bill his *father* once introduced—and you had the making of a tour de force.

Hillary had expected health care reform to be a tough fight. But flying west from Washington, she read an article in the *New York Times* that suggested the fight was nearing an end, almost before it had even begun. "Hillary Rodham Clinton dazzled five Congressional committees last week," reported the *Times*, "advocating health care legislation in the most impressive testimony on as complete a program as anyone could remember, and raising hopes that an issue that has stymied Congress for 50 years was now near solution."

Maybe this was going to be easier than she had thought?

Of course, that would depend on Republicans, particularly in the Senate, where the Clintons needed sixty votes to defeat a filibuster.

"The single most puzzling question after the first week of Congressional consideration of the issue," the *Times* article noted, "was where are the Republicans going?"

Later That Fall, 1993—Washington, D.C.

As Phil Gramm walked with his colleague John McCain out of their meeting and toward the Senate floor, he knew what needed to be done. He needed to slow Hillary Clinton's momentum. He needed to show that the passage of HillaryCare was not inevitable. And he needed to inject some steel into the spine of the Republican Party.

"If you're wrong on this," said McCain, "you can give up any idea of running for president."

Gramm was favored to be one of two or three leaders in any Republican presidential primary field in 1996. But personal ambition was the last thing on Gramm's mind that day.

"John," he said, "if we lose this issue, it won't do any good for me to become president, because I can't fix this thing."

Once HillaryCare was passed, there could be no going back— for quality medical care, for the federal budget, for the nation Gramm loved.

That's why Gramm walked straight to the floor of the United States Senate, delivered a no-holds-barred critique of Hillary Clinton's plan to socialize American medicine, and finished with a rallying cry for conservatives suddenly energized by his words. "The Clinton health care bill," declared Phil Gramm, "is going to pass over my cold, dead political body!"[37]

Early the Next Year, January 1994—Washington, D.C.

Hillary had been to this rodeo before. Her husband, always eager to please everyone, didn't want to take a stand. Others at today's Oval Office meeting—advisors such as David Gergen, Rahm Emanuel, and John Podesta—were encouraging his instincts. Sellouts, she almost certainly was thinking to herself!

The item up for debate was the president's upcoming State of the Union address—specifically, whether he should raise a writing pen during the speech and threaten to use the pen to veto any legislation that did not mandate and pay for universal health insurance.

The Gergen crowd argued it made little sense to limit the president's room to compromise. Already, his plan was losing a bit of momentum. Conservatives like Phil Gramm were blitzing the country with town hall meetings, radio interviews, and television appearances to inform Americans about the problematic details, shaky financials, and troubling consequences of Hillary Clinton's health care plan. Would the president really veto a bill that was 99 percent perfect? What about one that was 98 percent perfect?

But Hillary wasn't about to bend to their second-rate minds, or their old-school politics. These advisors were part of the system. When her husband left office, health care would be a memory for them. For Hillary, it would be her legacy.

So at today's meeting, Hillary argued forcefully for the dramatic veto threat, and at the end of the day, her husband gave her what she wanted. When it came to health care, he always did, especially in recent weeks when he was hoping to make amends after an *American Spectator* exposé about his sexual infidelities in Arkansas.

Later that month, when Clinton waved his veto pen and vowed to "come right back here and start all over again" if Congress didn't give him universal health care, the First Lady looked on from the gallery.

And smiled.[38]

Two Months Later, March 4–5, 1994—Annapolis, Maryland

By the beginning of March, five months after the *New York Times* had gushed over Hillary Clinton's charm offensive, the momentum had shifted. After Phil Gramm's "cold, dead political body" speech galvanized his fellow conservatives, they had led the effort to inform Americans about the truth behind HillaryCare's promises, and Americans did not like what they learned. Its alliances were too bureaucratic. Its numbers didn't add up. Its employer mandate could crush small businesses.

Whereas supporters had once outnumbered opponents by almost a two-to-one margin in public opinion polls, opponents now narrowly outnumbered supporters.[39] But the public's opposition wasn't yet large enough for Phil Gramm to declare victory, especially because his own party was still flirting with HillaryCare.[40]

Gramm was in Annapolis that day for his caucus's health care retreat, and Senator John Chafee, one of the Senate's most liberal Republicans, had organized the meeting around presentations by liberal pollsters and consultants.[41] Chafee was the author of the individual-mandate bill Gramm called "socialism with a smile."[42] The Rhode Island liberal had recently predicted, "We will have major health reform this year."[43]

Gramm had a single goal for the retreat. It was not to figure out how to fix Chafee's bill. It was not to fix Clinton's bill. It was to show his colleagues, in particular Bob Dole, that passing a government-run health care bill was terrible for the country and dangerous for their political futures.

On price controls and rationing, Gramm believed "they have been employed in all times, in many places, and never, ever, have they worked."[44]

On alliances, he liked to ask, "If consumer cooperatives the size of states can be efficient, why don't we see them operating in any other market?"[45]

On employer mandates, Gramm could quote studies estimating that the unaffordable mandates would kill "3.1 million jobs."[46]

On central planning, he would ask, "Where on this planet does the government do a good job of running anything or controlling the cost of anything?"[47]

On federal spending for new entitlements, Gramm was sure "this is basically a health care plan that could bankrupt the government."[48]

More than anything, Gramm believed, "When my 'mawma' gets sick, I want her to talk to a doctor and not a government bureaucrat."

Speaking more than anyone else at the retreat, Gramm made clear that, in his words, this was "not a battle that was going to end in a whimper." If Bob Dole wanted to run for president (he did), and if he faced Phil Gramm in a Republican primary (he would), Dole would have to answer for any support of HillaryCare, Chafee-Care, or any other nod toward socialized medicine. The fight over health care was "a real war," said Gramm, and "if they got in the line of fire, they were going to get hit."[49]

Gramm knew his strategy at the retreat had succeeded later that month, when Bob Dole abandoned John Chafee's "socialism with a smile."[50]

Three and a Half Months Later, June 20, 1994—Washington, D.C.

Hillary Clinton was angry. Very angry. She had expected liberal special-interest groups to help her impose HillaryCare on the American people. Big labor was supposed to be on her side. So were so-called consumer advocacy groups. But their political performance had been, up to this point, unacceptable, at least so far as Hillary was concerned.

Today she had called them to the Executive Office Building's Indian Treaty Room for a dressing-down. Pounding her podium so hard it was shaking, she scolded them as if they were schoolchildren.[51]

For too long, they had been "taking it for granted that Congress will pass a bill." That assumption was now highly dubious. Support was plummeting. An increasingly informed public was turning against them. And Hillary knew who to blame: her allies.

The problem was that the people in the Treaty Room were greedy. They were supposedly the plan's proponents. But they kept "asking for this and that" to be added to it. They wanted "parochial victories." They weren't "on message."

As her anger built and built, as her podium continued to shake, the First Lady never considered the possibility that the problem wasn't the plan's proponents.

It never occurred to her that the problem was the plan.

One Month Later, July 19, 1994—Boston, Massachusetts

By mid-July, support for HillaryCare was in free fall. Only about a third of the country supported it.[52] If the Clintons didn't make some course corrections between now and 1996, they would lose more than the health care debate. They'd lose the White House.

Bill Clinton was too clever a politician not to realize this. He knew Congress was too frightened of public opinion to pass his wife's plan in its purest form. So, after an address to the National Governor's Association, in answer to a question by then-governor Ben Nelson, Clinton backed away from the uncompromising veto threat he had made in January. No longer would he reject, sight unseen, any compromise that did not include a mandate and funding for universal coverage.[53]

Instead, he would accept coverage "somewhere in the ballpark of ninety-five percent upwards." He was also "open to any solution" on funding it. "There may be some other way than an employer mandate," he conceded.[54]

The president probably believed he was just stating the obvious. Compromise had been in his nature all along. It was now plainly necessary. Who could object?

After his question-and-answer session was over, Clinton walked away from the podium. The looks on the faces of his aides, racing toward him, were the first sign that he was in trouble. A message from the White House operator was the second: His wife was on the phone.[55]

The president put the phone to his ear and heard a tone of voice with which he was all too familiar. The First Lady was furious.

"What the f**k are you doing up there?!" she roared.[56]

The next day, he retracted his statement. He once again promised to veto anything that didn't mandate and fund universal coverage.[57]

Little did he know that this was one promise he could keep—because Congress would never give him the opportunity to sign HillaryCare, Clinton-lite, or anything in between. It was all way too much big government for Congress's increasingly informed and adamant constituents.

Three and Four Days Later, July 22–23, 1994—
Portland, Oregon; Seattle, Washington

For Hillary Clinton, July 22 was supposed to be the beginning of the last great battle of her health care crusade. She was in Portland that day to personally launch the "Health Security Express." Its purpose was to send an unmistakable signal to America's representatives in Washington. It would soon accomplish that purpose, but not in the way Hillary had intended.

Taking a page out their 1992 campaign playbook, the Clintons had decided on a quartet of cross-country bus tours to rally support for health care reform. Departing for the nation's capital from Portland, Dallas, Independence, and Boston, each bus would make frequent campaign-style stops to tout health care reform. With live rock bands, Hollywood celebrities, testimonials from carefully recruited "Reform Riders," and all the balloons and stagecraft special interest money could buy—the caravans were funded by labor unions and left-wing political action organizations—each carefully designed stop would create the impression that the American people loved HillaryCare.[58]

At least, that was the plan.

The problem was that the protesters at Hillary's opening speech almost outnumbered her supporters.[59] They carried signs that said, "Beware ClintonCare!" and "Do you enjoy the *compassion* of the IRS and the *service* of the Post Office . . . if so, you'll love Government-Run Health Care!"[60] Overhead a plane flew a banner warning, "Beware the Phony Express."[61] This was not the image Hillary had hoped to create for tonight's network news.

Things only got worse when the caravan hit the road. "When the first buses reached the highway, they found a broken-down bus wreathed in red tape symbolizing governmental bureaucracy and hitched to a tow truck labeled 'This is Clinton Health Care.' "[62]

And when the buses reached their next stop, Seattle, the Clintonites knew something was *really* wrong.

Back in 1992, Bill Clinton had drawn a crowd of about seventy-five thousand people in Seattle. But today, only about twelve hundred people showed to hear the First Lady—not counting the many protesters.[63] Seattle was her Waterloo.

Looking down on her opponents—literally and figuratively—Hillary refused to see them as patriots concerned about the course of their country. She couldn't. Instead, she told herself they were "unbalanced" and "alienated" and "mean-spirited."[64] How could they not be? They disagreed with *her*.

But regardless of whether she was right about their character (she wasn't), there was no denying their numbers. Portland and Seattle were just the tip of the iceberg. Across the twenty-seven-hundred-plus miles between Seattle and D.C., Hillary's opponents were a majority. And in the face of a bus tour choreographed to create an inflated appearance of support for the Clintons, the real majority was not about to remain silent. They didn't just dislike HillaryCare. They *hated* it. And they were prepared to punish at the ballot box anyone, of any party, who supported it.

The "Health Security Express" quickly turned into a debacle. Sometimes only about twenty people showed up for HillaryCare rallies. At other times, opponents vastly outnumbered supporters. Frequently, stops were canceled entirely, so the press couldn't take embarrassing pictures showing how many more people opposed the Clintons than supported them.[65]

By the time the four beleaguered bus tours arrived two weeks later on the steps of the Capitol—where once again, turnout was meager[66]—two lessons were clear, one political, one philosophical. First, as Congressman Porter Goss explained, "Contrary to what the White House war room and political consultants might believe, government is not like a campaign. Every time you run into trouble, you cannot just climb aboard a bus and run over the truth."[67]

That was a political lesson, and it was, for Hillary, unexpected. But the second lesson probably surprised her even more: Americans don't want government-run health care.

Hillary could still, if she chose, believe she was the smartest person in every room. She could even believe she knew what was best for 260 million Americans. But those Americans—we Americans—still have a voice, because we still have a vote. The men and women we send to Congress still have to answer to us every two years. And the "Phony Express" made crystal clear that we did not want what Hillary Clinton was trying to sell us.

HillaryCare was dead.

HillaryCare's official obituary was written two months later, when Democratic majorities in both houses of Congress declined to hold any vote on any health care legislation. "I am very sorry that this means Congress isn't going to reform health care this year," read a written statement released by President Clinton on September 26, 1994.

Phil Gramm was not sorry at all. "I think it was the most positive thing we have done in many years in the Senate," Hillary's chief foe said with his heavy drawl. On some days, his office had received more than a thousand calls demanding that Congress reject HillaryCare. "This is American democracy at its best."

Later that fall, voters threw the Democratic majority out of Congress in an election in which health care, according to Gramm, was "the dominant factor." Not a single Republican incumbent lost. The repudiation of the president, the First Lady, and their party was complete.

★　★　★

Unfortunately, the American people's victory over socialized medicine was far from final. Two decades later, Congress passed, and

President Obama signed, the Orwellian-named Patient Protection and Affordable Care Act.

Quickly dubbed ObamaCare, it looked a lot like HillaryCare.

Like HillaryCare, ObamaCare has an employer mandate.

Like HillaryCare, it kills small-business jobs.

Like HillaryCare, it vastly expands the welfare state.

Like HillaryCare, it raises taxes.

Like HillaryCare, it raises many purchasers' premiums.

Like HillaryCare, it decides what must be included in an insurance policy.

Like HillaryCare, it establishes new federal bureaucracies that stand between patients and their doctors.

Although there are some differences between HillaryCare and ObamaCare—in many ways, ObamaCare is even worse—the most significant difference is this: HillaryCare is history, and ObamaCare is the law. Because the president had just enough Democratic senators to defeat a Republican filibuster of ObamaCare, and was willing to use parliamentary maneuvers and tricks even after they lost the election to replace Ted Kennedy, its dangers are not theoretical; they are clear and present. It raises premiums on the individual market by twenty-one hundred dollars per family; kicks 4.7 million Americans off their health plans; burdens our budget deficit with $2 trillion in new spending; raises taxes by $1 trillion; and reduces the number of workers in the American workforce by 2.3 million.

The next president must do everything possible to change that.

To fix ObamaCare, we must begin by repealing it. Not just some of it. Not just most of it. All of it—which requires us to eliminate all of its eighteen tax increases and not replace its $1 trillion in raised revenue with new tax hikes.

To fix ObamaCare, we must also recognize that by many measures, the American system of health care is the best in the world. It is a source of incredible innovation at the cutting edge of medical science, providing high-quality care to people who need it. We have some of the best doctors, nurses, researchers, and provider systems on earth. When world leaders need complex surgery and lifesaving treatment, they often fly to us. It is here, in America, where treatments are discovered, methods are improved, and diseases are cured. We cannot jeopardize what is right about our health care.

But to fix ObamaCare, we must also look with open eyes at measures by which the American system of health care is the worst of both worlds—and that was true before ObamaCare. For starters, it is extraordinarily expensive. This is partly because Americans aren't interested in just managing pain, but in curing diseases; partly because market-warping government policies and regulations drive costs higher and incentivize monopolization over competition; partly because Americans have a limited choice of health insurance options; and partly because patients and providers are insulated from the true costs of health care services.

This last cause of soaring expenses is particularly problematic. Most people have no incentive or opportunity to shop and compare prices and services as they do in nearly every other market. And government policies and sweeping regulations have only served to make it worse. It's long past time that we step back, look at what's wrong with our system, and ask what we want it to look like if we tear down the existing market-warping problems and start afresh.

I put together a plan to make health care more affordable by pushing it toward being a true competitive marketplace; to create a solid safety net for the poorest of the poor and the sickest of the sick, including those with preexisting conditions; and to enhance patient choice by removing obstacles to portability and consumer selection.

The principle behind this proposal is that, rather than trusting the government to fix problems and get everything right, we should trust the American people to know what's best. It focuses on controlling the health care issue that matters most to Americans—skyrocketing health costs—through free market principles, rather than HillaryCare-style price controls, which lead to rationing. It also empowers the states to enact reforms that can bring down costs, while guaranteeing access for individuals with pre-existing conditions. Rather than stifling states with additional regulations from Washington, my plan offers them incentives to improve their insurance markets in ways that offer more choice and lower costs.

The upshot is that Americans will enjoy new avenues to buy portable health insurance they can own themselves—through their church, alumni group, or trade association—and lower premiums, too. In fact, the Congressional Budget Office previously analyzed reforms similar to my proposals and found that they could reduce individual health insurance premiums by thousands of dollars per family.

Recently, the Left gave us an instructive lesson on why this debate about a conservative alternative is so important. The advocacy group Families USA—one of the special interest organizations that funded Hillary Clinton's disastrous "Health Security Express"—released a report calling for a veritable orgy of new ObamaCare-related spending: new subsidies, insurance mandates, and even a proposal to extend subsidized insurance to illegal immigrants. It's an important reminder, first that the Left will always want more government intrusion in health care—of the kind Clinton proposed and Obama passed—and second that conservatives can never hope to outspend the Left by acting as cheap liberals. That's why it's so important for our party to outline a conservative—repeat, *conservative*—vision for health care.

I recognize there are other ObamaCare alternatives out there; I welcome their ideas, and relish a debate about market-oriented alternatives to the administration's government-centered approach.

But I would caution that conservatives need to focus on truly conservative health reforms and not merely a slightly-less-liberal plan. History tells us it's critical to fashion smart conservative policies, policies that stand up for freedom and the rights of patients, rather than trying to function as cheap liberals, expanding government slightly less than the Left.

We won this war of ideas in the battle against Hillary Clinton's government-run health care plan. It is not too late to win it in the battle against Barack Obama's.[68]

PART III

DIVISION AND INDECISION

7

★ ★ ★

A PARTY DIVIDED

The Great Republican Crack-Up of 1912

I once commented that the GOP needs to "stop being the stupid party." When I said that, my comment was directed at the participants and party elites who in 2012 had guided Republicans to another embarrassing defeat against one of the most unpopular and rudderless presidents in memory. Our party leaders are pretty good at saying "no" to liberals' misguided answers to the nation's problems, but too often our party stops there, rather than offering answers of our own. They rightly resolve to repeal ObamaCare, but they don't offer a health care proposal of their own. Nor do they offer detailed plans for energy independence, school choice, or a stronger foreign policy where our friends trust us and our enemies respect and fear us. We need to be a party of solutions, and until we are, we will be, to a degree, the stupid party.

At some point since Ronald Reagan left office, the Republicans had become the party that protected the well off so that they keep their toys. We had become the party that propped up big businesses and big banks, while supporting big bailouts and big corporate loopholes. We had become the party that wrote off millions of

Americans—the "47 percent"—as too dense and too short-sighted to vote for us.

The same was true of Republicans one hundred years earlier, and the result was an epic crack-up of the GOP that forever changed history.

Nineteen-twelve had none of the makings of a pivotal year in American politics. There were no wars on the horizon. The economy was strong. Since the Lincoln administration, Republicans had held the White House for forty-four of the previous fifty-two years.

And yet events, and a combination of outsized egos, conspired to make 1912 one of the most consequential elections in American history, one that ushered in a century of progressivism and a fundamental transformation of the relationship between individual citizens and their government. This came about largely because the Republican Party was split in two, and neither Republican candidate made an effective case for "small r" republican government. As a result, Woodrow Wilson came to power with just 42 percent of the vote, ushering in a broad expansion of power for Washington, implementing the first income tax, and putting forward an idealistic peace plan after World War I—the League of Nations—that, if ratified by the Congress, would have subjugated America's national security to a foreign body.

The election not only brought Woodrow Wilson to office, but laid the groundwork for a century of leftist politics that continued with FDR, LBJ, and Barack Obama. It inculcated into both parties the assumption that Washington bureaucrats could handle problems best, and that an ever-expanding government was a good thing. Aside from a brief eight-year period under Ronald Reagan, the tide of big government continued, even under Republican administrations and Republican Congresses.

This is that story.

September 15, 1910—Princeton, New Jersey

At 5 p.m., the conservatively dressed president of Princeton University rose at the Trenton Opera House before the New Jersey Democratic Convention to accept his party's nomination for governor.[1] Though Woodrow Wilson had spent his career in academia, he could deliver a fine speech, and tonight, in front of the grandees of the New Jersey Democratic Party, proved no exception.

Thomas Woodrow Wilson had grown up the son of a minister in rural Virginia. He had studied law, which appealed to his precise nature, and then turned to a career in academics, eventually teaching political science at Princeton. On becoming president, he had fought to turn Princeton into a first-rate university modeled along the lines of Oxford and Cambridge. But his uncompromising— some would say self-righteous—approach had largely alienated everyone who mattered in Princeton's power structure. He had always longed for a career in politics, and was getting out of academia just as his welcome at Princeton was cooling.

His path to the statehouse in Trenton had been greased by New Jersey's big-money Democratic Party bosses, who sought to move the party from what they viewed as the excesses of the populists who had led the national party into the political wilderness. Democratic fortunes had been particularly low since the rise of William Jennings Bryan, the great orator who had led the party to defeat in 1896, 1900, and again in 1908. Men such as *Harper's* editor Roger Harvey, whose New Jersey seaside home gave him a strong base in the state's politics, and former U.S. senator Jim Smith saw in the dignified academic with the prominent chin a respectable face at the top of the Garden State's Democratic ticket. But they really didn't know their man, or his talent for telling people what they wanted to hear.[2]

With the nomination delivered on a silver platter by the party machinery, all that was left was for Wilson to deliver his acceptance speech. When he did, the Princeton president stunned supporters and detractors alike.

Wilson delivered a forceful address, calling for "a renaissance of public spirit, a reawakening of sober public opinion, a revival of the power of the people." He also envisioned a massive expansion of governmental control—an agenda his backers neither contemplated nor desired. Public utilities needed to be strictly regulated by state commissions! The big monopolies that called New Jersey home needed more controls! Finally, he set straight those who thought he was a tool of special interests. "If elected I will enter the governorship with no pledges of any kind!"[3]

The reaction was pandemonium.

Nervous party bosses tried to reassure each other that this was simply smart politics, and that Wilson had not snookered them. Stunned progressive delegates, who had disapproved of the Wilson choice, rose to their feet, shouting that "a leader has finally come, thank God!" Mobbing the Princeton president, the delegates attempted, awkwardly, to carry the dignified, aloof Wilson onto their shoulders. They would have carried him to the governor's office, if Wilson so desired.

But even on the eve of his first political victory, Wilson had another office in mind.

A Year and a Half Later, January 1912— Oyster Bay, Long Island

Edith Roosevelt had heard enough.

"You can put it out of your mind, Theodore," she told her impatient husband. "You will never be President of the United States again."[4]

That was her hope, at least.

Eleven years earlier, at the age of forty-two, Theodore Roosevelt had become the youngest president in American history upon the assassination of William McKinley. TR finished his predecessor's term, and then won election to a second. Vowing to follow the Washington tradition, the popular president had refused to run for a third term.

Now, not yet fifty-five, he was out of the limelight, craving attention, restless, and bored. He had already written one book about his grand safari to Africa and published a collection of the speeches he had delivered in Africa and Europe. A third book espoused his political philosophy. And he had two more on the way. This was in addition to his articles for *Outlook*, a weekly magazine of news and opinion published in New York City, where Roosevelt maintained an office. But that was not enough to busy the manic Roosevelt—not nearly enough at all.

He was relentless in his complaints about William Howard Taft, his onetime friend and handpicked successor. Taft had the misfortune of trying to replace a man whom many people in the country greatly admired, and none of them admired Roosevelt more than Roosevelt admired himself.

As for his replacement as president, two men could hardly have been more different.

Taft was a distinguished lawyer and judge. The son of a former secretary of war and attorney general and the beneficiary of his brother's financial largesse, Taft was conservative and cautious by both nature and training. He retained a nineteenth-century view of the Constitution, which featured a president who mostly existed to execute the laws enacted in Congress. In his view, the president's powers did not exist outside of what was explicitly written into the Constitution or granted by act of Congress. He was not a natural politician who could command the masses with spellbinding rhetoric. Once asked by a journalist how the president-elect would fare, Roosevelt himself offered what he undoubtedly considered the most cutting thing that could be said about another man: "He means well and he'll do his best. But he's weak."[5]

Weakness was not a word that was often associated with Theodore Roosevelt. Boisterous and confident, Roosevelt had stood astride the world as a colossus, leading the nation with a modern view of the president's outsized, activist role in national and global affairs.

Ever since he was little, however, the animating principle in Theodore Roosevelt's life had been to "Get Action." A sickly yet boisterous child, he went to the Badlands of the Dakota Territory and became a rancher after his first wife died. In the process of riding the range, driving cattle, and apprehending outlaws, he had physically remade himself from a wheezing asthmatic into an indefatigable force of nature that would dominate every room he entered.

His daughter, Alice, summed up Roosevelt's need to be at the center of attention: "He wants to be the bride at every wedding, the corpse at every funeral, and the baby at every christening." Alice herself was such a handful that when it was suggested to Roosevelt that he needed to exert more control over her, all he replied was: "I can either run the country or I can attend to Alice, but I cannot possibly do both."[6]

After his western sojourn, he had returned to New York and resumed a political career that resembled nothing quite so much as a knight in search of dragons to slay. Late-nineteenth-century America had plenty of them. Political bosses, industrialists, muckraking journalists. There was no end of battles to fight. Roosevelt had fought them first as a New York assemblyman, and after his return would do so again as a civil service commissioner, president of the New York City Police Commission, assistant secretary of the navy, and governor of New York.

Roosevelt's zeal for reform was such that by 1900 the vice presidency under William McKinley was seen as little more than a political rubber room where he could bounce around without doing any real harm to himself or others (particularly the big business interests that had been carrying increasing sway over the GOP since the time of Ulysses S. Grant). The political bosses had not foreseen the anarchist's bullet that would not only end McKinley's presidency, but also radically alter the course of the nation.

Despite his initial pledge to continue McKinley's policies, the Rooseveltian prime directive—"Get Action"—soon kicked in. On February 18, 1902, he ordered the Justice Department to file suit against the latest attempt to monopolize a vital element of American commerce. J. P. Morgan's Northern Securities Company had sought to control all the rail traffic between the Midwest and the West Coast. When he learned about it, a shocked Morgan rushed to the White House, telling Roosevelt that such action was unnecessary. "If we have done anything wrong, send 'your man' (by whom he meant the Attorney General of the United States standing in the room with him) to my man and they can fix it up."[7] This was the first of more than forty lawsuits the Roosevelt administration would file against the big trusts that dominated the American economy, using their size and scope to dictate prices, wages, and hours to American consumers, farmers, and laborers while driving smaller, often less efficient competitors out of the market.

His attitude toward the constitutional role of the president was quickly put on display when the United Mine Workers went on strike just before winter. The price of coal rose from five to forty dollars per ton, raising the specter of homes going unheated just before the 1902 elections. In an unprecedented act, Roosevelt summoned the union officials and mine owners to meet in Washington, and when the owners refused to accept arbitration he threatened to keep the mines operating with federal troops. A shocked congressman asked Roosevelt about the Constitution.

Roosevelt grabbed him by his lapels like a cowhand caught pilfering a calf. "The Constitution was made for the people. Not the people for the Constitution."[8]

In his postpresidency, Roosevelt called for a "New Nationalism" that put him to the left of even the Democrats. Casting himself in the guise of Lincoln, he laid out an extension of the "Square Deal" principles that had guided his presidency. American democracy had not yet lived up to its promise because of what he termed "special privilege"—men who enjoyed power, wealth, and position "which has not been earned by service to his or their fellows." The big "combinations" or trusts that "controlled the necessities of life, such as meat, oil, and coal" were an immutable result of economic laws. Efforts at prohibiting them from coming into being had failed. "The way out lies . . . in completely controlling them in the interests of the public welfare."[9] He called for a sweeping expansion of government—a graduated income tax and an inheritance tax, compensation of workmen for their injuries, and regulation of child labor. Congress needed to hand over the setting of tariffs to a commission insulated from special-interest politics. The federal government's authority to regulate business engaged in interstate commerce needed to be greatly expanded, as did the role of labor unions.[10] To make all of this function required a rethinking of fundamental aspects of American constitutional government, such as federalism and the separation of powers. Roosevelt conceded that this approach represented a strong break with the past, requiring "a policy of a far more active government interference with social and economic conditions in this country than we have had," but such changes were now necessary.[11]

By the beginning of 1912, despite Edith's admonitions, Sagamore Hill, the Roosevelt estate on the north side of Long Island, was already becoming a political mecca with more and more visitors hoping to convince "Colonel Roosevelt," as he now preferred to be called after the rank he had attained in the Spanish-American War, that he needed to return to political life and wrest the Republican nomination from the man to whom he had virtually handed the office. Not that the Colonel needed much convincing.

To reporters clamoring for him to enter the race, he announced that while he would not actively campaign for the nomination, if it "comes to me as a genuine popular movement of course I will accept it, and that is all there is to it." Everyone knew what that meant.

Three Months Later, April 16, 1912—The White House

William Howard Taft sported a ruddy complexion and legs that seemed too short for his torso. His most distinctive feature, of course, was his enormous girth. His 340-pound, five-foot-eleven-inch frame had required the installation of a new bathtub large enough for four men in the White House, to which he had been elected a year earlier, supposedly after he had found himself trapped in the original one.

The usually cheerful Taft could make jokes at his own expense. When he was once offered an endowed chair of law in his name, he responded that a "Sofa of Law" would be more suitable given his frame.[12]

But the early months of 1912 had not been joyous ones for him. And today's news, so out of the blue, hit him hard.

The RMS *Titanic* had sunk one day prior.

Aboard the doomed liner was his military aide and close friend Major Archie Butt, a man the president had considered close to a younger brother.

Taft had been buoyed by initial reports that the *Titanic* had been held afloat and was struggling toward Halifax. Those reports soon turned out to be untrue. The president then spent the previous evening waiting for news by telegraph that Butt was on the list of survivors. His name never appeared. Some fifteen hundred souls who boarded the greatest ship ever constructed were lost at sea, including famous names like John Jacob Astor and Benjamin Guggenheim. But Archie Butt was the loss that stung.

"It's hard to believe he's gone," the president said somberly. As he spoke, Taft looked as if he'd been physically stricken. "I expect him to walk in at any moment."[13]

Butt, who had worked tirelessly to help Taft fend off the looming Roosevelt challenge, had come to the president with second thoughts about going on his European trip. But Taft had insisted that he go. As Roosevelt ran against Taft in primaries across the country, Butt had cut his trip short to return to Washington as soon as he was able. That was why he'd boarded the "unsinkable" *Titanic* in the first place. (In later days, Taft would learn that Major Butt had led efforts to help women and children off the doomed ship.)

In the wake of this colossal tragedy, it was perhaps not a day for personal concerns. But those concerns could not be avoided. The hard fact was that Taft's presidency was meeting its own iceberg, Theodore Roosevelt.

Taft had served his country with great distinction, he felt, as solicitor general, a federal judge, governor of the Philippines, and secretary of war, and had been a loyal Roosevelt lieutenant. Indeed, the two men had a friendship that Taft described as "one of close and sweet intimacy."[14] If only Roosevelt had followed through on his plan to appoint Taft to the Supreme Court, a job that better suited his talents, all of this could have been avoided.

But that was not what had happened. The ever-persuasive Roosevelt—and Taft's wife, Nellie—had urged him to seek the White House. It was a job he didn't want, and one that he never felt he'd be good at.

But Roosevelt was insistent, and persuasive. He had assured Taft that no other man was better qualified for the job. As a member of the cabinet, Taft was often seen as Roosevelt's stand-in as president, and had played a key role in many of the administration's successes. But Taft knew his limits. He was a good supporter and foot soldier, not necessarily a good political leader.

When Taft announced for the presidency, in 1907, his comments were so milquetoast and so uninspiring that they almost sounded as if he'd decided to drop out. "I wish to say that my ambition is not political," he had declared. "That I am not seeking the presidential nomination, that I do not expect to be the Republican candidate."[15] But if "the opportunity to run for the great office of president were to come to me," he added, he would not decline it.

During his four years in the White House, he presided over a Republican Party that had grown comfortable in government and its alliances with big-business donors. Increasingly the rotund, golf-loving Taft was becoming a caricature in outlets like the influential *Collier's Magazine*, which called him "the toy of the politicians, money makers, with whom he golfs, walks and eats."[16] It was one thing for the press to believe that. The bigger problem was that Teddy Roosevelt, bored and restless, decided to believe it, too.

But in truth, Taft didn't really know whose side he was on. He called himself a progressive—a moderate progressive, one who acted within the Constitution's limits. He was not against many elements of the progressive agenda. For one thing, he proposed income taxes on corporations.

Unlike his predecessor, he was slow to criticize big businesses. At the same time, he filed more antitrust suits against corporations than TR had done in his entire presidency. One suit was against the behemoth U.S. Steel Corporation for its acquisition of a company during the Roosevelt administration. Unfortunately for the oblivious Taft, one of the people named in the suit was an infuriated TR himself. Newspaper headlines—such as "Roosevelt Was Deceived"—embarrassed the former president and set him into a fury against Taft.[17]

The only thing of which Taft was certain was that Teddy Roosevelt should not be the Republican nominee in 1912. In his years out of office, TR had become more extreme in his positions. Taft labeled him a "dangerous egoist" and a "demagogue" who threatened the very foundations of American democracy with an expansive view of presidential authority and power. Roosevelt had supported proposals that could win some Republican support, child labor laws and worker's compensation among them. But in Taft's view, Roosevelt had gone so far as to put forward the radical proposition that the American public should be able to overturn a decision by the judges "if they think it wrong." That, the judicious Taft feared, would mean that the Supreme Court could no longer rule a presidential decision "unconstitutional" out of fear of being overruled by the people.

But rather than make the case for his own policies, Taft largely defined himself by what he was against. Taft labeled the progressives who supported such reforms as extremists who "would hurry us into a condition which I would find no parallel except in the French Revolution. . . . Such extremists are not Progressives, they are political emotionalists or neurotics."[18] Their proposals were completely out of step with the founders' perception of the need for checks "upon hasty popular action which made our people who found the Revolution and who drafted the Constitution, the greatest self-governing people the world had ever known."[19] And, to Taft's astonishment, Teddy Roosevelt had cast his lot with them. He feared a third Roosevelt term could cause great danger to the republic, particularly when led by such a charismatic, insistent, and persuasive man as Theodore Roosevelt.

"The truth is I am not very happy in the renomination and re-election business," Taft confided to his brother. "I have to set my teeth and go through with it as best I can."

Perhaps more than the thought of losing the presidency, the idea that his treasured friendship with Roosevelt was in jeopardy was for the president a source of agony and discomfort.

"He was my closest friend," Taft said sadly. Then his eyes filled with tears.[20]

Two Months Later, June 15, 1912—Chicago, Illinois

At 4:00 p.m., Teddy Roosevelt stepped off the *Lake Shore Limited*, the train that had departed New York City nearly twenty-four hours earlier, taking him and his entourage to the Republican National Convention in Chicago. Accompanying them were his diminutive English secretary Frank Harper, progressive millionaire Regis Post, and a few staffers from *Outlook*, the small but influential journal for which Roosevelt penned articles and columns. When they spotted Roosevelt wearing his trademark "Rough Rider" hat, the waiting crowd burst through the barricades, surrounding him. Roosevelt was escorted to his hotel while a band playing "There Will Be a Hot Time in the Old Town Tonight" trailed behind.

The song was an appropriate one. The convention was in virtual deadlock from the get-go. The GOP nomination would largely turn on the bitter procedural wrangling over whether to seat the pro-Roosevelt delegates largely selected in popular primaries or the pro-Taft delegates selected by party bosses.

Upon arriving at the Congress Hotel, Roosevelt turned to the crowd, waved his hat for quiet, and shouted, "Chicago is a mighty poor place in which to try and steal anything! The people have spoken, and the politicians must learn to answer or understand. They will be made to understand that they are the servants of the rank and file of the plain citizens of the republic!" Fighting to make himself heard over what was now a deafening crowd roaring its approval, he concluded, "It is a fight against theft. And the thieves will not win!"[21]

Two Days Later, June 17, 1912—Chicago

Roosevelt addressed the assembled convention in a standing-room-only Chicago Auditorium, urging delegates to reject the rules by which the Republican National Committee proposed to run the convention.

His rhetoric became increasingly buoyant, fueled by the thunderous ovation:

> *Assuredly the fight will go on whether we win or lose. . . . What happens to me is not of the slightest consequence; I am to be used, as in a doubtful battle any man used . . . and then cast aside or left to die . . . this fight is too great to permit us to concern ourselves about any one man's welfare. . . . The victory shall be ours. . . . We fight in honorable fashion for the good of mankind; fearless for the future; unheeding of our individual fates; with unflinching hearts and undimmed eyes; we stand at Armageddon, and we battle for the Lord!*

Yet despite the euphoric rhetoric and rapturous applause wherever Roosevelt went or spoke, the result was never really in any doubt.

The Next Day, June 18, 1912—Chicago

"It is almost incredible to hear at a national convention," the *Washington Post* opined, "the question seriously discussed if there will be firearms used and whether blood will be shed, but one can hear this at every step in the frightful jam and welter in the hotel lobbies."[22]

The convention's first decision—the choice of chair— foreshadowed the rest. When conservative New York senator and corporation lawyer Elihu Root was elected over Francis E. McGovern of Wisconsin as convention chair, there could be no doubt as to how the procedural points on which the delegate seating, and therefore the nomination, would be settled. Root, formerly one of Roosevelt's best friends and closest confidants, would side with Taft.

At the Congress Hotel, Roosevelt seethed. His old friend Root was no more than "a receiver of stolen goods."[23] The Taft forces, now concerned with the prospect Roosevelt would bolt the convention, sought to placate him. Some progressives came to urge just that. Others, such as Senator William Borah, urged Roosevelt to put party unity first. After the others finally left at two in the morning, Roosevelt was left with Frank Munsey and former J. P. Morgan partner George Perkins. Munsey and Perkins promised to personally finance an independent Roosevelt with their own fortunes if he chose to run.

Four Days Later, June 22, 1912—Chicago

Henry Allen White of the Kansas delegation rose to deliver an authorized message from Roosevelt. The forty-five minutes of racket that followed made it difficult for the newsmen to capture a good deal of what he said, but what was heard was clear: "The convention is in no proper sense any longer a Republican convention representing the real Republican Party. Therefore, I hope the men elected as Roosevelt delegates will now decline to vote on any matter before the convention." The convention proceeded to nominate Taft.

Meanwhile, at Orchestra Hall, a new Progressive Party—quickly labeled "the Bull Moose Party" after TR proclaimed himself "fit as a bull moose"—was being called into being in an atmosphere quite different from that of the Republican convention. One reporter compared traveling from the latter to the former as "stepping from a board meeting of railroad directors, from a post mortem in a coroner's office on a corpse, into a Zuni snake dance."[24]

No one was quite so downhearted, though, as Republican convention chair Root, whose carefully reasoned rulings and parliamentary mastery had cemented the convention for Taft. "I care more for one button on Theodore Roosevelt's waistcoat than for Taft's whole body," he said despondently.[25]

Six Weeks Later, August 5, 1912—Chicago

Two days before Woodrow Wilson would deliver his acceptance speech as standard bearer of the Democratic Party, the apostate Republicans returned to Chicago, this time for the sole purpose of forming a new political party and nominating Roosevelt for president. With the zeal of missionaries, the delegates sang hymns that elevated Roosevelt to an almost Christlike figure.

Theirs was a convention unlike any before. Jews and Catholics mixed freely with immigrants. Numerous delegations contained African-American delegates.

Most conspicuous was the presence of women not just as wives but as delegates with equal rights. Jane Addams, the great social reformer, seconded Roosevelt's nomination once he had made clear he supported the vote for women unconditionally. Political reforms, labor rights, conservation, civil rights for women, and social insurance were all prominent aspects of the convention's platform.

Notably absent were mentions of protections for the rights of African-Americans. Despite his record of appointing African-Americans to government posts, Roosevelt's fondest hope had been to crack the "solid South" of the Democrats, and he now held on to the grandiose delusion that somehow he could do this while advancing their cause as well.

Roosevelt and his running mate, Senator Hiram Johnson (R-Calif.) appeared onstage at the convention to accept their nominations—something unprecedented in American politics, and something that would not be repeated until Roosevelt's worshipful cousin Franklin accepted the Democratic nomination in 1932.

Although he had grown stockier, and there were now gray flecks in his closely cropped hair, he was the Roosevelt of old: "Whatever fate may at the moment overtake any of us, the movement itself will not stop. Our cause is based on the eternal principle of righteousness, and even though we who now lead may for the time fail, in the end the cause itself shall triumph," Roosevelt told his audience.

Three Weeks Later, August 28, 1912—Sea Girt, New Jersey

Woodrow Wilson had come to the conclusion that the race was not between the Republicans and Democrats, but between himself and Roosevelt. Roosevelt and Taft had reached the same conclusion. After winning the party's nomination, a depressed and intimidated Taft, who'd never wanted the presidency in the first place, barely bothered to campaign. When asked about Taft, the ever-quotable Roosevelt quipped, "I never discuss dead issues."

It was essential that the race be one of ideas, concluded Wilson. For if it were to come down to a popularity contest, the sober-

minded governor and ex–college president knew full well that his
political career would be one more skin on the wall at Sagamore
Hill.

His challenge was to develop a plan that would provide voters a
strong contrast with the ex-president's progressive "New Nationalism," one that stole much of the Democrat's reforming thunder,
stopping just short of Socialist candidate Eugene Debs's in many
respects. As he had in winning the support of party bosses to gain
his nomination for governor, Wilson decided to position himself
as a candidate of the right. At least when compared with the "activist" Roosevelt.

On Labor Day, Wilson relaunched his campaign in a speech
before ten thousand workers in Buffalo. He praised the progressives for having aims similar to his and the Democrats', but there
was an important difference between Roosevelt's "New Nationalism" and what Wilson dubbed the "New Freedom." Roosevelt
wanted to legalize monopolies and welcome them as a means of
increasing national power while controlling them via licensing and
regulatory commissions, Wilson said. But such an approach would
not get to the root cause of the trusts: unregulated competition.
Wilson proposed instead to restructure competition, which would
accomplish the ends he sought: the destruction of monopoly rather
than its regulation. "Ours is a program of liberty; theirs is a program of regulation."

Throughout the fall, Wilson put forward detailed policy proposals to reform the banking system and reduce tariffs as the
means to restore a competitive free market. Appealing to the Jeffersonian strain in American life that embraced a country of small
entrepreneurs, the Virginian Wilson told his audiences that the
difference between his New Freedom and Roosevelt's New Nationalism were fundamental ones. It was industrial freedom ver-
sus industrial absolutism—what Wilson derided as a "government

of experts" as opposed to a government that would listen to the people and speak "for them." If people truly needed the government to tell them what to do rather than the other way around, "then we are not a free people," he told his audiences. "The history of liberty is a history of limitation on governmental power, not the increase of it."

This led to the odd specter of the Democrats fighting for limited government and a former Republican arguing for a broad expansion of federal power. Seeing what he perceived as yet another turn in Wilson's philosophy, Roosevelt seized upon Wilson's recommitment to limited government. Reminding his audience of Wilson's ivory tower background, he labeled Wilson's new approach to governance a "bit of outworn academic doctrine which was kept in the schoolroom and the professional study for a generation after it had been abandoned by all who had experience of actual life. It is simply the laissez-faire doctrine of English political economists three-quarters of a century ago."

Two Weeks Later, September 14, 1912—San Francisco

Teddy Roosevelt believed that Woodrow Wilson was not really a progressive, and in his first full-frontal assault on the Democratic campaign, he accused Wilson of being a phony. The truth, Roosevelt claimed, was that Wilson was a closet conservative. The real progressive, Roosevelt claimed, was Teddy Roosevelt.

Finally out on the campaign trail, Roosevelt was reinvigorated. Nothing would deter him. Not his former party. And certainly not his marginalized successor and former friend.

Roosevelt cited a quotation he culled from a Wilson speech to support his argument: "The history of liberty is the history of the limitation on governmental power, not the increase of it."

Such a view was anathema to the Bull Moose progressive, who no longer believed, if he ever did, in limits on government power. A view of governmental limits would, TR charged, lead to "the undoing of every particle of social and industrial advance we have made." Wilson's view, claimed Roosevelt, was that "every railroad must be left unchecked, every great industrial concern can do as it chooses with its employees and with the general public; women must be permitted to work as many hours a day as their taskmasters bid them."

Roosevelt offered the ominous promise of using the federal government to right all wrongs—as Roosevelt defined them. Roosevelt vowed to use "the whole power of the Government to protect all those who . . . are trodden down in the ferocious, scrambling rush of an unregulated and purely individualistic industrialism."

Of course, the idea that Woodrow Wilson was some sort of conservative in progressive clothing was as outlandish as it was untrue.

Wilson of course believed no such thing. Like Roosevelt, Wilson seemed to believe the constitutional checks on government and the separation of powers were quaint relics of a distant past.[26] If trained properly, civil servants could be disinterested administrators, and therefore needed no constitutional restraints. Whereas the founders, such as James Madison, saw political conflict as inevitable (factionalism is "sown in the nature of man"), most progressives believed that politics, in all its ugliness and self-interest, had been transcended by humankind's progress and enlightenment. "The period of constitution-making is passed now," Wilson had declared, "we have reached a new territory in which we need new guides, the vast territory of administration."[27] This was what Woodrow Wilson called "the Living Constitution." No document from 1776 or 1788 could possibly anticipate the needs of the people it governed one hundred years later. Therefore the

Constitution needed to evolve, and in some cases, be dismissed and ignored altogether.

Such fine points did not matter much to TR on the stump.

Now with Taft all but out of the campaign, the 1912 campaign became a fight between two left-wing progressives.

And of the two, Wilson seemed the more acceptable and least dangerous. At least to William Howard Taft.

Two Weeks Later, September 27, 1912—Boston

In a private suite on the fifth floor of the Copley Plaza Hotel, President Taft cordially greeted the man seeking to remove him from office.

The meeting has been instigated by Governor Wilson, who had heard that Taft happened to be in the city on the same day to give a speech, one of Taft's few speeches during the entire campaign. In fact, the president had yielded to the tradition of incumbents' not campaigning for re-election. Taft was content to leave his record to the judgment of the voters. Besides, he knew he was probably going to lose. His victory, he believed, was keeping the radical Roosevelt off the Republican ballot.

Wilson knew Taft was out of it as well, which was why he was happy to meet with him. The two shared a common cause in wanting to stop Roosevelt's election. Wilson in fact had grown so confident of his potential victory that he was poking fun at the prospect of Roosevelt back in the White House, bereft of any Bull Moose supporters in Congress or the judiciary.

"Don't you think he'll be pretty lonely?" Wilson asked his audience. "Not that he'll mind it, because I believe he finds himself rather good company."[28]

The late-night meeting between the two anti-Roosevelt contenders was amiable. "I hope the campaigning has not worn you out," the president told Wilson.

The governor admitted that his voice had gotten hoarse form overuse.

Well, Taft replied with a smile, I can sympathize with that.

The two men parted company that evening in the best of spirits.

"It was a very delightful meeting," Wilson told reporters. "I am very fond of President Taft."[29] And he was overcome with the belief that he would soon be visiting Taft again, this time as the president-elect.

Two and a Half Weeks Later, October 14, 1912— Milwaukee, Wisconsin

Roosevelt's campaign train, *The Mayflower*, pulled into Milwaukee at 6:00 p.m. The campaign had taken a heavy toll on the candidate, who had been barnstorming the country, delivering lengthy orations that had reduced his voice to barely a whisper.

Around 8:00 p.m., he rose from a nap at the Gilpatrick Hotel, folded up his speech, and placed it in the inside right pocket of his suit coat. He descended the staircase to the lobby with supporters and a small security detail. Emerging from the hotel, he made his way into a waiting car.

As the excited crowd converged near him, Roosevelt stood to doff his hat. At that moment a man only seven feet away aimed a pistol at Roosevelt and fired, at point-blank range, hitting Roosevelt in the right side of his chest. A shocked Roosevelt fell into his seat.

As the assailant prepared a second shot, campaign stenographer Elbert Martin leaped upon him, forcing the gunman to the ground and attempting to strangle him. Two of Roosevelt's security men piled on while a third drew an automatic pistol, threatening to shoot anyone who approached the Colonel.

"Lynch him!" members of the crowd shouted at the assailant. "Kill him!"[30]

Amazingly, Roosevelt regained his composure and rose to his feet.

"Don't hurt him!" Roosevelt ordered Martin and the others who now had complete control of a prostrate John Schrank. "Bring him here. I want to see him."

Roosevelt took Schrank's head in his hands, staring at his face to see if he recognized his assailant. "What'd you do it for?" Roosevelt demanded.

But only a dull-eyed insane look covered the man's face.

"Oh, what's the use? Turn him over to the police," Roosevelt commanded.

While his aides frantically searched his coat for a bullet hole, Roosevelt reached inside his jacket, and withdrew a bloody hand.

Scurry Terrell, a physician attending Roosevelt to minister to his aching throat, instructed the driver to head to Milwaukee Emergency.

But Roosevelt shook his head. "You get me to that speech," he rasped.

The car headed to the auditorium through a crowd largely unaware that anything was even wrong.

Only when he was safely in the auditorium did Roosevelt allow Terrell to perform a cursory exam. There was a bloody hole an inch below and to the right of his right nipple, the right side of his body entirely black. Roosevelt ignored renewed pleas to get immediate medical attention, simply putting a fresh handkerchief over his wound. He pulled down his shirt and headed for the stage.

By then, word had spread about the attempt on Roosevelt's life. Others gasped when Roosevelt himself told the crowd the news.

"It's true," he told his listeners. "But it takes more than that to kill a bull moose!"

He then unbuttoned his coat and allowed his audience a look at his bloody shirtfront. When he pulled out his speech, he realized that the bullet had pierced it. That Roosevelt was longwinded might have been a blessing—the thick, fifty-page speech tucked into his pocket, along with a metal eyeglass case, undoubtedly slowed the bullet and may well have saved his life.[31]

For the next eighty minutes, Roosevelt delivered his written remarks, defending his policies on trusts and organized labor. As he spoke, his face grew pale. His heart raced and he felt what he later described as a "knifelike pain in his ribs." Only after he let the last page of his speech drop from his hands did he declare that he was ready to go to the hospital.

After being treated in Milwaukee, Roosevelt boarded *The Mayflower* and returned to Chicago, where he was met by one of the nation's leading chest surgeons. Before he could be taken to the hospital, a flash went off from a newspaper camera.

"Ah, shot again," he quipped.[32]

Taft and Wilson quickly sent off sympathetic telegrams, and suspended their campaigns until Roosevelt was well again. On October 27, Roosevelt was well enough to return to his New York home, and gave notice that he would return to the campaign trail in seventy-two hours.

The shooting of the former president garnered international headlines. And for the Democrats, the fear was palpable that the attack on the popular Roosevelt, just days before the election, might somehow turn the race.

Woodrow Wilson had offered to suspend his campaign until Roosevelt's release. But the hard-charging TR, true to form, would hear nothing of it. "The fight should go on to its conclusion," he declared, "just as it would in case of battle, even though the commanding general might be struck down."

Two and a Half Weeks Later, November 1, 1912—Washington

As Taft sat down with the *New York World* reporter, his view of his own prospects in Tuesday's election was grim. But the end of the campaign, and his presidency, seemed to cheer him.

Asked to explain how the election had come to this, with the Republicans expected to lose for the first time in twenty years, Taft said simply that the Republican Party had "naturally divided itself."

The party, Taft reasoned, had finally split in two between the eastern business establishment and populists in the West.

Taft wasn't sure if Roosevelt would have gone through with his campaign had he known it would mean the utter defeat of the GOP, as polls seemed to indicate. But then he didn't know that Roosevelt wouldn't have done it anyway. He is simply a man who "acts from day to day," Taft said bluntly.[33]

The president held out hope that he might be able to beat the Bull Moose Party in terms of electoral votes, but that would be cold consolation in any event. Even the attempt on TR's life hadn't changed the dynamic. Woodrow Wilson was slated to be the next president of the United States. And America was on the verge of becoming a radically different place.

Four Months Later, March 4, 1913— East Portico, United States Capitol

On the steps of the Capitol building, Chief Justice Edward White stepped forward to administer the oath of office to the president. Woodrow Wilson and the assembled crowd were likely comfortable given the fifty-five-degree temperature that prevailed in the nation's capital. Dressed in his frock coat, sporting a rose-colored tie and silk top hat, Wilson placed his hand on

the same Bible he had used when sworn in as governor just two
years earlier.[34]

He had been elected with a vast majority in the electoral college (435 votes to 88 for Roosevelt and a scant 8 for Taft). The
popular vote was a different story. Wilson garnered just 42 percent
of the votes cast. Roosevelt and Taft had combined for just over
50 percent (27 percent for Roosevelt and 23 percent for Taft). The
Socialists had garnered 6 percent for Eugene V. Debs, the largest
share before or since for a Socialist candidate.[35]

Despite his victory, Wilson was in a somber rather than celebratory mood. For the first time since 1853, there would be no inaugural ball, such frivolity not being in sync with the tone Wilson
sought to set. For the election had resulted not only in a progressive Democratic president, but in a progressive Democratic Congress as well, completing the work that had begun in 1910 with the
election of a Democratic House. It was this theme around which
Wilson's inaugural address would revolve.

"There has been a change in government," Wilson began.
His address sounded more like a lecture as the former college professor told his audience that the purpose of his address
would be to explain that change and what it would mean for the
country.

A lower tariff, banking, and currency regulation, stronger control of industry to the benefit of workers, agriculture, and resource
conservation were all on the table, Wilson told them. Men, women,
and children needed to be "shielded from the consequences of great
industrial and social pressures which they cannot alter, control, or
singly cope with." But this was to be done in accord with America's
own traditions. "We have made up our minds to square every process of our national life again with the standards we so proudly
set up at the beginning and have always carried at our hearts. Our
work is a work of restoration."[36]

★   ★   ★

To a large extent, we still live in the age of Theodore Roosevelt's and Woodrow Wilson's progressive vision of government, with the federal government taking more and more responsibility, states becoming increasingly marginalized as administrative entities, and constitutional checks and limits on the executive all but ignored.[37]

The idea of representative government itself is subject to question. Both parties in Congress increasingly set broad policies, leaving most of the details to unelected administrative agencies, and not the public's elected representatives.

The 1912 election should not have resulted in the victory of Woodrow Wilson. That outcome was the direct consequence of a Republican Party that was unable to define itself or its vision to the voters, and whose unofficial leader, Theodore Roosevelt, embarked on a vanity third-party campaign, propelled by a convoluted notion of presidential authority under the Constitution. We can learn much from the split in the Republican Party that brought elitist progressivism to power. Republicans must not simply become cheaper Democrats, sacrificing our conservative principles for illusory electoral gains. We must eschew vanity campaigns, wobbly conservatism, and political candidates who are unable to define their ideology and their vision with courage and clarity.

Although Taft was the most conservative of the three major candidates running in the election, it was clear from the outset that he had neither the vision nor the willingness to make the conservative case. As a result, no one effectively articulated the case for limited government or federalism under the Constitution. Taft in fact modeled himself after his idol, Roosevelt, and indeed considered himself a "moderate" progressive.

The 1912 election is a cautionary tale. If in 2016 the Republican nominee fails to make the case for constitutional principles and goes along with the belief in an ever-expansive federal government to solve the nation's problems, then there is every chance another leftist will come to office and build on the disasters that Barack Obama has brought the nation. Indeed, if the Republican Party is divided among the comfortable ruling class and grassroots conservatives, then we cannot win.

8

THE TRUMAN AFTERTHOUGHT

How Indecision and Recklessness
Almost Lost the Cold War

It was 1946, and Winston Churchill was once again out of power. In the what-have-you-done-for-me-now nature of politics, the man who vanquished Hitler was swept out of office by a war-weary British electorate. Thus, as he arrived at an obscure college (Westminster) in a small town (Fulton) due east of Harry Truman's home in Independence, Missouri, Churchill had no formal authority, save the moral authority he had earned by standing alone against Hitler a decade earlier. In that era of appeasement, he was a voice crying out in the wilderness. Now he intended to do it again.

"From Stettin in the Baltic," Churchill said, in remarks that were transmitted over the radio and reported widely in American newspapers, "to Trieste in the Adriatic, an Iron Curtain has descended across the continent." Behind the Iron Curtain lay "Warsaw, Berlin, Prague, Vienna, Budapest, Belgrade, Bucharest, and Sofia." According to Churchill, "all these famous cities and the populations around them" were under the "control of Moscow." Elsewhere, "far from the Russian frontiers," the Soviet Union's "fifth columns" imperiled "Christian civilization."[1]

Sir Winston's call to action against the growing threat of Soviet communism was warmly received in Fulton, and many parts of the United States, where public opinion of the Soviets under Joseph Stalin quickly plummeted. But in other quarters, the remarks provoked outrage. Churchill was labeled an imperialist. A warmonger. A relic. The police were called out to contain protests against him in New York City. And in Washington, D.C., Henry Wallace, who only two years earlier had been the vice president of the United States, shared the Left's disgust.

Wallace considered himself an expert on Russia. He had tried to learn the language. He had read Marx and Lenin. And as vice president, he had returned from a lengthy tour of Siberia in 1944, with more exposure to the Soviet system than any high-ranking government official in American history. In Wallace's opinion, almost everything Winston Churchill said in Fulton—and almost everything Harry Truman would do to combat communism in the next seven years—was dangerously wrong. And he intended to rebut it all in a speech in New York City.

"Never have the common people of all lands so longed for peace," he scrawled on his notepad. "But the price of peace is the price of giving up prejudice, hatred, fear, and ignorance." We must not hate communists, he would argue. Or fear them. Or "get tough" with them. " 'Getting tough' never brought anything real and lasting—whether for schoolyard bullies or businessmen or world powers. The tougher we get, the tougher the Russians will get."

And the former vice president of Franklin Roosevelt thought that little could be gained for America by maintaining an alliance with the British. "Certainly we like the British people as individuals," wrote Wallace in his notes, "but to make Britain the key to our foreign policy would be the height of folly."

The solution, the "way to peace," required several steps.

First, the United States must butt out of the struggles of the people behind the so-called Iron Curtain and "recognize that we have no more business in the political affairs of Eastern Europe than Russia has in the political affairs of Latin America, Western Europe, and the United States."

Second, the United States must keep Germany weak so that the Soviet Union is "assured that never again can German industry be converted into military might to be used against her."

Third, the United States must cease "our excessive expenses for military purposes."

Fourth, the United States must "close our ears to those among us who would have us believe that Russian communism and our free enterprise system cannot live, one with another, in a profitable and productive peace."

Fifth and finally, the United States must relinquish control of, and give to the United Nations, our "atomic bombs . . . strategically located air bases . . . guided missiles and military aircraft for bombing purposes."[2]

When he was finished with his rough draft, the former vice president leaned back in his chair. He was satisfied with his effort and his eloquence. But he was pained by the thought that when he delivered the speech, it would be as a mere cabinet secretary in the administration of another man. A lesser man.

Wallace thought back to a time, less than two years earlier, when it looked as if *he* would be the commander-in-chief. If only Franklin Roosevelt had kept Henry Wallace on the ticket, "the way to peace" would now be clear.

But Roosevelt had dumped his vice president. He had made Harry Truman his successor. And that unlikely choice of an obscure senator from the Midwest did more to change history than any decision Franklin Roosevelt made, from the New Deal through World War II.

The first and arguably most important decision of the Cold War—Franklin Roosevelt's selection of Harry Truman as vice president in 1944—almost didn't happen at all. The chaos and uncertainty surrounding the decision itself was a textbook example of how not to lead, especially during a time of war.

Up until the very last moment, it appeared in 1944 that the Democrats would select as the nation's future president either a communist sympathizer or a segregationist. Few knew much at all about the man who actually did get the job—a relatively obscure, blunt-spoken former haberdasher from Missouri who would go on to change the world.

This is the story of how that happened.

Spring 1944—Kolyma, U.S.S.R.

The region of Kolyma, in eastern Siberia, was the "pole of cold and cruelty." So said the most famous witness to Kolyma's gulags, Aleksandr Solzhenitsyn. On a warm day, its average winter temperature was two degrees below zero. For two decades, its vast network of concentration camps put millions of political prisoners and "class enemies" to work in its gold mines, sweat shops, and collective farms. With little food, rest, or shelter, a quarter of the brutalized slave-laborers died every year—most from starvation and disease, others from torture and execution.

When Vice President Henry Wallace landed in Kolyma in May of 1944, there were clear signs that he was about to embark on a tour of human captivity and monstrous cruelty. In a *Reader's Digest* article, Wendell Willkie, the Republican who lost to FDR in 1940, described his trip through Kolyma and reported being denied access to areas that may have been concentration camps.[3] Similarly, Britain's minister of production, Sir Oliver Lyttelton, flatly told

Wallace over dinner at the British embassy that some 16 million prisoners were toiling in Siberia's concentration camps.

None of these claims made much of an impression on Wallace. Willkie was a reactionary. Lyttelton was an imperialist. These were not his people.

Far more to Wallace's liking was Sergei Goglidze. Once commissar for internal affairs in the republic of Georgia, Goglidze was by 1944 the Soviet secret police's highest-ranking general in Siberia. Already responsible for ordering hundreds of thousands of death sentences in Georgia, he was now a Soviet version of Germany's Adolf Eichmann, in charge of Joseph Stalin's "gulag archipelago."

Wallace had no inkling of this. He knew only that Goglidze was Stalin's "intimate friend." The Soviet butcher seemed to Wallace "a very fine man, very efficient, gentle, and understanding with people."[4]

With Goglidze, the vice president spent twenty-five days touring Kolyma. At a factory, seemingly happy workers applauded the American visitor. At a gold mine, strapping young men chatted amiably with him. At a collective farm, lovely young girls tending the pigs laughed at Wallace's jokes, although they seemed baffled by the former agriculture secretary's rather elementary questions about farming.

Wallace never once suspected that this workers' paradise—the factory, the mine, the farm, and all that he saw in between—was a façade. In fact, the "workers" he saw were often the guards, pretending to work in factories and mines. The "farmers" were police clerks, with no clue how to answer Wallace's questions about raising pigs. Most of the real laborers, emaciated and diseased, were kept out of sight. So were the guard dogs, the watchtowers, and the searchlights. On the occasions when Wallace was allowed near actual prisoners, Goglidze ensured that they were among the better fed, that they could not speak English, and that they were never left alone with the American visitor.

If Wallace had found a moment alone with a typical worker, that worker could have told the American what a survivor later wrote—that every time the gulag's guards brought them soup, "it made us all want to cry." He would have explained, "We were ready to cry for fear that the soup would be thin. And when a miracle occurred and the soup was thick we couldn't believe it and ate it as slowly as possible. But even with thick soup in a warm stomach there remained a sucking pain: we'd been hungry for too long." In Kolyma, as Russian author Varlan Shalamov noted, "all human emotions—love friendship, envy, concern for one's fellow man, compassion, longing for fame, honesty—had left us, along with the flesh that had melted from our bodies."[5]

A more skeptical visitor might have wondered why, when Wallace absentmindedly strolled up a ridge by himself, a major in the secret police frantically chased after him, yelling, "Come down at once!" But Wallace always thought the best of people (aside from conservatives and imperialists). He did as he was told, taking his interpreter's word for it that the major was merely announcing that "dinner is ready."[6]

For Henry Wallace, the lesson of his trip to the Soviet Union was clear: "Free people, born on free expanses, can never live in slavery." At the end of Wallace's twenty-five-day tour, he told a crowd in Irkutsk, "There are no more similar countries in the world than the Soviet Union and the United States of America."[7]

And it was to the United States that Wallace had to admit he'd given increasing thought. If only because he knew he was at risk of losing his job.

The Day Wallace Returned Home,
July 10, 1944—The White House

For forty minutes, Vice President Wallace sat quietly and patiently as he awaited his appointed meeting with the old man. He was exhausted, having just returned from his fifty-one-day trip to the Far East. But the meeting with Roosevelt took precedence over the human need for sleep, which is why he made a point of visiting him only hours after his return home.

Earlier this very day, at Wallace's lunch with Roosevelt advisor Harold Ickes, Ickes pressed the case that Wallace's nomination would cost the ticket too many votes, and his candidacy should be withdrawn. It was hard to imagine the loyalist Ickes would have rendered that advice to Wallace without some sense that he was speaking for the president. But Wallace said he would not step down as vice president, not without FDR's direct guidance that he wanted him to do so.

In this, Wallace had an advantage. The wily Franklin Roosevelt was not often direct, especially in matters of politics and personnel. This crucial meeting with the president, scheduled for four-thirty in the afternoon, was ostensibly a briefing on Wallace's trip to China.[8] But both men knew it was about much more.

Welcoming the vice president into his study, Roosevelt was warm and gracious, even if he was also gray and tired. His voice still carried the strength that failed the rest of his body.

After a long discussion of Wallace's recent trip, FDR turned the conversation to politics, with the direction that, should anyone ask about their meeting, the vice president should say no politics were discussed.[9]

"I am now talking to the ceiling about political matters," the president proclaimed with a wink.[10]

Franklin Roosevelt contemplated his imminent death almost

as often as he contemplated his vice presidents—which is to say almost never. But even the über-confident FDR had to acknowledge that the Republicans were putting forth a worthy contender that year. Tom Dewey was an appealing stalking horse for a war-weary nation also growing tired of one-party rule. It was assumed by many pundits than any other Democrat would lose to Dewey in the election this year. Of course, as FDR knew, he was not any other Democrat.

Sitting with Wallace, FDR admitted frankly there indeed had been talk of changing the ticket. But there was nothing to fear, FDR assured him.

Indeed, the president gave every indication he was firmly in Wallace's corner. He intended his fourth term to be "very progressive," Roosevelt said, and he needed Wallace to help him carry that out.

Of course, Roosevelt added with perhaps a slight twinkle, there were "political folks" urging him to consider a different direction. Some even thought that Wallace on the ticket might cost 2 or 3 million votes from conservative Democrats and middle-of-the-roaders.

The vice president was well prepared for this argument, and his response. And he was prepared to take a gamble.

"Mr. President, if you can find anyone who will add more strength to the ticket than I, by all means take him."[11] Wallace knew FDR well enough to know that the president rarely made such definitive declarations. A natural contrarian, FDR often responded in the opposite manner when encouraged to make a choice.

And that, indeed, is what happened.

"Oh, I have no basis for a judgment of my own," FDR demurred. "Still, it is mighty sweet of you to offer to withdraw. I would not for a moment accept it, however."[12]

FDR doubled down on that sentiment, telling Wallace he'd be willing to make a statement to that effect.

Wallace's eyes widened. Would you, he asked the president, be willing to say, "If I were a delegate to the convention I would vote for Henry Wallace?"

FDR did not hesitate. "Yes," he said firmly. "I would."[13]

The Next Day, July 11, 1944— Mayflower Hotel, Washington, D.C.

In 1944, Franklin Roosevelt was the most powerful man in the world. Elected in three landslides, he had almost single-handedly transformed his country, and most especially his political party. Where it took an army and armada to exert his will against Hitler at Normandy, it had taken only a few words to impose his will over the Democratic National Convention four years earlier.

The Democratic Party's big-city bosses and Jim Crow enthusiasts had disagreed with Roosevelt's selection of the ultraliberal Henry Wallace as vice president in 1940. But the stakes had been minimal. Vice presidents were powerless. Roosevelt was in good health. It didn't really matter who he wanted for his running mate.

Four years later, much was the same. At least on the surface. Roosevelt's popularity was still high. Vice presidents were still an afterthought. But one thing was different, something certain to affect the fate of every human being on earth:

The president of the United States was dying.

No one but the president and his doctor knew the specifics of the heart disease that what would, in just a year, kill him. And the ever-confident FDR did not for a moment believe the diagnosis.

But everyone around Roosevelt saw the symptoms. He never seemed to have any energy, despite routinely sleeping twelve hours a night. His once radiant face was gaunt, and his once sun-tanned complexion was gray. He still had his trademark smile, the mischievous twinkle in his bespectacled eyes, and a voice still capable of reaching the majestic notes that rallied a nation after Pearl Harbor and carried millions through the Great Depression. But now they were accompanied by trembling hands, a low cough, and a chronic upset stomach.

Though the three men meeting clandestinely in Washington that night did not know the particulars, they knew there was a chance, and a good one, that FDR would not survive a fourth term. That would leave them, the party, and the country, with President Henry Wallace—an alienating radical, in their view, who would lurch the party to the far left and alienate the rest of America. Most worrisome, it would likely end the lock of the Democrats on political power in Washington, as the nation turned to the appealing young New York governor running against FDR that year, Tom Dewey. One sentiment was clear among the men: Henry Wallace should not continue as vice president of the United States.

The men had settled on their consensus choice, the candidate among the Democrats to garner the least opposition. Senator Harry Truman of Missouri.

There were only two problems, but they were both surmountable. One was that Roosevelt didn't really want to give Truman the job. And Harry S. Truman didn't want it either.

That Evening, July 11, 1944—Oval Study, The White House

To the men watching the president closely that evening, but pretending not to, the old man looked both tired and unsettled. Still, he was in a jovial, if odd, mood.

At one point, FDR was his familiar self, reveling in the men's reviews of his famous martinis, a point of great pride to the president. At other times, he seemed strangely preoccupied by the presence of an unfamiliar butler, who seemed to hover every time the president spoke. After the butler was gone, FDR speculated about his own security and the risk that his food might be poisoned.[14]

When they adjourned after dinner to the blue oval room on the second floor of the mansion, talk finally turned to the business at hand. With the Democratic convention scheduled to begin in eight days in Chicago, FDR was being pressed to settle the vice-presidential matter once and for all. And it was not a secret that the group before him—including Ed Flynn, the Democratic leader from the Bronx and a longtime Roosevelt confidant; Bob Hannegan, the national Democratic Party chairman, who hailed from St. Louis; and Mayor Ed Kelly of Chicago—were in league against the sitting vice president of the United States, whom many in the room seemed to believe might even be a communist.

No matter what he'd said to Wallace the day before, Roosevelt had no reservations about dumping Wallace from the ticket. In fact, he'd been secretly discussing dumping Wallace for months.

Roosevelt watchers speculated that one of the reasons for the vice president's long trip to the Far East was to disrupt efforts to rally support for another term.[15] Perhaps in keeping with his propensity for mischief, FDR included on the vice president's itinerary stops in Outer Mongolia and Siberia so he could jest to friends, "I sent Henry to Siberia."[16]

But though FDR was happy to toss his vice president overboard—he done that same thing before to his first VP, John Nance Garner—a successor was a question mark. Gathering with the president, the conspirators were finally free to engage him directly.

Battling the oppressive Washington heat, the men gathered in shirtsleeves while cool drinks were passed around. That Wallace needed to go was hardly under dispute within the group, and Roosevelt made no effort to defend him.

For a brief moment talk centered on Associate Supreme Court Justice William O. Douglas, whom FDR liked for his youth (he was forty-six) and what was considered a Boy Scout quality that would play well with the media.

"Besides," FDR said with a smile, "he plays an interesting game of poker."[17]

There was little enthusiasm for Douglas in the room. "What about Harry Truman?" someone offered, referring to the senator from Hannegan's own Missouri. Truman was an ideal compromise candidate. He supported the administration on the majority of issues and was liked by the unions. But the conservatives liked him, too. He was the least offensive candidate anyone could think of.

FDR said little. He hardly knew the man. When he finally did speak up, his only concern was Truman's age.

"I think he's near sixty," FDR said, though he wasn't sure. Roosevelt himself was sixty-two. By contrast, Tom Dewey was a robust forty-two.

Another name popped up in Roosevelt's mind—his friend Jimmy Byrnes. James Byrnes was a former congressman and senator, representing his beloved South Carolina. He also had served a year on the Supreme Court before resigning during the war to head the Office of Economic Mobilization.

Byrnes was the perfect choice, FDR asserted, "because he knows more about government than anyone around."[18] As was often his habit, FDR overlooked inconvenient facts in his arguments—such as the fact that Byrnes was sixty-two, two years older than he thought Truman was.

In the room, the Byrnes balloon was met with uncomfortable looks and a notable shifting in seats. FDR knew why, of course. The race business again. Byrnes had tried to stop antilynching legislation while in the Senate, believing that lynching was necessary "in order to hold in check the Negro in the South." The reason for most lynchings in the South, Byrnes had claimed, was that so many blacks were rapists.[19]

Finally, FDR turned to Hannegan. He was tired and ready to be done with this. "Bob, I think you and everyone else here want Truman," he said. He instructed the men to notify Wallace and Byrnes that they were out.[20]

That evening the men left the president feeling like their coup had succeeded. Hannegan, however, still felt a little uneasy.

Two Days Later, Morning, July 13, 1944—The White House

"Mr. President, all I have heard around this White House this week was Negro," Jimmy Byrnes protested. "I wonder if anybody ever thinks about the white people."[21]

Byrnes had been delighted to hear from intermediaries that he was far and away FDR's first choice for the vice presidency, though the choice was hardly a surprise. He had been FDR's go-to guy on so many things during the administration that he was sometimes dubbed FDR's "assistant president."

He had no regrets about quitting the Supreme Court after a year. That place had been a mausoleum—he needed interaction with people. Which was why working at the White House for FDR during the war effort was ideal. He had quickly gained Roosevelt's esteem and trust. His trick was to show the contrarian FDR that he didn't need him. Whenever it suited Byrnes, he threatened to the president that he'd resign. Which of course only made FDR value him more.[22]

As he met with FDR at the White House, and talked turned to the vice presidency, FDR shared his dilemma. "I'm having trouble with Wallace," he said. He explained his promise to give the vice president a letter of support, but said it would be lukewarm. "I had to do at least this for Wallace. But don't you worry. Everyone assures me you will be nominated without any trouble."[23]

"All of us agree you are the best qualified man and all of us would rather have you than anyone else," FDR said. But his advisors—well, some of them—thought Byrnes on the ticket could cost two or three hundred thousand "Negro votes."[24]

Byrnes scoffed. He wasn't worried about this issue at all. He showed the president a press clipping of Mrs. Roosevelt surrounded by smiling black faces. "You can't tell me that because you have a southerner on the ticket that these people are going to turn on Mrs. Roosevelt," he said.

FDR did nothing to cool Byrnes's ardor. He wanted an open convention, he told Byrnes. "You are the best qualified man in the whole outfit and you must not get out of the race," he said firmly. "If you stay in, you are sure to win."[25]

Byrnes left the president sure of two things: that he had FDR's total support for the vice presidency and that Henry Wallace was a goner. To nominate him at the convention, now six days away, Byrnes had the perfect candidate in mind, the only person who might conceivably cost him the job.

Same Day, Lunchtime, July 13, 1944—The White House

The vice president came to his Thursday lunch with the president loaded with good news. First, he presented FDR with a list of nearly three hundred state delegates ready to renominate him at the convention.

In response, FDR emitted a whistle.

He also handed him the latest Gallup poll, which showed Wallace the overwhelming preference for vice president among the party faithful. The result was indeed impressive. Wallace had

65 percent support. Senator Alben Barkley was a distant second at 17 percent. Harry Truman was dead last at 2 percent.

Roosevelt's eyes widened and he seemed to marvel at the result. "Well, I'll be damned!" Roosevelt replied, before repeating an earlier promise to draft a letter to the convention recommending Wallace.[26]

"That's very generous of you, Mr. President," Wallace replied. Still there were all these rumors going around.

"Mr. President, is there any chance you would need an alternative candidate to the convention?"

"No," FDR assured him, with a broad smile. "I won't."[27]

Henry Wallace had served FDR for the entirety of his term, first as secretary of agriculture and then for the past four years as vice president. He admired FDR, revered him even, but he still didn't trust him completely.

As he left their lunch Wallace approached the president. "Well, I'm looking forward with pleasure to the results of next week," he said. He was not able to stop himself from adding a skeptical, "No matter what the outcome."

Roosevelt clasped the vice president's hand and pulled Wallace close to him.

"While I cannot put it just that way in public," he assured Wallace, "I hope it will be the same old team."[28]

Then FDR flashed his famous toothy grin, the smile that charmed millions and hid a powerful bite.

The Next Day, July 14, 1944—
President Hotel, Kansas City, Missouri

Harry Truman was annoyed. The Missouri senator had told everyone who'd asked him he had no interest in the vice presidency, yet the idea kept popping back in front of him like a bad movie review. He couldn't imagine in a million years why the Washington journalist crowd seemed to take the idea seriously. He hadn't even seen President Roosevelt in a year and even then hardly said two words to the man. That FDR wanted him to be next in line to be leader of the free world was not only preposterous, but frightening. What the hell would he do if he were president of the United States?[29]

"I don't want to be vice president," he'd told anyone who asked. "The Vice President simply presides over the Senate and sits around waiting for a funeral."[30]

The idea of a vice presidential candidacy caused other discomforts. Truman feared that people would bring up his alleged ties to the corrupt Pendergast Machine, which had sprung him into politics in Missouri. Or that someone would focus on the fact that his wife, Bess, was on the Senate payroll. Truman could have a volcanic temper when it came to criticisms of his family.

He knew, of course, that his name was being tossed around. But so were many others. Most everyone in the Senate had gossiped that it would be Wallace again. Then a few days later that Byrnes had it sewn up. Someone mentioned Senator Alben Barkley as a possibility. Personally, he believed Wallace would be in for another four years. That evening, however, he received a call at the hotel that changed his mind.

"Harry, it's Jimmy Byrnes," said the voice on the other end. "Were you serious about not wanting the vice presidency?"

"Yes," Truman replied. Absolutely. He was not a candidate and did not intend to be.

Byrnes informed him that he had "a 'go sign' from FDR." The vice presidency was his. Would Truman mind delivering his nominating speech?

If Jimmy Byrnes wanted the job, then best wishes to him.

"I'd be happy to rally the Missouri delegation behind you,"

Truman replied. No more vice presidency talk for him. And that, he thought, was that.[31]

Not long after he committed himself to Byrnes, Truman received a call from Alben Barkley. He was going to be vice president, Barkley told him. Would Truman nominate him?

Truman was baffled. What the heck was going on?

The Next Day, July 15, 1944—Chicago Rail Yards

The *Ferdinand Magellan* weighed 285,000 pounds, a wartime traveling fortress so impenetrable that it was said if a substantial cache of dynamite blew up on the tracks directly beneath it, the rail car would not budge.[32] The window glass was three inches thick, believed impervious to bullets. Now the mighty machine, carrying the president of the United States, was en route to San Diego. But it had made an unscheduled stop just outside Chicago, where its chief occupant might have one more visit with his convention planners.

When Bob Hannegan and Mayor Kelly entered the car, they greeted Mrs. Roosevelt and a speechwriter, and then met the president for a private conversation.

The mood at the convention site was worrisome. Wallace forces in Chicago were thick in number, a spirited bunch, backed by labor unions. And if there was one thing labor unions knew how to do it was organize. Wallace himself was expected to personally rally support. Even FDR was not immune to the power of the unions.

But even then it wasn't clear who FDR supported. "You know that Jimmy Byrnes had always been my first choice," FDR said. "Go ahead and name him."

But then FDR gave a seemingly contradictory order. "Be sure to clear it with Sidney," he ordered, meaning Sidney Hillman, who headed the political action committee for the powerful CIO, one of the nation's largest labor unions.

Hannegan knew there was no way Hillman would support a southern conservative like Jimmy Byrnes, especially against Henry Wallace. So, presumably, did FDR.

Before exiting the train, Hannegan asked for one more thing: another letter from Roosevelt that made his support for Truman plain. FDR agreed to it, but then added yet another name to the list of possibilities.

"Dear Bob, You have written me about Harry Truman and Bill Douglas. I should, of course, be very glad to run with either of them and believe that either one of them would bring real strength to the ticket."[33]

If they had hoped their visit with FDR would clarify things, they were disappointed. Hannegan and Kelly left the train believing that the vice presidency was still almost anyone's prize.

Two Days Later, July 17, 1944—Chicago

Jimmy Byrnes arrived in Chicago preparing to take on the burdensome but honorable mantle of the vice presidency of the United States. In a phone conversation, Roosevelt personally had told him that he was always his first choice for the job. Indeed, FDR asserted, of the men being mentioned for vice president, Byrnes was the only one who was a friend.

Yes, FDR had conceded, the pros were saying only William Douglas or Harry Truman were the safe choices. "I did not express myself," FDR lied.[34]

FDR's letter, the one he'd promised Wallace, was released in Chicago that day, and in Byrnes's assessment, did nothing to slow his juggernaut.

"I personally would vote for [Wallace's] re-nomination if I were a delegate to the convention," the letter read. That might have been all well and good, but FDR didn't leave it at that. "At the same time, I do not wish to appear in any way as dictating to the Convention. Obviously the Convention must do the deciding. And it should—and I am sure it will—give great consideration to the pros and cons of its choice."

As one wag put it, unwittingly summarizing FDR's indecisiveness throughout the process: "If you want him, well, OK. If you don't, well, OK." Another reporter labeled the letter "the coolest and cruelest brushoff in all the long Roosevelt career."[35]

The letter's thud coincided with a call from Bob Hannegan, who confirmed to Byrnes that he was FDR's choice and that the party had the "green light" to secure his nomination. There were even "Roosevelt-Byrnes" placards being ordered.

Mayor Kelly had called Byrnes separately to tell him FDR was no longer worried about his effect on "the Negro vote."[36]

Nothing, Byrnes believed, could stop things now.

The Next Day, July 18, 1944—Blackstone Hotel, Chicago

Twice Bob Hannegan had obtained letters from Roosevelt endorsing Harry Truman for vice president. And on more than one occasion, FDR had told him directly that he wanted Truman on the ticket. And yet Jimmy Byrnes was now the likely vice president of the United States.

Hannegan had told this to Byrnes himself the night before, even though there was no earthly way he could see labor unions blessing a Byrnes selection.

But Hannegan had given up. As he went to put the machinery in motion, one of his fellow conspirators stopped him.

"We couldn't have Byrnes. He'll hurt the ticket. We need to try the old man again."

One by one they reached Roosevelt on the train as it made its way to San Diego, each making the case for Truman.

Finally, FDR had heard enough. His games, if that was what they were, were over. "All right," FDR replied. "Tell Byrnes he's out. Go all out for Truman."[37]

The men looked at each other with relief. Of course, there was still a wrinkle, they told the president. Truman himself.

FDR knew how to take care of that.

The Next Day, July 19, 1944—Blackstone Hotel, Chicago

With Truman perched on one of the room's twin beds in Hannegan's suite, Hannegan called FDR's train in San Diego. Before long, everyone could hear the president's booming voice on the other end, carrying the strength that his body could no longer muster.

"Bob, have you got that fellow lined up yet?" Roosevelt called, fully aware that Hannegan was not the only person in the room.

Hannegan glanced at Truman. "No, he's the contrariest god-damned mule from Missouri I've ever dealt with."

"Well," came FDR's booming voice through the line, "you tell the senator if he wants to break up the Democratic Party in the middle of a war, that's his responsibility."[38]

The Missouri senator was stunned. "Oh, shit," Truman blurted out. "Well, if that's the situation, why didn't he say so in the first place?"[39]

What none of the men knew was that Henry Wallace might still have a chance to be president of the United States after all.

The Next Day, July 20, 1944—
Aboard the *Ferdinand Magellan*, San Diego

The president was on his way to review an exercise of the Fifth Marine Division as it prepared for its Pacific operations when the seizure struck.

Roosevelt's face turned white—deathly white. His voice faltered, and he gasped for air.

He motioned toward his son. "Jimmy, I don't know if I can make it," he managed to utter. "I have horrible pains."[40]

His son looked upon his stricken father, a giant of history who was now succumbing to illness and age. "Is it your heart?" he asked.

FDR shook his head. He refused to consider the possibility that he was having cardiac arrest.

"Should I call a doctor?"

Again the president shook his head. Reporters accompanying the train would be alerted, and FDR didn't want to cause a stir. It was digestive pains, he was certain. It would pass.

He needed to lie down, flat on the floor. That would ease the pain.

As Jimmy helped his father to the floor of the rail car, he watched in horrified silence.

He didn't want to, but the worst thoughts crept into his mind. For a moment it looked as if Henry Wallace might become president of the United States, just as he was about to be fired.

And then, as suddenly as the attack came on, the moment passed. Color returned to the president's face. Perhaps through sheer will, or stubbornness, FDR pressed on.

"We have an event to attend," Roosevelt said to his astonished son. "Let's go."

Later That Evening, July 20, 1944—
Chicago Stadium, Convention Hall

"We want Wallace!"

It first started as a faint cry in one section of the audience. But it became louder.

"WE WANT WALLACE!"

And louder still.

"WE WANT WALLACE! WE WANT WALLACE!"

The voices spread until the entire convention floor seemed to be screaming the name of the vice president of the United States.

Calling into the convention from his train, FDR delivered a short speech that brought the hall to its feet. Judging from his firm, familiar tones, no one had any sense he had seemingly come so close to death that very morning.

The attendees kept celebrating, waving signs that read ROO-SEVELT AND VICTORY. Then suddenly the attention turned to his running mate.

Hannegan and other party leaders suspected that union workers had infiltrated the convention to start the chants for Wallace. Whatever the case, there was no denying that Wallace had the support of the majority of the hall. A mania seemed to take over the crowd. Even the convention organist, a loyalist for Democratic Party heads, joined in, playing the "Iowa Corn Song" in honor of Wallace, the state's native son.

Standing on a chair in the Florida delegation, Senator Claude Pepper waved his arms and shouted at the top of his lungs and waved the Florida placard to get the attention of the convention chairman. He wanted to call for an immediate vote on the vice presidential nomination, a vote that, considering the mood of the assembled crowd, he was certain his man, Henry Wallace, would win.

But his microphone was turned off and the convention chairman, acting on orders of Hannegan and others, pretended not to see him. The Democratic leaders were in a panic; as it looked as if Wallace supporters would storm the convention.

Undaunted, Pepper marched to the convention rostrum to make his motion before the entire convention. As they watched Pepper inch closer, Hannegan screamed at the convention chairman: "Adjourn the session!"

"I can't," the chairman replied. "This crowd is too hot."

"You're taking orders from me," Hannegan snapped. "And I'm taking orders directly from the President."[41]

With that statement, the chairman relented. Before an angry and frustrated crowd, the proceedings were adjourned for the night. And with that, Henry Wallace's mounting hopes to return to the vice presidency finally ended.

The Next Day, July 21, 1944—Chicago Stadium

Nobody had an exact total of how many deals were struck, how many promises made, how many jobs offered, how many perks awarded, in the hours after Henry Wallace almost returned to the vice presidency.

But by the time the convention reconvened, the revolt was over. The die was cast. And Harry Truman, having done almost nothing to attain the job and not even wanting it, was nominated vice president of the United States.

Winning the nomination on the second ballot, Truman went to the platform and delivered before the convention the least stirring and perhaps shortest speech in Democratic Party history.

Missouri was honored by this nomination, a slightly bewildered Truman told the crowd. But he accepted it "with all humility."

Looking through his round wireless glasses, Truman added, almost shyly, "Now give me a chance."[42]

★   ★   ★

As it happens, I have some personal experience with the vice-presidential selection process. In 2008, Senator McCain asked me to submit myself for vetting by his campaign so that he could consider whether to select me as his running mate. I of course do not presume that he ultimately would have chosen me. But I knew at the time that Senator McCain was unpredictable and unconventional enough that he just might pick a young, conservative, first-term governor, whom most of the country had never heard of. And I didn't want it to be me.

I politely declined to be considered in 2008 because I felt I had work to do in Louisiana. I had been elected on a platform of significant policy reforms. I had already led successful fights for ethics reform, tax cuts, and a better budget. But there was a lot more that I wanted to accomplish. I hadn't run for governor in order to *be* something; I had run in order to *do* something, and too many of those things were not yet accomplished.

In hindsight, I now know that even if I had allowed myself to be considered, and even if Senator McCain had selected me, I would not have become vice president, because the Republican ticket still would have lost. No Republican ticket was likely to win the White House in 2008. But in other years, in other political environments, the vice-presidential selection can make a difference. It probably did in 1960, when John F. Kennedy needed LBJ's Texas. It might also have mattered in 1992, when Bill Clinton's choice of a fellow southerner, Al Gore, may have helped him win close races in the South.

Vice-presidential selections can also make a difference after the election, and not always in a good way. Lincoln's choice of Andrew

Johnson in 1864, perhaps the worst decision of our greatest president, helped lead to a century of Jim Crow segregation. McKinley's choice of Theodore Roosevelt led to a leftward shift in the Republican Party and, indirectly, to the eventual election of the disastrously progressive Woodrow Wilson. Eisenhower's choice of Richard Nixon led indirectly to Watergate.

We will never know with certainty what would have happened if Franklin Roosevelt had chosen someone other than Harry Truman to join his ticket in 1944. We will never know, for example, if President James Byrnes, a southerner who once defended lynching, would have decided, as Truman did in 1948, to desegregate the U.S. Armed Forces. But we do know that President Henry Wallace, a Soviet accommodationist, would have made many of the wrong decisions in the early days of the Cold War. As president, Wallace would have had a naïve, wrongheaded view of Stalin and his aspirations. He would not have come to the defense of Europeans or spoken out on behalf of dissidents trapped in Soviet gulags. How do we know this? Wallace said so himself.

In the fall of 1949, Wallace met with Vladimir Petrov, who escaped from the Soviet gulag Wallace had once visited. Petrov told Wallace the truth about his imprisonment and the Soviet regime, and Wallace was stunned.

In September 1952, eight years after he came so close to the presidency, Wallace published a book entitled *Where I Was Wrong*. The book was in effect an apology for his pro-Soviet leanings. He said he labored under illusions.

He wrote, "I had not the slightest idea that there were many slave-labor camps in Siberia in 1944 and that of these the most notorious was Magadan," which he visited. "What I did not see was the Soviet determination to enslave the common man morally, mentally, and physically for its own imperial purposes.

"My analysis failed utterly to take into account the ruthless nature of Russian-trained Communists." With language that could have been borrowed from Ronald Reagan, the left-wing former vice president wrote, "More and more I am convinced that Russian Communism in its total disregard of truth, in its fanaticism, its intolerance and its resolute denial of God and religion is something utterly evil."

If Wallace had been president, this realization would have come too late, because by 1952 the damage would have been done and the Cold War perhaps lost.

Fortunately for the nation, Harry Truman took his place— a man who initiated the Truman Doctrine to stop the spread of communism and defend free people under siege; the Berlin Airlift, which saved West Berlin from Soviet takeover; the defense of Korea, which led to one of the world's strongest economies and one of our strongest allies in Asia; and the Marshall Plan, which saved Western Europe from postwar devastation and helped its nations become critical allies in the Cold War. It was Truman's administration that set in place the architecture that over the next forty years helped America and the West win the Cold War, led the Soviet Union to dissolution, and brought liberty to tens of millions trapped behind the Iron Curtain. And it was Truman who maintained the "special relationship" between America and Great Britain, which has proven time and again to be the anchor in the battle against terrorism and tyranny.

But in 1946, none of those policies were obvious. The Western world was tired of war. The United States had reduced the size of its military by 90 percent. The Soviet Union was remembered as an indispensable ally. Few Americans believed there was a Cold War to fight. Though far from intuitive, Harry Truman's decisions affected the security of the entire world. But the chaotic and even reckless manner in which he was given the opportunity to do so could have changed history dramatically and, almost certainly, for the worse.

PART IV

QUESTIONS OF FAITH

9

★ ★ ★

GREAT AWAKENINGS

Abolition and the Hidden Hand of God

Religion has always been part of American politics and governance. The Declaration of Independence, our founding document and the philosophical blueprint of our liberty, tells us that our natural rights to "life, liberty, and the pursuit of happiness" are rights with which we are "endowed" by our "Creator."[1]

Those words express the very core of who we are as a country. Unlike France, or China, or Germany, ours is a nation founded on ideas, not race or ethnicity. It is our principles, as outlined in the Declaration and detailed in the Constitution, that bind us.

And from the very beginning, our core principles—our natural rights—were declared to come from God.

I care so much about religious liberty and the necessity of religious people's participation in American government, business, and civic life that I delivered an entire address about the subject in February of 2014 at the Ronald Reagan Library. It is among my proudest moments. Most politicians go to the Reagan Library and talk about their life stories. They see it as their big chance to connect their careers and ambitions to the Gipper's. But I didn't want to use that great stage to talk about me. I wanted to talk about God and God's place in the United States of America.

Today, many on the Left argue that religion has no place in the public square. The Constitution, they say, creates a "wall of separation between church and state."[2] This belief is based on a misinterpretation of the First Amendment to the U.S. Constitution.[3] In fact, nowhere in the Constitution does it use those words, which are actually from a letter by Thomas Jefferson.

It is clear that the founders were staunchly against the creation of a state religion. They were also deeply committed to preventing the government from restricting faithful citizens from exercising their religious beliefs. Today's liberals conveniently forget about this second part, and push for policies that use government to suppress public expression of private religious belief.

The vast majority of the founders clearly identified themselves as Christians and applied Judeo-Christian principles to the creation of our great nation. And even those who were unorthodox in their faith or were enamored of a more general, Enlightenment-inspired "deism" would have found the idea of liberal secularism both preposterous and dangerous.

A free people must have a moral foundation from which to act as responsible citizens. To the founders, religion provided this foundation. In the context of their time and place, that meant Christianity. They did not want the government to interfere with private belief or expression—of the people, or of those elected by the people.

And thank God this was so. If it weren't for religion, many of the great moral victories of U.S. history, from the abolition of slavery to women's suffrage to the civil rights movement, would never have happened. The abolitionist movement would have been impossible without the public religion and Christian fervor of the Second Great Awakening. The Christian revivalism and activism championed by leaders of the Second Great Awakening, such as Lyman Beecher, made plain the sinful nature of slavery, and called on all Christians to work for its abolition.

Among those who answered this call were titans of United States history: Frederick Douglass, William Lloyd Garrison, Horace Greeley, Wendell Phillips, Harriet Tubman, and of course, Lyman Beecher's two most famous children—Harriet Beecher Stowe and Henry Ward Beecher.

This is their story.

September 3, 1817—Boston

The summer was waning, but the fields and earth were still warm with the glow of August. This was the best time of year to be in New England: not yet cold, no longer stifling, with a small promise of crisp autumn on the air. Traveling the rough roads from Litchfield, Connecticut, to Boston, Massachusetts, Lyman Beecher considered the weighty task in front of him. Now in his forties and one of the nation's most famous ministers, he felt every root and rut along the way.

Arrival in Boston was as strange as always, with farmlands, forests, and meadows giving away suddenly to the great city. He could see the steeple of his destination—Park Street Church—from the road.

Stepping out of the carriage, he looked up at the huge edifice before him, a magnificent structure, all for the glory of God. Entering, he surveyed the massive crowd. Beecher paused before beginning.

It was one thing to give a sermon, yet another to preach the Gospel at the ordination of your great friend, and the son of your recently deceased spiritual mentor. Timothy Dwight had been a giant—writer, theologian, president of Yale University. He had had a tremendous impact on his students, especially the young Lyman Beecher, who followed him into the ministry.

Dwight's son Sereno had at first chosen a different path, tutoring students after he graduated from Yale, and then practicing law in New Haven. But the call of the ministry found him as well, early enough for his father to know his intentions, though not to see him ordained. His father had died of cancer just eight short months earlier.

On this day Sereno would be officially ordained at Park Street, famed for its devotion to Christ and to bringing the Gospel alive through good works and moral action, themes that closely hewed to Beecher's own Christian philosophy. Both men wished the missing father could have been there to witness it, but at least Lyman was there.

Beecher was nearly as bereft as Sereno over their loss. He once wrote of Dwight: "Oh how I loved him! I loved him as my own soul, and he loved me as a son."[4] Facing the large congregation in the massive, elegant church in the heart of Boston, he waited, silently praying before beginning.

As a minister of deep experience, he began with practical advice to his friend, and now colleague: "Your duty is plain," he said. "It is simply to explain and enforce the laws of the divine moral government contained in the Bible."[5]

For the rest of the sermon, he returned to familiar themes: the glory of God, the Scriptures as moral laws, faith, and repentance. And over and over, he started a new lesson with a forceful "Dare to think for yourself."[6] And then cautioned against prideful overreach.

In conclusion, he spoke the soul of the matter at hand plainly, giving voice to his own theology, which had stirred countless hearts to Christian action across the country.

"Set your heart upon the great blessing of a revival of religion!" he thundered. "Desire it speedily and constantly pray for it without ceasing, and stir up the members of your church to concentrate on, this point, the whole importunity of the prayer of faith."[7]

Twelve Years Later, July 4, 1829—Boston

Walking along the surprisingly cool and rainy streets on Independence Day, William Lloyd Garrison focused on his task—a great speech at Park Street Church in Boston on the evils of slavery.

Garrison was the latest in a long line of abolitionists invited to deliver speeches at Park Street Church on every Independence Day, a tradition begun there by its pastor, Sereno Dwight.

The church was only a handful of blocks from William Lloyd Garrison's boardinghouse, and despite the cool weather, his hands were sweaty. He knew he was right, but was he the right messenger? Today, and the many days that followed, would tell.

Born into poverty, Garrison was raised by a strict Baptist mother who taught the young William the virtues of moral fortitude and the Christian faith. Arriving in Boston in 1826, when the Second Great Awakening was at its height, he began his search for meaning in life. His religious wanderings brought him eventually to Lyman Beecher.

Garrison would join what Beecher called a "disciplined moral militia."[8] And even if Beecher himself eventually found Garrison's approach too radical—and Garrison in turn criticized Beecher for what he saw as accommodation—without the Awakening and Beecher himself, Garrison may not have found his true purpose.[9]

Garrison called slavery a "national sin"[10] and saw emancipation as redemption for the country's trespasses. Christianity was, after all, a faith of second chances. Galilee's tax collectors and prostitutes had received such chances. So had Peter. So would America—*if* she mended her wayward ways.

Entering the church, Garrison was both terrified and gratified by the size of the crowd. For a moment, his knees locked together, and he was momentarily unable to move forward, such was his shock.

He was steadied, however, by the beautiful and thrilling abolitionist hymn sung by the Park Street Church choir. Who was he to linger over stage fright when millions toiled in bondage in his own country? He must steady himself, and look to the memory of his old minister Lyman Beecher for an example of rhetorical poise.

Unlike the enthusiasm of other preachers whose passion burned brightest in their youth, Garrison's grew with age. At a tender and bespectacled twenty-four, he believed in gradual emancipation, a position he would soon strongly denounce from a platform whose reach would one day extend to states that did not yet even exist.

But on this July 4, Garrison had yet to make a name for himself. He would today. "It is natural," he said, referring to his nation's Independence Day, "that the return of a day which established the liberties of a brave people should be hailed by them with more than ordinary joy; and it is their duty as Christians and patriots to celebrate it with signal tokens of thanksgiving." [11]

But was this celebration truly deserved? Gaining confidence, he warmed to his address, declaiming, "I speak not as a partisan or an opponent of any man or measures when I say that our politics are rotten to the core." On he went, adding: "*We* boast of our freedom, who go shackled to the polls, year after year, by tens and hundreds and thousands!" [12]

The crowd was enthralled. Who was this young firebrand, speaking with such power and eloquence in the very heart of abolitionism? Throughout the sermon, Garrison held the crowd, bound by his logic, vigor, and most of all his passion.

Pulling the crowd with him to his final rhetorical climax, he stated, "I call upon the ambassadors of Christ everywhere to make known this proclamation: Thus saith the Lord God of the Africans. Let this people go, that they may serve me."[13]

Nearly breathless, Garrison ended with a forceful call for Christian action: "On this subject, Christians have been asleep; let them shake off their slumbers, and arm for the holy contest."[14]

Five Years Later, November 1834—Washington, D.C.

The bold, stern-faced minister faced a different kind of congregation tonight. Dressed in his finest clothes—not as fine as some, on his smallish income—Lyman Beecher had come to address the American Colonization Society, which was dedicated to encouraging the immigration of free blacks "back" to Africa.

Lyman Beecher believed in the righteousness of abolition but worried that large numbers of free blacks posed an insurmountable challenge to white American society. If emancipation came, as it must, integration would be all but impossible, especially with the size of the slave population.

But most of all, he wanted Christian unity; he had seen how the bitter enmity between colonization supporters and full abolitionists—who opposed colonization—could rend otherwise peaceful brothers in Christ. This very question had nearly destroyed his own beloved Lane Theological Seminary, back in Cincinnati.

Steadying himself, he began his address, speaking slowly but with force. From the hundreds of sermons and speeches he had delivered in his work as a minister, he knew how to draw in a crowd. He called for those assembled to not work at cross-purposes with the abolitionists, to see that their goals were largely one and the same.

"There would be great danger," he said, that a collision between the two antislavery groups would "degenerate into party spirit, depreciating each other's success . . . and bring a deep reproach, over which angels must weep, upon our common Christianity." Are not both sides "agreed in most of the great principles which command the entire subject"?[15]

Warming to his topic, he continued, driving home the point that both sides agreed on the most important principles: "That slavery is wrong, and a great national sin and national calamity, and that as soon as possible it is to be brought to an end, not however, by force, nor by national legislation, nor by fomenting insurrection, nor by the violation of the Constitution and the dissolution of the union, but by information, and argument, and moral suasion."[16]

This was the key point, not just for slavery, but for bettering the world through Christ. This was the theology that made him famous. He believed deeply that a republic of free men must be peopled with those imbued with both personal and civic virtue through the vehicle of Christianity. Christian activism through righteous volunteer associations would keep the great American experiment from degenerating into chaos.

"There can be no doubt that slavery, through the world, is destined to cease . . . the day hastens, when every yoke shall be broken, and the oppressed go free!" Beecher exclaimed.[17]

Beecher concluded with a plea for the souls of Africa—that they should receive the Gospel, either by free Christian blacks "returning" to the continent, or by other missionaries. "If I forget thee, O Africa," he thundered, "let my right hand forget her cunning. If I do not plead thy cause, let my tongue cleave to the roof of my mouth."[18]

Sixteen Years Later, February 1851—Brunswick, Maine

Maine has the hardest of Februaries. Brittle, isolating, so distant from spring it feels as if warmth never existed. You don't so much see your breath on the air as feel it solidify as it leaves your lungs.

Harriet Beecher Stowe, strong-featured, smart, deeply religious, and still mourning the death of her eighteen-month-old son,[19] dead from cholera caught the previous year, sat attentively in pew number 23, at First Parish Church. She prayed and sang with singular focus, meditating on God and suffering.

Born in the summer of 1811, in Litchfield, Connecticut, Stowe was the beloved daughter of the famous minister Lyman Beecher, and sister to the even more famous minister Henry Ward Beecher.[20] When the minister called the congregation to join the Eucharist, Stowe did so with a small sliver of joy. Her boy was gone, but gone to Christ. She must remember that.

As she took Communion, her vision blurred, but she was steady. Before her, almost tangible, was a horrible scene: a brutal slave master standing over two slaves, forcing them to whip a third, much older slave. To death.[21]

She did not know how long the vision lasted, but it burned in her mind's eye. It expanded her inner vision. She could hardly wait for services to end, because she was in such agony. She was sure she could relieve the agony only by making a difference in the battle over the freedom of these slaves. By doing *something* for their cause.

She *had* to do *something*.

She *had* to get *home*.

She *had* to start *writing*!

God had sent Stowe the vision so that she could more deeply understand the horror that was human bondage, and further the cause of moral suasion her father, Lyman, preached of so often to help free the slaves. Hurrying up Federal Street, she was finally back home. Rushing to her desk, she found pen, ink, and paper, and began to write the story of her vision, about a slave called Tom.

Published first as a serial in 1851 and 1852 in the Washington, D.C., abolitionist newspaper the *National Era*, and then in 1852 as a book, *Uncle Tom's Cabin* told a deeply moving story of slavery, the quest for liberty, and how deep religious faith can sustain one in even the worst circumstances. Tom's powerful devotion to Christ was a reflection of her own, and reminded many otherwise disinterested Americans of their duties as Christians. "I did not write it. God wrote it. I merely did his dictation," she would say.[22]

Uncle Tom's Cabin was more than a sensation—it was an earthquake. It brought the horrors of slavery directly into the parlors and studies of the once apathetic. Like her father's preaching, it set the hearts of many aflame. *Uncle Tom's Cabin* sold ten thousand copies in just its first week. Within a year, three hundred thousand copies were on American bookshelves.[23] Within five years, more than two *million* copies had been sold.[24] The book reshaped the slavery debate[25] and spread the abolitionist movement in the North to people of all walks of life, many of whom would find themselves wearing Union uniforms a decade later in a war triggered in part by the words of Harriet Beecher Stowe.

Eleven Years Later, July 22, 1862—Washington, D.C.

The meeting's start was typical. As his cabinet and top advisors shuffled into President Abraham Lincoln's office, talking quietly in pairs or threes, the president surveyed them, calculating their probable reactions to the hammer of news he was about to drop upon them.

This large, but cozy, office was the center not only of Lincoln's administration, but of the country itself. Cabinet meetings, strategic decisions, military appointments, diplomatic wranglings—all took place in this surprisingly unkempt room. Today's meeting would be more momentous than almost any other, save one.

The wallpaper was patterned, in places covered with maps. Various upholstered and wooden chairs, horsehair couches, and desks were scattered around the room, all resting on an ornate carpet. Rickety gas lamps lit the room, and near the president's desk hung a corded bell for Lincoln to beckon his aides. On the west wall was a fireplace, over which hung a portrait of Andrew Jackson, who had warned South Carolinians who threatened to flout federal authority, "If one drop of blood be shed there in defiance of the laws of the United States, I will hang the first man of them I can get my hands on to the first tree I can find."[26] That was one way to preserve the Union.

Looking out the tall windows draped with heavy curtains, Lincoln could see the stub of the Washington Monument, still under construction, and the freezing Potomac. He could also see Union army camps—a constant reminder of the great task at hand, and the weight of it.

Dominating the room near its center was a long walnut table, piled high with papers, maps, books, and letters.[27] As the president's advisors settled into their typical places, they discussed several matters of various import.

Rising from his chair, Lincoln commanded the attention of the room. He announced that he had prepared a new document— a proclamation—to free the slaves in states in rebellion.

Holding up a handwritten piece of paper, Lincoln read the Preliminary Emancipation Proclamation aloud. With particular emphasis, he declared, "That on the first day of January, in the year of our Lord one thousand eight hundred and sixty-three, all persons held as slaves within any State, or any designated part of a State, the people whereof shall then be in rebellion against the United States shall be then, thenceforward, and forever, free."[28]

Standing before his closest advisors, most of whom were

shocked by what they were hearing, Lincoln continued, watching the alarm grow on the faces of many of his cabinet. "The Executive Government of the United States including the military and naval authority thereof, will recognize and maintain the freedom of such persons, and will do no act or acts to repress such persons, or any of them, in any efforts they may make for their actual freedom."[29]

When the president finished, he looked around the room. Then discussion resumed, and in earnest. Some voiced their strong support, others their disapproval—it either went too far or did not go far enough. What about slaves within the Union? What would the reaction be in Europe?

But Lincoln was firm in his resolve. He brooked no argument but one: the shrewd secretary of state, William Seward, said, it would be better to "postpone its issue, until you can give it to the country supported by military success."[30]

Two months later, a victory, or at least something approaching one, was won along a little stream in Maryland called Antietam Creek. In the bloodiest day in American history, the Union army checked Robert E. Lee's march into Union territory and sent his Army of Northern Virginia back across the Potomac to the fields and forests that gave Lee's army its name. Five days later, Lincoln published the Preliminary Emancipation Proclamation.

Five Months Later, December 2, 1862—Washington, D.C.

It was damp and cold, but Harriet Beecher Stowe burned nonetheless with a fiery passion. Today, she would meet the president, Abraham Lincoln, her hope and perhaps her folly. The man was too slow on the great issue of the day, slavery. Stowe believed Lincoln mistakenly thought the war a political crisis, and his main obligation preventing dissolution of the United States. But clearly,

Stowe felt sure, it was a moral crisis. The soul of the nation was at stake. Why was Lincoln dragging his feet on the slavery question? She would soon find out.

She had invited herself to the presidential mansion to tell Mr. Lincoln what she thought of his pace, and of the war, emancipation, and few things otherwise. But her primary mission was to find an answer to the burning question of the day: Would he soon issue the final Emancipation Proclamation as had been promised months earlier?

Entering the White House, Stowe found the experience thrilling, but the mansion mundane. A fine building for certain, but a building still. She had been in many as grand, or nearly as grand. After being led through a labyrinth of corridors and doorways, she walked into the cozy room that held both the president and Secretary of State Seward. He, at least, had been a forceful abolitionist in his time. Had he been despoiled, she wondered, by Lincoln's pragmatism?

Lincoln sat before a smoldering fire. Slowly, he rose, as if stiff from many labors, as Seward made the introductions. Approaching with all his height, and with the look of warm, homespun intelligence that had won him this very house, he said, "Why, Mrs. Stowe, right glad to see you."

He paused, his eyes crinkling.

"So," he said, "you're the little woman who wrote the book that made this great war!"[31]

Sitting back in front of the fire, Lincoln warmed his hands, turning them slowly to distribute the heat. After some pleasantries, Harriet Beecher Stowe explained her true reason for coming. "I want to ask you about your views on emancipation."[32]

The conversation made its way around many a topic, from the placement of high officials to her enlisted son Frederick's well-being. Through it all—and it could justifiably be called a quiet tirade—the president was attentive, kindly, and patient. Before leaving, he faced the famous writer and said with weary regret about the war: "Whichever way it ends, I have the impression that I shan't last long after it's over."[33]

She had not accomplished her mission exactly; she was not explicitly told the proclamation would be signed on January 1. But she was confident it would be, and ever more confident in the man who would sign it.

One Month Later, January 1, 1863—Washington, D.C.

Waking on a cold, sunny New Year's Day, Abraham Lincoln was weary, but determined. Good work would be done today, though many would curse him for it. Though it still stung, he was used to the cursing, from both sides of most arguments. After dressing and breakfasting, Lincoln retired to his office to await the arrival of Secretary Seward. At 10:45 a.m., he arrived, and brought with him the momentous document. The rebels had been duly warned in September. Months had passed, and none had laid down their arms. So be it then—emancipation.

As he signed the proclamation, Lincoln noticed a small mistake. Sighing, slightly frustrated, he asked Seward to have it fixed. It would not do to have an error in a document that would almost certainly be remembered and read for generations. The signing would have to wait until after the day's traditional White House New Year's celebration. Steadying himself, weary, Lincoln headed down for the reception.

Standing with his wife, Mary Todd Lincoln, the president was distracted. His love for the American people was real, but he was exhausted. Physically. Emotionally. Spiritually. In every way possible. He once said of these occasions that "the tax on my time is heavy," but "no hours of my day are better employed than those which thus bring me again within the direct contact and atmosphere of the average of our whole people."[34]

He continued: "Many of the matters brought to my notice are utterly frivolous, but others are of more or less importance, and all serve to renew in me a clearer and more vivid image of that great popular assemblage out of which I sprung, and to which . . . I must return."[35] A good lesson for anyone in the White House to learn well.

Today, he would rather not have spent hours glad-handing. But even the president—most of the time, it felt like *especially* the president—was not master of his own time. The signing would have to wait, the hands would have to be shaken, and the kindly smile would have to be repeated, hundreds of times.

The president and Mrs. Lincoln began the work of greeting visitors at 11:00 a.m. Diplomats and foreign attachés in their finery—fancy clothes, gold lace, feathers, and much else—came first. Then came the military officers. Like the president, they hoped the New Year would be better than the last.

It would. The decisive battles of Gettysburg and Chattanooga later in the year, and the capture of Vicksburg on the Mississippi, would mark the beginning of the end of the Confederacy.

At noon, the White House opened to welcome the citizenry. Waiting, some patiently and some not, was a mass of people and carriages. At one point, Lincoln thought he saw Congressman William Kellogg of Illinois sporting a torn coattail from the melee of entry.[36] He chuckled. You must take your small joys when and where you can find them.

Surrounded by police and soldiers on the ready to deal with any trouble, the teeming crowd was generally peaceful, if not exactly calm. Though no doubt the pickpockets would do a good business in this tightly packed, distracted group. Most—burly workers, dapper businessmen, fine ladies in their dresses and bonnets—simply wanted a glimpse of the lanky president, his wife, and the White House itself during the New Year's Day celebration.

Entering in groups and delving deep into the storied abode, down a hallway to a suite of rooms for reception, bachelors, couples, and families righted their crowd-disheveled hats and clothes. Then another line in which to stand, but more orderly, and leading right to the great man. Guest after guest approached the president and First Lady, first giving their name to Lincoln's friend and unofficial bodyguard U.S. Marshal of the District of Columbia Ward Hill Lamon,[37] who passed the name along to the president. Lincoln smiled graciously while shaking hands with each of his fellow citizens, and tried to say a few kind words in his surprisingly high-pitched voice.

Departure was swift. Through the richly decorated East Room, and then out past a corps of cavalry officers and back into the milling crowd of the New Year's reception itself.[38] Lincoln watched them all go, wishing he, too, could be freed from the tyranny and tedium of official business. After many wearying hours, the reception ended, and the president finally turned his attention to the real work of the day. Though his love for his fellow citizens was genuine, he was also reserved, perhaps even introverted. The day's mingling depleted him greatly, loath though he was to admit it.

By early afternoon, Lincoln made his way to his office to sign perhaps the most important document of his presidency—or any presidency. He planned no fanfare. He was not one for self-congratulation. This was a sober occasion for a solemn duty. With Seward and some of his staff, Lincoln sat down at the huge office table, ready to review the corrected draft. Looking over at Seward, he marveled at the steady trust between them. It had not always been so. Once, not too long ago, they were political rivals. They couldn't be more different. Lincoln was tall and gangly, a westerner of humble origins with the customary beard and bushy eyebrows. Seward, an Eastern blue blood with an aristocratic mien, had been the favorite for the Republican nomination in 1860. But the relatively unknown Lincoln snatched it away. The two had learned to greatly admire each other in the years since.

Lincoln and Seward were also different in their approach to abolition: Seward was a lifelong abolitionist whose New York house served as a stop on the Underground Railroad. Lincoln, no friend of slavery, nonetheless famously wrote to the abolitionist editor of the *New York Tribune*, Horace Greeley, in the months before the proclamation that he would do anything to save the Union, even preserving slavery:

My paramount object in this struggle is to save the Union, and is not either to save or to destroy slavery. If I could save the Union without freeing any slave I would do it, and if I could save it by freeing all the slaves I would do it; and if I could save it by freeing some and leaving others alone I would also do that.[39]

This letter no doubt dismayed the staunchly abolitionist Greeley, who had repeatedly pushed for Lincoln to end slavery by any means possible, including by executive fiat. Greeley, who had earlier been aligned with Seward but switched his support to Lincoln in 1860, had helped found the Republican Party expressly on the slavery issue.[40]

Lifting his pen, Lincoln dipped it gingerly into the waiting inkwell and prepared to write. But his hand was trembling—not from fear or hesitation, but from exhaustion. Shaking hands with hundreds of visitors earlier in the day had taken its toll, even on this experienced campaigner.

Lincoln paused briefly to steady his hand, lest it "appear as if I hesitated."[41] For a moment, he couldn't control his arm, and he worried that a larger power was giving him pause, or a signal. Then he thought about those hundreds of people he had shaken hands with over the previous several hours and realized, with a small smile on his face, that it was not God, but exhaustion, that made his hand tremble.[42]

"I never, in my life, felt more certain that I was doing right than I do in signing this paper,"[43] he said, and then signed. Looking up, smiling, he added: "That will do."[44]

Secretary Seward then signed in his fine style. The official seal was affixed. And with that, the proclamation became the enforceable law of the United States.

Though the Emancipation Proclamation was only a partial victory for abolition—it freed only the slaves of those areas in active rebellion—almost everyone saw it for what it was: the death knell of slavery in the United States.

It was late afternoon when the great document was finally ready to release to the press, and 8 p.m. before it went out over the wires to newspapers around the country. Citizens waited across the nation, nervous, as the news was late in coming. Anxiety increased with each passing minute. They waited. And waited. And waited.

Nowhere was the anxiety higher than in Boston, the center of American abolitionism, where a host of the movement's leading lights gathered in churches, homes, and public halls.

It would be worth the wait.

Same Day, January 1, 1863—Boston, Massachusetts

"Will he actually sign it?" That was the only question on the minds of the many abolitionists gathered around Boston, waiting for the good news.

Many who had fought longest and hardest for emancipation

gathered in Boston's Music Hall for a celebratory concert and to wait for the news. The atmosphere was tense. After decades of work, abuse, and threats of legal actions and physical harm, the elusive goal was at hand. Or so they hoped.

Few had slept well the night before, tossing and turning in worry that the next day would bring disappointment instead of exultation. Standing in the music hall that day, many, perhaps most, remained fearful. All the work, hopes, dreams, and prayers of those assembled came down to this moment: would he or wouldn't he? Was freedom, or at least the promise of freedom, finally at hand? Would the stain of the great "national sin" finally be expunged? Would we finally repent as a nation for our crimes against our fellow man, and God?

The wait was excruciating. Each moment of silence from the telegraph office confirmed the crowd's worst fears. Their worries that the president would make a change at the last minute to help the war effort seemed justified. "Why hasn't it come?" they asked.

Little did they know that their agony had been prolonged by a simple clerical error. How the fate of the world sometimes hangs on the mundane.

Among those waiting for news from Washington were many leading lights of New England. Ralph Waldo Emerson read his "Boston Hymn," written especially for the occasion. From the point of view of God himself, the poem boomed with righteous indignation:

> *My angel, his name is Freedom,*
> *Choose him to be your king;*
> *He shall cut pathways east and west.*
> *And fend you with his wing . . .*
> *I break your bonds and masterships,*
> *And I unchain the slave:*

Free be his heart and hand henceforth,
As wind and wandering wave . . .
My will fulfilled shall be,
For, in daylight or in dark,
My thunderbolt has eyes to see
His way home to the mark.[45]

During intermission, in between performances of the works of Beethoven, Mendelssohn, and Handel, the news finally arrived: Lincoln's proclamation was burning up the wires to Boston!

The massive crowd surged, exploding with rapture and relief. Laughter mixed with tears, joy with a wondrous disbelief. Calls of thanksgiving filled the air. Those standing stood taller still. Those sitting jumped to their feet. Almost as one, their joyous voices joined in the cacophony. To be sure, the word wasn't yet official. No newspapers were yet reporting it. But they would be, soon.

The crowd, so recently wary of Lincoln and his pragmatism, burst forth with nine cheers for the president, and then three cheers for William Lloyd Garrison. The abolitionist stood joyful and unbelieving in the music hall's gallery. Few in the country deserved such plaudits at this moment as much as Garrison. His zeal for and work in the abolitionist movement had grown exponentially since his first major public speech on the topic in 1829 at Park Street Church. His daughter, next to him, believed the joy in his heart was so intense it was "akin to pain."[46]

Before long, the crowd began to chant the name of "the little woman who wrote the book that made this great war." Finally, Harriet Beecher Stowe came forward, proud and humbled by the moment. For years, her book had been a best seller. But only now was her mission, so long in the making, nearly complete.[47] The beginnings of freedom were finally, blessedly, at hand.

Later That Month, January 1863—Brooklyn, New York

A few days after the proclamation, at Plymouth Church in Brooklyn, Henry Ward Beecher, son of Lyman, brother of Harriet, and the most famous of the three, faced his congregation. His task today was both heady and difficult: deliver a sermon celebrating the proclamation, yet underscoring its shortcomings. Few were as fiery in their devotion to both faith and abolition as Henry Ward Beecher, after whom so-called "Beecher's Bibles" were named. This was a nickname given to the Sharps rifles Beecher helped provide to antislavery migrants to "Bleeding" Kansas in the years before the Civil War.[48]

All of the hopes, fears, and frustrations President Lincoln brought out in the abolitionist community were personified in Henry Ward Beecher. For years, he had severely criticized the president's slowness and pragmatism on the slavery issue. This criticism had an impact on the president, who twice sought out Beecher for spiritual counsel.

Like his father, Henry was not averse to using theatrics to convey his moral message, such as dragging the actual chains that held John Brown in captivity onto his pulpit. He was famous for holding mock "slave auctions" to raise money to buy the freedom of those in bondage. Today, the huge, fortresslike church was overflowing, and warm despite the cold outside; its gallery creaking under the weight of the many come to hear Beecher's judgment of the proclamation, and Lincoln.

He did not disappoint, pulling the crowd along with his moral reasoning, praising the man and the deed while also emphasizing the work left to be done. Summing up the impact of the proclamation with brevity, he declared: "The Proclamation may not free a single slave, but it gives liberty a moral recognition."[49]

It did the same for the great war itself.

Later that year, an exhausted Beecher would be sent to Europe for a rest. But in England, where many favored recognition of the Confederacy that was a main source of the cotton badly needed in British mills and factories, demand for the famous American preacher's views on slavery, abolition, and the war was too powerful to resist. He was, first and foremost, a man of God, but he did not mind the spotlight.

Relenting, Beecher delivered a series of speeches supporting the Union and abolition, and describing the horrors of slavery. Much as with his sister's publication of *Uncle Tom's Cabin*, the impact was massive. The British public was swayed, and Britain remained neutral in the battle between its former colonies. Beecher's tour through Britain was decisive. Its continued neutrality, coupled with the increasing effectiveness of the Union blockade of Southern ports, meant that the vast British empire could no longer supply the Confederacy with enough of the goods it needed to wage war. It would take time, and many, many more deaths in battle and from disease, but England's decision effectively set the stage for the South's defeat.[50]

★   ★   ★

Like millions of Americans, I had my own personal awakening. And it changed me forever. The son of two parents from India, I had grown up in a Hindu household. It wasn't all that different from what my I knew of my friends' faith. They went to church on Sundays. We didn't. But we believed in God and the values of the Ten Commandments, although ours felt more like philosophy and less like a faith tied to Scripture. I prayed a great deal. But I found it was a bit like talking to Santa Claus: If God gave me this or that, I would promise to behave. Every prayer was a deal. In return for good deeds, I expected something in return. By my early teens, I realized my prayers—my faith—felt incomplete to me.

So I began reading the Bible and praying harder. I went to a church musical to see a friend perform, and saw a video of the Passion of Christ, with Jesus nailed to the cross, suffering unbearable pain. This was the Son of God who had died for me, for my sins. Despite all my doubts and misgivings, and after years of searching, I did not hesitate when the youth pastor invited anyone who had not accepted Jesus Christ as his or her personal Lord and Savior to contact him. I don't know why it happened at that moment, but God hit me harder than I have ever been hit before.

My parents were none too happy to learn of my conversion. They were proud Hindus, and initially saw their faith as inseparable from their heritage. Why, they wondered, was I turning my back on it? My only answer was that I had found Christ. A year later, when I was sixteen, I totaled my father's brand-new car. It was a mangled wreck, and miraculously I had come out of it unscathed. "Which God do you have to thank for your safety?" my mom asked me. Despite our religious differences, I love my parents. The more I studied Scripture and the more I read of history and philosophy, the more I recognized the transformative power of Christianity. Not just in my own life after I had professed my faith in Christ and converted to Catholicism in college, but also in the life of our amazing country, which has been buoyed and transformed in generation after generation by the redemptive power of faith.

I think back to Lyman Beecher: His mission was to transform the soul of American Christianity into an engine of civic activism, not limited to abolition. Through his teachings—and his many children, the sons and daughters of "the father of more brains than any other man in America"[51]—Beecher created the spiritual framework for numerous national moral victories, from the abolition of slavery, to women's suffrage, to the civil rights movement of the twentieth century.

The First Great Awakening helped set the stage for the Revolutionary War and the founding of the republic. The Second Great Awakening created an army of Christian activists bent on social and moral reform, ultimately helping the Union win the war and abolish slavery. The Third Great Awakening built on the work of the first and second, driving the successful women's suffrage movement and other social causes.

To those who doubt it, I'd recommend the following anecdote: According to a former aide, Confederate general Robert E. Lee firmly believed that without the publication of Harriet Beecher Stowe's *Uncle Tom's Cabin* and a series subsequent speeches by Henry Ward Beecher in England, both England and France would have recognized the Confederacy. In Lee's mind, had they done so, it would probably have meant a Southern victory.[52] Whether this is actually true can never be known for sure. But it rings true to those who understand history. Lyman Beecher, perhaps unbeknownst to him, had quite literally sired two of the mightiest weapons deployed against slavery. For the accomplishments of his life and of his children, he should always be remembered, and venerated, even if his positions on gradual emancipation and his anti-Catholicism are offensive to modern sensibilities.

The story of the Beecher family and abolitionism is very much relevant today, when secular liberals are working hard to relegate religion itself to history. Let us be clear: There has never been a wall between church and state, nor should there be. The First Amendment prohibits the formation of a state religion in the United States, and guarantees religious freedom for its citizens. It does no more. It does no less.

The liberal position on religion and government is based on a myth: that the Constitution states and the founders believed that religion should be left out of government and the public square entirely. That is simply not true. Our faith can and should inform what we think about government and how we go about trying to improve it. The abolitionists understood that. So did the Reverend Martin Luther King, Jr. The millions who have marched for life in the last thirty years comprehend it as well.

Public servants and edifices need not be completely devoid of religious influence. In fact, by demanding that religion be banned from the public square, liberals are themselves being religiously intolerant. In some parts of the country, liberals may as well hang signs on voting booths that say, "Christians need not apply." They have taken the founders' wisdom—to reject an official religion of the United States—and twisted it into a ban on faith in governance, or any other part of public life. Liberals even want to tell private companies such as Hobby Lobby what they can and can't do with their own faith. This is both ludicrous and dangerous, requiring people of faith who want to be public servants somehow to not let their deepest religious convictions affect their decisions. This is akin to asking liberals to not let their own deeply held convictions about human rights, social justice, or multiculturalism affect how they govern. It's impossible, unnecessary, and frankly more than a little foolish.

The truth is, liberals are not bothered by many forms of faith in the public square. They are bothered by conservative faith, particularly evangelical Christianity, in politics and government. For liberals have their own doctrines that they "cling" to with religious-like zeal. They want their own faith—secular humanism—to be the unofficial state "religion" of America. And in many ways, if we are frank with ourselves, we must admit that secular humanism has indeed become the de facto state religion of our nation, which has led to an understandable backlash in the late twentieth century and early twenty-first century that some scholars have termed the Fourth Great Awakening. The Christian zeal of the Beecher family and other great religious reformers of American history was rekindled in reaction to the degradation our society suffered in the decades after World War II, and continues to suffer, as faith and public morality are pushed farther and farther from the center of not only politics, but our culture in general.

Liberals will try to persuade us otherwise, but Billy Graham and Martin Luther King, Jr., are part of the same, broad movement of Christian activism in the twentieth century. They are both the direct descendants of the powerful voices of the First, Second, and Third Great Awakenings: from Jonathan Edwards to Lyman Beecher to William Lloyd Garrison.

Today, a new generation of awakened Americans has risen to once again fight for their faith and freedom. Today, Beecher's spiritual descendants are fighting to save the lives of the unborn and for traditional values, while also helping to relieve the suffering from poverty, disease, and war across the globe. The irony of the liberal position on religion is that many of the causes championed by religious activists were considered "liberal" in their day. In fact, it was the Christianity of the reformers who took on these causes that made them "liberal." That today the people who call themselves liberal have not just abandoned this faith, but are actively working against it, makes little historical sense (then again, liberals don't make much sense in general these days).

Liberals like to claim that the Republican Party of today is too Christian, and too illiberal. They need a history lesson. It is not too much to say that the Republican Party was founded specifically to achieve one religiously inspired goal: to prevent the growth of slavery. Personal freedom and individual liberty were at the core of Republican values from the beginning. The party, with some deviations over time, has worked hard to stick to these values. It is liberalism as defined today that has abandoned reason and logic, not the Republican Party.

The Republican Party didn't abandon liberalism. Instead, liberalism was redefined to mean government control, secular humanism, and a rejection of traditional values. Meanwhile, today's "conservatives" have taken up the mantle of liberty and freedom: personal, economic, and religious. The labels have changed, but the values haven't.

Somewhere along the way, liberals lost their faith, and with it their way. Many liberals have become not just agnostic, but actively antagonistic to faith, despite the fact that it was in large part the faith of their forebears that helped lead to the great moral (and in the context of time "liberal") victories of U.S. history.

Today, we are once again in a fight for personal and religious liberty. That's why I spoke about religious freedom at the Reagan Library last year, and why I have spoken frequently on the subject across the country since then. There is today a silent war being waged for the hearts, minds, and souls of the American people. Our existence as a nation depends on a moral victory in this battle for the essence of our great republic. While we have worked hard and won many battles, right now the secularists are winning the larger war. If you doubt this, simply engage with any kind of mainstream media, whether news programming or entertainment. Christian beliefs are at best belittled, and at worst defined as bigoted. The free expression of religion guaranteed by the Constitution is disparaged, and sometimes it is outright prohibited.

The Obama administration's antipathy to the Christian faith was on full display in the crafting of ObamaCare. The law requires that employers who provide insurance to their workers cover contraception, including some abortifacients, regardless of the fact that some Christian denominations expressly forbid the use of abortifacients.

The Green family that started and owns retailer Hobby Lobby felt the law infringed their religious rights. The administration then filed suit to force Hobby Lobby—a private company in the

United States of America—to enforce a measure that directly contradicts its owners' religious beliefs. Fortunately, the Supreme Court ruled in favor of the Green family and Hobby Lobby. What the Court understood—and what President Obama, a former constitutional law professor, somehow did not—is that the attempt to force Hobby Lobby to adopt the administration's own secular liberal position on a key issue of faith strikes at the heart of free expression of religion as defined in the United States since the ratification of the Bill of Rights.

But this is just one case of religious intolerance in secular America. In my own life, I've had countless "open-minded" liberals insinuate that my own conversion to Christianity was for political expediency, not for faith. In 2013, for example, the *Huffington Post* said that "Jindal . . . converted his religion to become less different from the dominant white Christians of his party."[53] Apparently, someone who isn't "brainwashed" since birth could never actually believe in something as backward and illogical as Christianity, right? I've been happy to prove them wrong time and time again.

Those who claim that the Republican Party is too religious, too Christian, fail to understand that the Republican Party was forged in faith. Without the deep Christian devotion of those in the Second and Third Great Awakenings, which inspired the growth of the abolitionist movement and thence the GOP, we would have no Republican Party. Now certainly, the Republican Party and America rightly welcome Christians, people of other faiths, people of no faiths, and we don't tolerate discrimination against anyone. But we must always remember that the United States of America did not create religious liberty; religious liberty created the United States of America.

Today's Republicans, not so-called "liberals," are the ones faithfully carrying out the founders' vision as perfectly encapsulated in the Declaration of Independence: support for life (for all humans, including the unborn), liberty (personal, economic, and religious), and the pursuit of happiness (the opportunity to build the life you want without government interference). So long as we are willing to trace those rights back to the Creator who endowed us with them, our faith and our republic's future will always have a fighting chance.

10

RELIGION AND THE SCHOOLS

How Religious Bigotry Has Punished American Students

At the corner of Seventh Avenue and Twenty-eighth Street in Manhattan exists a very peculiar room. In it are New York City schoolteachers so bad that they're no longer allowed in a classroom. Known officially as the "Temporary Reassignment Center," it's more often referred to as "the Rubber Room."[1]

The six hundred New York teachers in the Rubber Room and six others like it are there for any number of reasons. Misconduct. Abusing students. Abject incompetence. The average teacher in the Rubber Room has been there for three years. So long as they show up, they continue to accumulate pay and benefits, sometimes in excess of one hundred thousand dollars annually. When they retire, their time in the Rubber Room will count toward computing their pensions.

Before the educational reforms of school chancellor Joel Klein, most of these teachers, perhaps all of them, would have been in the classroom, teaching whichever students were unlucky enough to live in the ZIP code assigned to these teachers' schools. Even more alarming, not every teacher who should be removed from the classroom is. Only 1.8 percent of those who have received an "unsatisfactory" rating are actually there.[2] The rest? Still teaching our children.

Abraham Lincoln once said "the leading object of the government" was "to afford all an unfettered start and a fair chance in the race of life."[3] He understood that in our republic, government doesn't guarantee equality of results, but at its best, it should guarantee equal opportunity. In the words of our Declaration of Independence, government doesn't provide happiness, but it does protect "the pursuit of happiness."

The sad reality is that in America today, this promise remains a hollow one because we do not provide an equal opportunity in education. This is an indisputable point, even an inconvenient truth. If families have the means to live in areas with good public schools, to send their children to private schools, or to homeschool them, their kids can receive a first-rate education. But if not, there is an alarmingly high chance that their kids will never have the opportunity for a first-rate education. They will not begin the "race of life" with an "unfettered start and a fair chance." Instead, those kids will have a much harder time for the rest of their lives.

The problem for kids trapped in failing schools is that our education system is set up as a collective, rather than a free market. It is a series of interlocking, coercive monopolies that assign children to a single school based on where they live. If that school is low-performing, unsafe, or lacking the elective course a child needs, the child typically must attend anyway.

At the center of the solution to this Soviet-style quagmire is the creation of an individual-driven ecosystem of freedom and choice where people willingly work together to accomplish their mutual goals. Giving families, parents, and students more choices will lead to better results. In fact, in my state of Louisiana, particularly in New Orleans, it already has. After Hurricane Katrina destroyed

much of the city and its schools, the citizens of New Orleans realized that they had a chance to build an education system from the
ground up, so they chose a mixture of traditional public schools,
charter schools, parochial schools, and private schools.

All these schools are a vital part of the mix, for they give parents a true choice in their children's education. We constantly hear
that we want parents to be "involved" in their kids' education by
the educrats who run the public schools. But, it turns out, not *too*
involved. For, generally speaking, they do not want them to have a
choice in *where* their child attends school. As one former Louisiana
state teachers' union leader candidly stated, he believed that low-
income parents had "no clue" about choosing the right school for
their children.

Unfortunately, this sentiment is not new. Since at least 1875,
there has been a concerted effort by powerful coalitions with mixed
motives to keep children, particularly poor children, from Catholic
schools. It is a frustrating and tragic story that begins with violent
and virulent bigotry, continues with a presidential aspirant's political opportunism, and ends with a host of legal obstacles that stand
in the way of at-risk children who cannot afford the school of their
choice.[4]

This is that story.

October 14, 1854—Ellsworth, Maine

Father John Bapst had never known true terror. Sure, six years
ago, he had been afraid. How could he not have been? Assigned
to preach among Maine's Penobscot Indians, he had known his
chances of survival had not been great. Ten of his Jesuit predeces-
sors had been killed.[5]

But, in spite of an intra-Indian war and a cholera epidemic, he had survived his mission. And until today he had never felt the kind of true terror in which you believed—you *knew*—that you were probably, imminently going to die.

The sharp rail dug into Father John's body. He had heard of being ridden out of town on a rail. But he had never thought about what it really meant—excruciating pain, and unimaginable fear.[6]

The men who had pulled the clean-shaven, Swiss-born Jesuit out of his confessional were very angry.[7] They had screamed at him then. They were screaming the same things now, the most foul, vicious epithets they could think of. And why? All because he was Catholic, and believed Catholic children should not be[8] made to read a Protestant Bible in public schools.[9]

These were the same kind of men who had been vandalizing Catholic churches, burning Catholics' houses, and butchering innocent Catholics throughout the United States for the past decade.[10] They believed America was *their* country. A white country. A Protestant country. As it had been before these "papists" began to arrive, uninvited, on the nation's shores a decade or two ago. Didn't this foreign horde know there wasn't room here for millions of impoverished, illiterate Catholic immigrants who had been taking natives' jobs, raising cities' crime rates, and, perhaps worst of all, voting for Democrats?

When Father John's kidnappers arrived with their prey at a sufficiently isolated location, they ripped his clothes off him. The rain poured down on the terrified priest, as his captors tied him to a tree and smeared hot tar up and down his naked body. The tar burned his flesh, and he screamed in agony.[11]

The feathers came next. He had seen it coming. But he hadn't expected them to then pile brush around his feet. Was the torture of tar and feathers not enough? Were they really going to burn him alive?[12]

The rain was his only hope.[13] Perhaps God had sent it. The mob's matches were failing them. The brush wasn't catching fire. His skin would never completely heal. Nor would his mind, haunted by the horrifying memories of this murderous mob. But because the matches wouldn't light, he would survive the night.[14]

Protected by pitchfork-wielding supporters, he would somehow, amazingly, say Mass the next day. Twice.[15] He would even go on to become the first president of Boston College. But a quarter of a century later, the horror of that evening in Ellsworth returned, in dreams that became nightmares, and to a mind that slowly slipped from Father John's control.[16]

Seventeen Years Later, August 17, 1871—Saratoga, New York

James G. Blaine hadn't been particularly bothered by the attack on Father John, at least, not for Father John's sake. Anti-Catholic bigotry was simply a fact of life. There was no point in fighting it. The real question, at least for an ambitious newcomer to Maine with a Catholic mother and Catholic sisters, was how to avoid it. And channel it. And exploit it.[17]

In the past seventeen years, Blaine had learned how to do exactly that. Shortly after the tarring and feathering of Father John, in the pages of the newspaper Blaine edited, he had called "Slavery, Rum, and Foreigners" the "three greatest evils of the times and the worst foes of our liberties." "Foreigners" meant Catholics. It wasn't long before he was calling the anti-Catholic "Know Nothings" the "party of Progress and Reform."[18]

Since then—after electing governors in seven states, congressmen in seventy-five districts, and mayors in Boston, Philadelphia, and Chicago—the Know Nothing Party had merged with the nascent Republican Party. And now, having played his cards right, Blaine was the second-most-powerful member of that party, the Speaker of the U.S. House of Representatives, and frontrunner in the race to replace President Ulysses S. Grant, whenever the first-term president should decide to retire.

This night, around nine in the evening, the forty-one-year-old former professor with the thick beard and the long nose was listening to Wagner's New York orchestra perform just a few steps from his hotel. Before the orchestra was a large crowd of Republicans, all there to sing to their hero and then listen to the political rallying cry that was sure to follow.[19]

They were not to be disappointed. Stepping out from the Union Hotel and onto the grand piazza, Blaine gazed upon an audience of ten thousand. Had he dreamed there would be this many? Behind him, from every window and balcony of his hotel, throngs of supporters cheered his name and filled the summer evening with tremendous, prolonged applause. With acolytes like this, how could he not be the next president?

"To so much of this ovation as may be personal to myself," said Blaine when the cheering finally died down, "I tender you my most grateful thanks." He assumed "an invitation for me to speak to you, however briefly, upon the political questions and issues of the hour." And the "Magnetic Man"—a nickname Blaine's powerful oratory would earn him—was only too happy to oblige them.

The difference between the nation's two political parties was clear, he declared. In Washington, where Republicans were "in full power," the national debt was declining, and taxes were falling. At the same time, in New York City, where Democrats were in charge, "every dollar that can be raised or wrung from the groaning taxpayers above current expenses is faithfully applied to the benefit of a private ring of political speculators." In Boss Tweed's New York, "we have seen with consternation and alarm the increase of the municipal debt at such a rate as would involve at no long period the bankruptcy and ruin even of that gigantic Metropolis."[20] That was what happened when you put Democrats in charge.

Partisan as they were, Blaine's words had the ring of some truth.

Tammany Hall controlled New York. It was wasteful. It was corrupt. And it was the face of the Democratic Party.

But Blaine did not leave it at that. Amid interruptions of applause, he reminded his audience there was another problem with Democrats: They were beholden to Catholics.

The "recent conduct" of the Democratic government in New York City "threatens that most dangerous of all political excitements—a war of class and creeds." They had recently decreed "that a certain procession of Protestants should not march through the streets of the American metropolis." The march in question would have celebrated the victory of Protestants over Catholics at Ireland's Battle of the Boyne. "Protestant myself," Blaine assured them, "I stand for the rights of all; and while I concede the fullest rights of the Catholic Irish to celebrate St. Patrick's Day, I demand the equal right of the Protestant Irish to celebrate the Battle of the Boyne."

On its face, Blaine's position was sound. All groups have a right to assemble. All groups can march, even if the purpose of the march is to rub Catholics' defeat and subsequent loss of the British throne in their faces. But why was Blaine, a federal legislator from several hundred miles away, going off on a tangent about the politics around parade permits in New York City?

The answer, of course, was that Catholic-bashing was good politics, at least outside America's big cities. Catholics were still blamed for a whole host of societal problems, from low wages to high crime. They were still seen as second-rate citizens at best, and foreign slaves obedient to a puppet-master in Rome at worst.

Recently, Catholics had been causing even more trouble.

Like Father John in Ellsworth, they didn't think Catholic boys and girls in public schools should be forced to recite verses from Protestant Bibles. To make matters worse, they were asking for tax dollars to support the education of Catholic children in Catholic schools. And with machines like Tammany Hall on their side in places like New York City, Catholics weren't just demanding these things, they were starting to receive them.

The next day, the *New York Times* reported that Blaine's "Serenade Speech" was enthusiastically received by an audience excited "when reference was made to the honesty of the National Administration as compared with the Tammany rule in New-York."

These were high times for the Republican Party.

They would not last.[21]

Four Years Later, December 14, 1875—Washington, D.C.

The Republican Party was in big trouble. The Grant administration, whose "honesty" once contrasted so sharply with Tammany's corruption, was plagued by scandal. Nothing pointed directly to the president himself, but the men he had surrounded himself with were now synonymous with scandals like the Whiskey Ring and Crédit Mobilier.

The result of the scandals was the loss of Republicans' majority in the House of Representatives. Speaker James G. Blaine was Speaker no more. And if the Republican Party didn't get its act together, he could say good-bye to his chances of being president. So could every Republican.

To make matters worse, within the Democratic Party, the Catholic vote was growing, as was the power of the anti-Catholic vote within the Republican Party. That year's gubernatorial election in Ohio had shown as much. "We have been losing strength in Ohio for several years by emigration of Republican farmers and especially of the young men who were in the army," Blaine had told Ohio governor Rutherford B. Hayes. "In their place have come Catholic foreigners." Blaine's advice to Hayes was to connect

Democrats to plots by the pope against American democracy. "We shall crowd them on the school and other state issues," Blaine had written.[22]

This strategy had paid dividends when Hayes was re-elected a month before, and Blaine was sure it would work on a national scale. "The signs of the times all indicate an intention on the part of the managers of the Republican party to institute a general war against the Catholic Church," reported the *St. Louis Republican*. "Some new crusading cry thus become a necessity of existence, and it seems to be decided that the cry of 'No popery' is likely to prove most available."[23]

In light of the Grant administration's scandals, a "new crusading cry" was more necessary than ever. Republicans couldn't let Democrats capture the "reform" mantle. So, on December 14, when James G. Blaine introduced to the House what he hoped would be the first constitutional amendment since emancipated slaves were granted the right to vote, he did so under the banner of reforming one of the most important institutions in the American republic: public schools.

The Blaine Amendment provided that "no money raised by taxation in any State for the support of public schools, or derived from any public fund therefor, nor any public lands devoted thereto, shall ever be under the control of any religious sect."[24]

Those words would not, Blaine was sure, preclude Protestant teachings in the public schools. Christianity was no mere "sect." And Christianity meant Protestantism. Sects meant Catholics.[25] Or Mormons. Or Jews. Not that the latter two sects were powerful enough to require a constitutional amendment to keep them in check.

Catholics, however, were another story. There were so *many* of them, and they were so *different*. No English in the Masses. Heck, no English in many of their homes! It was easy to tell nativists that these foreigners were to blame for their problems. It would be simple to mobilize support for an amendment aimed at undermining their strange schools, taught by those strange nuns and priests in those strange outfits. It would be possible, Blaine believed, to ride this amendment, and all the anti-Catholic bigotry it represented, all the way to the White House.[26]

"Mr. Blaine has introduced his amendment," reported the *New York Tribune*, "and the chances are that he will be able to carry it."[27]

That would mean, Blaine believed, "the complete victory for non-sectarian schools."[28]

Eight Months Later, August 1876—Washington, D.C.

When the *New York Tribune* predicted victory for the Blaine Amendment, there were two things it didn't count on: the solidary of the Senate's Democratic minority, and the apathetic attitude of James G. Blaine toward the amendment that bore his name.

Last December, Blaine had seen his assault on Catholic schools as a springboard toward the Republican presidential nomination. But he had cared much more about using it than about passing it. And now, as debate on his amendment finally made it to the floor of the Senate, Blaine was nowhere near the Capitol dome.

Appointed to the Senate to fill a vacancy created when Maine's Senator Lot M. Morrill became secretary of the Treasury, Blaine could have been a leader in the Senate's debate over the amendment he had once introduced and championed. But instead, Blaine was still licking his wounds from a Republican convention in June where he had led on the first six ballots, and whose final ballot had put Rutherford B. Hayes on top.[29]

Thus, the debate proceeded without him, and for his supporters, it did not go well. Democratic senator Lewis Bogy of Missouri blasted the Blaine Amendment as "a cloak for the most unworthy partisan motives." He accused Republicans of trying to distract from the Grant administration's scandals by stoking anti-Catholic antipathies. Their only goal, he said, "is to arouse feeling against the Democratic Party, and make it appear that it is dependent upon the support of the Catholics for success."[30]

Other Democrats agreed with Bogy. Connecticut's William Eaton spoke for many in his party when he said, "This whole matter is brought up as an election dodge." In fact, he may have spoken for his entire caucus, because when the final votes were counted on August 17, 1876, every Democrat in the Senate voted against it.[31]

Two weeks before, the House had passed the Blaine Amendment almost unanimously. But in the Senate, the solidarity of the Democrats, perhaps feeling more protected against popular passions and prejudices in an era that preceded their direct election, left the amendment two votes short of the supermajority required for a constitutional amendment.

The Blaine Amendment was down.

But it was not out.

★   ★   ★

Eight years later, the political career of James G. Blaine once again intersected with the question of whether America's melting pot was big enough for the millions of Catholic immigrants who continued to find shelter in the United States from the poverty and repression of Europe. In 1884, after a second unsuccessful bid in 1880, Blaine finally obtained the Republican presidential nomination. He was on the cusp of victory until one of his supporters called the Democratic Party, in words reminiscent of Blaine's early editorial after the tarring and feathering of Father John Bapst, the party of "Rum, Romanism, and Rebellion."

The alliterative line convinced Catholics, especially Irish Catholics in New York City, to turn out in huge numbers to defeat Blaine. If he had won New York, he would have become president. He lost it by 1,047 votes. Not until George W. Bush's 537-vote margin in Florida would a presidential election be so close.[32]

But Blaine's legacy would outlast his failed presidential campaigns. Although his party didn't have enough votes in the Senate for a constitutional amendment in 1876, they had more than enough votes for a Blaine-inspired statute. And before 1876 was over, Republicans used their Senate majority to push through a statute requiring new states to add the Blaine Amendment to their state constitution before they could be admitted to the Union. By the time Hawaii became the nation's fiftieth state, thirty-seven states had a "Baby Blaine" in their state constitutions.[33]

As a plurality of the Supreme Court stated in 2000, the "hostility to aid to pervasively sectarian schools has a shameful pedigree," and the Baby Blaines are the products of that pedigree. More than a century after the federal Blaine Amendment's defeat, its progeny continue to be an obstacle, though not necessarily an insurmountable obstacle, to support for parochial schools that promise children a pathway out of poverty.

In some way, the Baby Blaine Amendments are even more dangerous now than they were in the late 1800s, because our education system is so broken today. Only 17 percent of Americans would give U.S. public schools an A or B. A plurality of American parents would prefer to put their child in a private school. Yet approximately 87 percent of children attend regular public schools.[34] This means millions of American families aren't getting what they want from the U.S. education system, at even the most basic level of what school to attend.

The heart of the solution to this problem is more choice, not simply more money. The United States already spends more on education than every other developed nation in the world. Meanwhile, the test scores of high-school graduates have not improved in the past forty-five years.[35]

School choice means that the money follows the student to any willing school his or her parent chooses, including charter schools, virtual school, course providers, traditional public schools, and private schools that accept publicly funded scholarships, regardless of whether that private school is religious. The Supreme Court made clear in *Zelman* v. *Simmons-Harris* that the Establishment Clause of the United States Constitution's First Amendment poses absolutely no obstacle to this kind of school choice.[36]

Choice is already working wonders in New Orleans, where over 90 percent of kids in the public-school system in New Orleans now attend charter schools, and across Louisiana, where more than seven thousand kids use our scholarship program to attend the schools of their choice. Whereas 65 percent of New Orleans public school students attended a failing school in 2005, now only 4 percent of New Orleans students attend a failing school.[37] The parent satisfaction rate among those in the scholarship program is over 90 percent; the percentage of students in the program who are proficient in third grade English has grown by twenty percentage points; and it has grown in math by twenty-eight percentage points. The program is so popular that it has grown by approximately 1,223 percent since lawmakers passed it six years ago.

To be sure, school choice is not the entire solution to fixing broken schools. Reform also requires returning education policy to state and local governments and freeing educators from the failed policies of powerful teachers' unions. But choice is uniquely important, because a system of full and genuine parent choice empowers parents to make high-quality choices for their children, regardless of their ZIP code, and brings natural, market-style accountability to education instead of outside, government-led "accountability" that is highly susceptible to manipulation and cronyism.

Many politicians say they support school choice—but only the "right" kind. For instance, President Obama's budget proposed defunding the D.C. Opportunity Scholarship Program, even though the program improved student graduation rates by twelve percentage points and more than 90 percent of its participants come from black, low-income, single-parent households. (Congress, in a moment of clarity, restored the funding.)

The Obama administration also attempted to block Louisiana's scholarships to low-income students at failing schools. Obama's Department of Justice asserted the program violates federal desegregation orders, although data show nearly 90 percent of scholarship recipients are minorities. President Obama's endorsement of public-school choices, such as charter schools and magnet schools, over other types, such as private schools, homeschooling, and privately operated course providers, reflects the educational-industrial complex's paternalistic view of taxpayer dollars as "government" money.

President Obama's paternalism denies choices to millions of children of all races and family incomes by setting the "right" and limited choices their parents can make. Lifting the mediocre level of education too many of America's students attain, and the shockingly substandard level of education America's poor students receive, demands a more humble and holistic approach. Every child deserves a better option, and every option should be considered, not just those options D.C. bureaucrats might deem worthy.

What would happen if we transcended the shortsightedness and self-interest of bureaucrats and unions? One estimate found that just closing half the distance between the United States' international test scores and high-scoring Finland's could add more than $50 trillion to our gross domestic product between 2010 and 2090.[38]

This is not just about money. It's about providing more opportunities for American citizens to maximize their happiness and pursue their dreams. Set aside the lost trillions and consider the lost opportunities. Who can quantify what millions of children and our entire society have lost? Who can restore the incalculable loss of freedom and dignity when parents have been forbidden to chart the course for the children they alone know best?

One way to understand this loss is to consider how well Americans can participate in civic life. In our country, public education exists because a self-governing republic needs responsible, knowledgeable citizens. When people manage their own affairs, they must be intellectually and morally capable of doing so. The very first American document to set aside a structure for public education, the Northwest Ordinance, famously explained why a country like ours needs a strong education system: "Religion, morality, and knowledge, being necessary to good government and the happiness of mankind, schools and the means of education shall forever be encouraged."

Good government requires civic knowledge. Yet today, a third of Americans cannot name a single one of the three branches of government. Another third cannot name all three branches. These are questions a grade-schooler might find on an easy quiz. Given that a republic must have an educated citizenry to survive, our failure to cultivate civic literacy is akin to a human neglecting to feed himself.

We're not only failing at our society's central task of cultivating young citizens, we're failing at far more menial instruction such as reading and math. Our education system pushes neither high performers nor disadvantaged children to be the best they can. Usually, it doesn't push poor children to even basic competency. Essentially, children's test scores parallel family income, and income has become even more important to achievement in the past forty years, meaning that American schools barely mitigate a child's disadvantages, and they've been getting worse at doing so.

Neither ZIP code nor family income should determine a child's chances in life. America must be an aspirational society. Circumstances of birth should not determine adult outcomes; if you work hard and get a good education, you should have the chance to do better than your parents. Research and history show that education—and some specific ways of arranging an education system—can help lift children above their circumstances. It's time to put that knowledge to work for the most vulnerable members of our society, to improve American life for all.

Reform along these principles, beginning with the kind of school choice that the Blaine Amendment's anti-Catholic bigots attempted to preclude, will restore the balance in education toward parents and teachers, and away from the bureaucracies that stand as obstacles to change. Most important, it will give parents the power to choose among many quality educational options, instead of taking away their power by keeping children in poor-performing schools.

These are the stakes: restoring freedom for parents to choose, and the freedom for children to develop the tools with which they can flourish in life. It's time for us to embrace this opportunity, because the opportunity of the next generation is too critical to waste. True, there are many roadblocks. But embracing the free market principles that have served so many other sectors of our nation so well and repealing thirty-seven Baby Blaine Amendments that stand in opposition to those principles would be a good place to begin.

CONCLUSION

2016: ANOTHER TURNING POINT

Forty-four years ago, my parents came to the United States of America, and for that choice I will be forever grateful. Of course, there were some things about having immigrant parents that weren't easy, from cultural barriers to assimilation issues. But among the many great things about being the son of parents who chose this country is that they taught me how precious freedom truly is.

Free nations too often take freedom for granted. But as President Reagan said, "Freedom is a fragile thing and is never more than one generation away from extinction. It is not ours by inheritance; it must be fought for and defended constantly by each generation."

The breadth of that freedom has hinged on the pivotal moments of our history, including the ten that I try to bring to life in this book. And next year, in 2016, America will face another turning point. I do not believe it is an exaggeration to say the next presidential election will present our nation with the most consequential electoral choice since the presidential ballot bore the names Lincoln and Douglas.

To be sure, much that is great about our nation has survived presidents whose elections were regrettable. But coming off two decades of intermittent drift under both Bushes and Bill Clinton, followed by eight years of the worst president in American history, I am not sure that we can survive another mistake of Obama-esque proportions.

In the near future, we will either elect a leader who sees us as citizens or one who considers us subjects. We will either strengthen our defenses or embolden our adversaries. We will either defend religious liberty or send people of faith to the back of the bus. We will either embrace the values of our forefathers or betray the hopes of our children. In short, in 2016, the voters will determine the proper roles of government, of American leadership, and of religious faith, perhaps forever.

I'd like to share a few thoughts about each of those three questions.

In 2016, the role of government will be on the ballot. In the previous chapters, a vision of limited government was advanced and defended by Delegate Melancton Smith, Governor Ronald Reagan, and Senator Phil Gramm. But in many ways, in recent years, the opposite vision of government has been ascendant, one inspired and enabled one hundred years ago by the victory of turn-of-the-century progressives.

If we were going to build our government from scratch, Washington, D.C., would be a lot smaller. It would only have about half of its government workers. Enormous sections of the federal bureaucracy would be eliminated, with a few good websites created in their place (and we wouldn't let Kathleen Sebelius build the websites). Americans would not be required to send trillions of dollars to a capital hundreds or thousands of miles away, where it winds its way through the conveyor belts of bureaucratic friction, only to return in some watered-down way, if at all, to the states that it came from, bogged down by arbitrary rules and conditions, like Gulliver trapped by the Lilliputians.

Just as our government is failing, so, too, is our political discourse. Politicians spend months fighting over the margins of an out-of-control federal budget and a regulatory state that would have been inconceivable to our founders. We need to move beyond and above this petty and shortsighted debate. The real question before us is not how to tinker with the machinery of the bureaucracy but rather how to empower ordinary Americans—like the oil boom's Edwin Drake, and like the energy innovators of today's oil and gas revolution—to do what bureaucrats and big-government liberals would consider the unimaginable and the impossible.

Americans like Edwin Drake risk. They build. They invent. They try and fail and try again. They don't need a government that picks winners and losers, and they don't want a government that throws up a hundred regulatory roadblocks along their way.

They do, however, want their children to have the same opportunities they enjoyed, which requires a school system that gives all our children the tools they need to succeed. Americans are sick and tired of our broken public-school system, where the child follows the dollars, rather than the dollars following the child. It is long past time for education solutions that focus on rescuing failing children, rather than rewarding failing teachers, administrators, and labor unions.

In 2016, the role of the United States in the world will also be on the ballot. Thomas Jefferson understood that role. Henry Wallace and Joseph Kennedy did not. Of the three men, each of them among the most prominent of their day, Jefferson alone knew that peace is possible only through strength, and he alone believed in American exceptionalism.

The product of Jefferson's vision for America was the peaceful purchase of half a continent. But what has been the product, in recent years, of the alternative vision of American leadership in the world?

We've seen that product in Iraq, where towns and territories liberated with the blood of our troops have been ceded to ISIS by an administration overly eager to withdraw from the world. We've seen that product in Syria, where a dictator who sponsors terrorism and butchers his people was emboldened by a red line drawn but not enforced. We've seen that product in Iran, where our secretary of state promised to lift sanctions without requiring Iran's America-hating theocracy to abandon its nuclear program. And we've seen that product in Russia, where a twenty-first-century czar is gobbling up the territory of his neighbors because he neither fears nor respects American power.

The United States and our allies need an American president who does not apologize for American power. We need a leader who is not afraid to call radical Islam by its name. And we need a commander-in-chief who keeps his word, who negotiates from a position of strength, and who knows that we have never won a war against a murderous enemy by concession.

Finally, in 2016, the role of religious faith in American society will be on the ballot. Just as Senator Blaine and anti-Catholic bigots once waged a war against Catholics and Catholic schools, there is a war against religious Americans who want the freedom to practice the faith that they preach.

Ours is a nation of many religions, and we are the better because of that diversity. Hindus make up only about one-half of one percent of the American population, but because every faith is welcome in America, my Hindu parents were free to come here without surrendering the callings of their conscience. And because of our country's religious freedom, I was free to convert to Christianity, an act that is not only criminal, but punishable by death, in some countries.

This diversity of religions is not only protected under our Constitution. It is the foundation of our Constitution. As John Adams wrote in 1798, "Our Constitution was made only for a moral and religious people. It is wholly inadequate to the government of any other."

And yet, today, a set of liberal elites is waging a war against religion on three fronts. First, they want to take away business owners' freedom to exercise their religion, as shown by this administration's threat to fine Hobby Lobby $1.3 million per day if it didn't pay for abortion-inducing drugs for its employees. Second, they want to take away religious people's right to build and sustain faith-based associations of disciples who share a common faith, as demonstrated by the argument, advanced by this administration before the Supreme Court, that religious organizations do not have the absolute right to select their own ministers. And third, they want to take away the freedom of religious expression, as evidenced by proposed legislation requiring churches to hold gay weddings unless they, in effect, shut their doors to nonmembers and withdraw from the communities they are called by their Creator to serve.

All three fronts of this war are of a piece. The liberal elites concede (perhaps grudgingly) that people of faith should be allowed to worship as they choose, but they fail to understand that religious Americans are called by their faith to do more than pray. They are called to practice what they believe. They are called to run soup kitchens, and parochial schools, and counseling services. They want the freedom to run a business without violating the tenets of their faith. And they believe, as Justice Scalia wrote more than two decades ago, that religion is not "some purely personal avocation that can be indulged entirely in secret, like pornography, in the privacy of one's room."

Like the abolitionists during the Great Awakening, religious people today desire to practice their faith in the public square. The First Amendment of the antifederalists' Bill of Rights was written to guarantee that we can do exactly that. When liberal elites tell religious Americans like us that we cannot, they are not only rejecting us; they are rejecting a principle that always was, still is, and must remain central to the basic identity of America.

In fact, each of the three issues listed above—illustrated by previous chapters, and on the ballot in 2016—go to the heart of what it means to be the United States of America. If we choose poorly, we might never be the same. That is the bad news. But here's the good news: Arrayed against the threat at our proverbial gates is the greatest force for liberty in the history of human civilization, the citizens of the United States of America.

Because I trust the wisdom and basic common sense of the American people, I've written a book for them that doesn't dumb down my ideas, traffic in cheap slogans, or package my message into thirty-second sound bites that are filtered through focus groups and tested by opinion polls. And because I trust the American people, I believe that in 2016 we will unleash a new dawning of the American Dream.

It is a dream for which my parents came to America.

It is a dream that remains the envy of millions trapped in tyrannies.

It is a dream that has been the hope of generations of pilgrims who believed in the promise of that wonderful word—tomorrow.

A better tomorrow is not inevitable. But it is attainable. All it requires is American Will.

NOTES

1. Individual Liberty: The Antifederalists and the Fight for a Bill of Rights

1 See generally Woody Holton, *Unruly Americans and the Origins of the Constitution* (New York: Hill and Wang, 2007); see also Pauline Maier, *Ratification: The People Debate the Constitution, 1787–1788* (New York: Simon & Schuster Paperbacks, 2010), p. xiv.

2 *The Papers of Alexander Hamilton: Volume V*, edited by Harold C. Syrett (New York: Columbia University Press, 1962), pp. 171–77. I have altered some punctuation in an attempt to reflect the speech's delivery.

3 Maier, p. 387.

4 Maier, p. 387.

5 Holton, pp. 4–10.

6 Maier, p. 64.

7 Maier, p. 64.

8 For a list of common trades of the era, see Maier, p. 212.

9 Although the "Federalist Papers" written by Hamilton, Madison, and Jay did not begin to appear until late October, other federalist essays were, by this time, already appearing.

10 "Federal Farmer Letter I," *The Essential Antifederalist*, edited by W. B. Allen and Gordon Lloyd (Lanham, MD: Rowman & Littlefield Publishers, Inc., 2002), pp. 78–86.

11 Smith supported more amendments than the ten ultimately found in the Bill of Rights, but those ten amendments captured most of the important substance of the amendments he proposed.

12 "Federal Farmer Letter IV," http://press-pubs.uchicago.edu/founders /documents/v1ch14s24.html.

13 "Federal Farmer Letter IV," http://press-pubs.uchicago.edu/founders /documents/v1ch14s24.html.

14 "Federal Farmer Letter IV," http://press-pubs.uchicago.edu/founders /documents/v1ch14s24.html.

15 http://www.accessible-archives.com/collections/the-pennsylvania -gazette/.

16 Jackson Turner Main, *The Anti-Federalists* (New York: W.W. Norton & Company, 1961), p. 251.

17 Maier, p. 100.

18 "Federal Farmer Letter VI," http://teachingamericanhistory.org /library/document/federal-farmer-no-6/.

19 "Federal Farmer Letter IX," quoted at Webking 513–14. There is some debate over the identity of the Federal Farmer, but the weight of evidence strongly supports the conclusion that the Federal Farmer was Melancton Smith. See generally Robert H. Webking, "Melancton Smith and the Letters from the Federal Farmer," *William and Mary Quarterly* (Vol. 44, No. 3, July 1987), pp. 510–28.

20 "Federal Farmer Letter VII," quoted at Webking, 514.

21 "Federal Farmer Letter VI," http://teachingamericanhistory.org /library/document/federal-farmer-no-6/.

22 Maier, p. xiv.

23 Maier, pp. 130, 132; see also Holton, p. 252.

24 For a portrait of Melancton Smith, see Maier, p. 347.

25 Census data at https://www.census.gov/population/www/censusdata /files/table-16.pdf.

26 Main, p. 250.

27 Main, pp. 250–52; http://history.house.gov/HistoricalHighlight /Detail/35264.

28 Robert Allen Rutland, *The Birth of the Bill of Rights 1776–1791* (New York: Collier Books, 1962), p. 180.

29 Maier, p. 333.

30 Maier, p. 333.

31 It is doubtful Smith could have won election in the federalist stronghold of New York City, but he still owned property in Dutchess

County, where he had lived for many years, so he was elected from there (Maier, p. 332).

32 Smith speech to convention on June 21, 1788, available at http://www .constitution.org/rc/rat_ny.htm.

33 Main, p. 288.

34 New Hampshire ratified three days earlier, but it took until June 24 for the news to reach Poughkeepsie (Maier, p. 361).

35 Rutland, p. 178.

36 Maier, p. 374.

37 Maier, p. 374; Robert Allen Rutland, *The Ordeal of the Constitution* (Boston: Northeastern University Press, 1983), p. 256.

38 "Melancton Smith Replies to Nathan Dane," July 15, 1788, in *The Debate on the Constitution: Federalist and Antifederalist Speeches, Articles, and Letters During the Struggle over Ratification—Part Two: January to August 1788* (New York: Library of America, 1993), p. 851.

39 "Nathan Dane Writes to Melancton Smith," July 3, 1788, in *The Debate on the Constitution: Federalist and Antifederalist Speeches, Articles, and Letters During the Struggle over Ratification—Part Two: January to August 1788*, pp. 844–50.

40 Maier, p. 389.

41 Maier, p. 390.

42 "Melancton Smith Speaks in Support of Ratification Without Condition," July 23, 1788, in *The Debate on the Constitution: Federalist and Antifederalist Speeches, Articles, and Letters During the Struggle over Ratification—Part Two: January to August 1788*, pp. 852–53.

43 Maier, pp. 466–68.

44 Maier, p. 425. Federalists did not recognize the legitimacy of this unofficial convention, but the convention is an indication of just how insistent the antifederalists were about amending the Constitution.

45 Mark Halperin and John Heilemann, *Double Down* (New York: Penguin Books, 2014), Chapter 4.

2. Defending American Sovereignty: Napoleon, Jefferson, and the Louisiana Purchase

1 Charles Cerami, *Jefferson's Great Gamble* (Naperville, IL: Sourcebooks, Inc., 2003), p. 7. ("In 1778, when Jefferson was well into his thirties, an amazing new volume came into his hands.")

2 Marshall Sprague, *So Vast, So Beautiful A Land* (Boston: Little, Brown and Company, 1974), p. 221.

3 Donald Barr Chidsey, *Louisiana Purchase* (New York: Crown Publishers, Inc., 1972), p. 113.

4 Sprague, p. 216; Cerami, p. 6.

5 Sprague, p. 275.

6 Thomas Fleming, *The Louisiana Purchase* (Hoboken: John Wiley & Sons, Inc., 2003), p. 31.

7 Alexander DeConde, *This Affair of Louisiana* (Baton Rouge: Louisiana State University Press, 1976), p. 109. ("The Jeffersonians thought Napoleon now had adopted that plan" to "acquire Louisiana, conquer Canada, and then unite the two empires into one.")

8 DeConde, p. 149.

9 DeConde, p. 103.

10 Chidsey, p. 134.

11 DeConde, p. 101.

12 DeConde, p. 101.

13 Fleming, p. 12.

14 DeConde, p. 101.

15 Cerami, p. 58.

16 Cerami, p. 58.

17 Cerami, p. 58.

18 Sprague, pp. 283–84.

19 Sprague, p. 284.

20 DeConde, p. 114.

21 Cerami, pp. 66, 68.

22 DeConde, p. 132.

23 DeConde, p. 157; Sprague, p. 289; Harlow Giles Unger, *The Last Founding Father: James Monroe and a Nation's Call to Greatness* (United States: Da Capo Press, 2009), p. 154.

24 DeConde, p. 117.

25 DeConde, p. 120; Fleming, p. 61.

26 The 1795 Treaty of San Lorenzo guaranteed the right of deposit for three years, and many Americans understood the treaty to imply a right of deposit indefinitely. We are assuming Napoleon was surprised by the reports.

27 Fleming, p. 57.

28 Sprague, p. 301.

29 Cerami, p. 93.

30 Sprague, p. 300.

31 Chidsey, p. 134.

32 Sprague, p. 300.

33 Sprague, pp. 301–2.

34 Sprague, p. 297.

35 Cerami, p. 175.

36 Chidsey, p. 135; Cerami, p. 175; Sprague, p. 304; Fleming, p. 115.

37 Sprague, p. 306.

38 Chidsey, p. 140; Sprague, p. xvii.

39 Fleming, p. 135.

40 Cerami, p. 209.

41 Bobby Jindal and Jim Talent, Executive Summary, Rebuilding the American Defense Consensus, America Next, http://americanext.org/wp-content/uploads/2014/10/Rebuilding-Defense-Consensus.pdf.

42 Cerami, p. 205.

43 Cerami, p. 220.

44 Bobby Jindal and Jim Talent, Executive Summary, Rebuilding the American Defense Consensus, America Next, http://americanext.org/wp-content/uploads/2014/10/Rebuilding-Defense-Consensus.pdf.

45 Bobby Jindal and Jim Talent, Executive Summary, Rebuilding the American Defense Consensus, America Next, http://americanext.org/wp-content/uploads/2014/10/Rebuilding-Defense-Consensus.pdf.

46 Rebuilding the American Defense Consensus, America Next, http://americanext.org/wp-content/uploads/2014/10/Rebuilding-Defense-Consensus.pdf.

47 Rebuilding the American Defense Consensus at p. 12, America Next, http://americanext.org/wp-content/uploads/2014/10/Rebuilding-Defense-Consensus.pdf.

48 Rebuilding the American Defense Consensus at p. 12, America Next, http://americanext.org/wp-content/uploads/2014/10/Rebuilding-Defense-Consensus.pdf.

49 Rebuilding the American Defense Consensus at pp. 11–12, America Next, http://americanext.org/wp-content/uploads/2014/10/Rebuilding-Defense-Consensus.pdf.

50 Rebuilding the American Defense Consensus at p. 12, America Next, http://americanext.org/wp-content/uploads/2014/10/Rebuilding -Defense-Consensus.pdf.

51 Rebuilding the American Defense Consensus at p. 8, America Next, http://americanext.org/wp-content/uploads/2014/10/Rebuilding -Defense-Consensus.pdf.

52 Rebuilding the American Defense Consensus at p. 11, America Next, http://americanext.org/wp-content/uploads/2014/10/Rebuilding -Defense-Consensus.pdf.

53 Rebuilding the American Defense Consensus at p. 11, America Next, http://americanext.org/wp-content/uploads/2014/10/Rebuilding -Defense-Consensus.pdf.

54 Bobby Jindal and Jim Talent, Executive Summary, Rebuilding the American Defense Consensus at p. 12, America Next, http://american ext.org/wp-content/uploads/2014/10/Rebuilding-Defense-Consensus .pdf.

3. Boom: The First Energy Revolution and the Rise of the American Entrepreneur

1 Dr. William R. Brice, "Myth, Legend, Reality: Edwin Laurentine Drake and the Early Oil Industry," available online: http://www .oil150.com/essays/article?article_id=106.

2 Quoted in Paul H. Giddens, *The Birth of the Oil Industry* (New York: The MacMillan Company, 1938), p. 48.

3 Judith Ann Schiff, "How Yale Launched the Oil Economy," *Yale Magazine*, November/December 2005. Available online: http://archives .yalealumnimagazine.com/issues/2005_11/old_yale.html.

4 Judith Ann Schiff, "How Yale Launched the Oil Economy," *Yale Magazine*, November/December 2005. Available online: http://archives .yalealumnimagazine.com/issues/2005_11/old_yale.html.

5 Giddens, p. 50.

6 Daniel Yergin, *The Prize: The Epic Quest for Oil, Money, and Power* (New York: Simon & Schuster, 1991), p. 10.

7 Yergin, p. 10.

8 Yergin, p. 8.

9 J. T. Henry, *The Early and Later History of Petroleum* (New York: J.B. Rodgers Company, 1873), p. 57.

10 Yergin, p. 5.

11 Edward Chancellor, "Whale of a future for oil industry," *Financial Times*, June 2, 2008. Available online: http://www.ft.com/cms/s /0/059fe970-303d-11dd-86cc-000077b07658.html#ixzz3PDUvGlRQ.

12 Yergin, p. 11.

13 Yergin, p. 11.

14 Giddens, p. 62.

15 Yergin, p. 13.

16 Yergin, p. 13.

17 Yergin, p. 13.

18 Quoted in Yergin, p. 12.

19 "Dramatic Oil Company," The American Gas & Oil Historical Society, available online: http://aoghs.org/editors-picks/the-dramatic-oil -company/.

20 "Dramatic Oil Company," The American Gas & Oil Historical Society, available online: http://aoghs.org/editors-picks/the-dramatic-oil -company/.

21 Bobby Jindal and Bill Flores, "Organizing around Abundance: Making America an Energy Superpower," America Next, p. 18. Available online: http://americanxt.org/wp-content/uploads/2014/09/Organizing -Around-Abundance.pdf.

22 Bobby Jindal and Bill Flores, "Organizing around Abundance: Making America an Energy Superpower," America Next, p. 15. Available online: http://americanxt.org/wp-content/uploads/2014/09/Organizing -Around-Abundance.pdf.

23 Bobby Jindal and Bill Flores, "Organizing around Abundance: Making America an Energy Superpower," America Next, p. 7. Available online: http://americanxt.org/wp-content/uploads/2014/09/Organizing -Around-Abundance.pdf.

24 Bobby Jindal and Bill Flores, "Organizing around Abundance: Making America an Energy Superpower," America Next, p. 7. Available online: http://americanxt.org/wp-content/uploads/2014/09/Organizing -Around-Abundance.pdf.

4. Preemptive Surrender: Joe Kennedy and the Perils of Appeasement

1 David M. Kennedy, *Freedom from Fear: The American People in Depression and War* (New York: Oxford University Press, 1999), p. 367.

2 http://www.newsweek.com/when-franklin-roosevelt-asked-joe-kennedy-drop-his-pants-283146.

3 David Nasaw, *The Patriarch: The Remarkable Life and Turbulent Times of Joseph P. Kennedy* (New York: Penguin Press, 2012), p. 291.

4 Peter Collier and David Horowitz, *The Kennedys: An American Drama* (New York: Encounter Books: 1984), p. 3.

5 Nasaw, pp. 289–90.

6 Nasaw, pp. 310–11.

7 When this conversation later became public, Joe Kennedy would deny von Dirksen's recollection.

8 Max Wallace, *The American Axis: Henry Ford, Charles Lindbergh, and the Rise of the Third Reich* (New York: St. Martins Press, 2003), p. 167.

9 Nasaw, p. 313.

10 Nasaw, p. 315.

11 Nasaw, p. 331.

12 Nasaw, p. 102.

13 The Lindbergh kidnapping was one of the reasons cited for Joe Kennedy's decision to give his daughter, Rosemary, a lobotomy. He and his wife, Rose, were afraid his differently abled daughter might wander off somewhere and be abducted. See, e.g., Nasaw, p. 266.

14 Nasaw, pp. 338–39.

15 Lynne Olson, *Those Angry Days: Roosevelt, Lindbergh, and America's Fight Over World War II, 1939–941* (New York: Random House, 2013), p. 18.

16 Will Swift, *The Kennedys: Amidst the Gathering Storm: A Thousand Days in London, 1938–1940* (Washington, DC: Smithsonian: 2008), p. 98.

17 Nasaw, p. 360.

18 Franklin Roosevelt, Public Papers of the President, 1938, Vol. VII, (Washington, DC: Office of the Federal Register), p. 597.

19 http://www.pbs.org/wgbh/americanexperience/features/primary-resources/kennedys-memo/.

20 http://www.pbs.org/wgbh/americanexperience/features/primary-resources/kennedys-memo/.

21 Nasaw, pp. 401–2.

22 Nasaw, pp. 401–2.

23 Graham Macklin, *Chamberlain* (London: Haus Publishing, 2006), p. 85.

24 Nasaw, p. 407.

25 Nasaw, p. 413.

26 Nasaw, p. 414.

27 Malcolm H. Murfett, *Fool-proof Relations: The Search for Anglo-American Naval Cooperation During the Chamberlain Years, 1937–1940* (Singapore: NUS Press, 1984), pp. 273–74.

28 http://www.jfklibrary.org/Asset-Viewer/Archives/JFKPP-002-011.aspx.

29 http://www.jfklibrary.org/Asset-Viewer/Archives/JFKPP-002-011.aspx.

30 http://www.jfklibrary.org/Asset-Viewer/Archives/JFKPP-002-011.aspx.

31 Nasaw, p. 441.

32 Nasaw, p. 474.

33 Alex Kershaw, *The Few: The American Knights of the Air Who Risked Everything to Save Britain in the Summer of 1940* (New York: Da Capo Press, 2006), p. 13.

34 Nasaw, p. 485.

35 Nasaw, p. 497.

36 http://www.pbs.org/wgbh/americanexperience/features/primary-resources/kennedys-democracy-finished/.

37 *Boston Sunday Globe*, November 10, 1940.

38 http://www.washingtontimes.com/news/2014/dec/5/hillary-clinton-empathize-enemies-remark-slammed/.

39 http://www.telegraph.co.uk/news/politics/9696402/Why-Winston-Churchill-will-always-be-the-last-word-in-political-wit.html.

40 Bobby Jindal and Jim Talent, AmericaNext, "Rebuilding the American Defense Consensus," available online: http://americanxt.org/wp-content/uploads/2014/10/Rebuilding-Defense-Consensus.pdf.

41 Jon Wiener, "Joe Kennedy, Cold War Critic," *Nation*, February 4, 2013.

5. In Defense of Federalism: Ronald Reagan and the Fight Against Richard Nixon's Welfare State

1 Lou Cannon, *Governor Reagan: His Rise to Power* (New York: Public Affairs, 2003), p. 350.

2 Franklin D. Roosevelt, "Annual Message to Congress," January 4, 1935.

3 Steven Hayward, *The Age of Reagan: The Fall of the Old Liberal Order, 1964–1980* (New York: Prima Publishing, 2001), p. 235.

4 Tom Wicker, "Nixon is Nominated on the First Ballot; Support for Lindsay in 2d Place Growing," *New York Times*, August 9, 1968.

5 Tom Wicker, "Nixon is Nominated on the First Ballot; Support for Lindsay in 2d Place Growing," *New York Times*, August 9, 1968.

6 Tom Wicker, "Nixon is Nominated on the First Ballot; Support for Lindsay in 2d Place Growing," *New York Times*, August 9, 1968.

7 Hayward, p. 238.

8 Hayward, p. 238.

9 Hayward, p. 238.

10 "Nixon and Reagan: Leaders of a Bygone Era," Available online: http://blog.nixonfoundation.org/2014/06/nixon-reagan-leaders-bygone-era/.

11 A National Review Book, *Tear Down This Wall: The Reagan Revolution* (New York: Continuum, 2004), p. 103.

12 Hayward, Location 5220 of 16528.

13 Hayward, Location 5220 of 16528.

14 Quoted in J. David Woodard, *Ronald Reagan: A Biography* (Santa Barbara, Calif.: Greenwood, 2012), p. 77.

15 Hayward, Location 5303 of 16528.

16 Hayward, Location 5237 of 16528.

17 Hayward, Location 5220 of 16528.

18 Ronald Reagan, interview with *California Journal*, December 16, 1970.

19 Robert Knight, "Income Inequality: How Reagan Handled It," *American Thinker*, January 31, 2014. Available online: http://www.americanthinker.com/articles/2014/01/income_inequality_how_reagan_handled_it.html#ixzz3S0QqytCT.

20 Hayward, p. 237.

21 James Madison, *Federalist* 45.

22 U.S. Term Limits, Inc. v. Thornton, 514 U.S 779, 838 (1995) (Kennedy, J., concurring).

23 NFIB v. Sebelius, 132 S.Ct 2566 (2012).

24 Avik Roy, "Oregon Study: Medicaid 'Has no Effect' on Health Outcomes vs. Being Insured," Forbes.com, May 2, 2013. Available online: http://www.forbes.com/sites/theapothecary/2013/05/02/oregon-study-medicaid-had-no-significant-effect-on-health-outcomes-vs-being-uninsured/.

6. From HillaryCare to ObamaCare: The Left's
Quest for Socialized Medicine

1 Jill Lepore, "Preexisting Condition," *New Yorker*, December 7, 2009.

2 Most of this introduction is taken verbatim from Governor Jindal's introduction to *The Freedom and Empowerment Plan: The Prescription for Conservative Consumer-Focused Health Reform*, http://americanxt.org/wp-content/uploads/2014/04/The-Freedom-and-Empowerment-Plan.pdf.

3 David Lauter and Robert Rosenblatt, "Clinton Spells Out His Plan to Curb Health Care Costs : Campaign : His reform package stresses free-market forces. But government would still play a major role," *Los Angeles Times*, September 25, 1992.

4 John Harris, *The Survivor* (New York: Random House, 2005), p. 112.

5 http://www.lyricsfreak.com/f/fleetwood+mac/dont+stop_20054276.html.

6 "First in his class" alludes to David Maraniss's biography of Bill Clinton, *First In His Class*, which refers both to Clinton's often being the smartest person in his class and also to Clinton's being the first of his generation to reach the White House.

7 David Lauter and Robert Rosenblatt, "Clinton Spells Out His Plan to Curb Health Care Costs : Campaign : His reform package stresses free-market forces. But government would still play a major role," *Los Angeles Times*, September 25, 1992.

8 Gwen Ifill, "The 1992 Campaign: The Democrats; Clinton Proposes Making Employers Cover Health Care," *New York Times*, September 25, 1992.

9 David Lauter and Robert Rosenblatt, "Clinton Spells Out His Plan to Curb Health Care Costs : Campaign : His reform package stresses free-market forces. But government would still play a major role," *Los Angeles Times*, September 25, 1992 ("Clinton generally avoids discussing [costs]").

10 David Lauter and Robert Rosenblatt, "Clinton Spells Out His Plan to Curb Health Care Costs : Campaign : His reform package stresses free-market forces. But government would still play a major role," *Los Angeles Times*, September 25, 1992.

11 Iver Peterson, "Clinton Hits Hard in New Jersey (Close), Relaxes in New York (Ahead)," *New York Times*, September 25, 1992.

12 Iver Peterson, "Clinton Hits Hard in New Jersey (Close), Relaxes in New York (Ahead)," *New York Times*, September 25, 1992.

13 Haynes Johnson and David Broder, *The System* (Boston: Little, Brown and Company, 1996), p. 310 (describing Cooper as "thin, soft-spoken, formal, and aloof").

14 Connie Bruck, "Hillary the Pol," *New Yorker*, May 30, 1994 ("sureness about her own judgment . . . is probably Hillary's cardinal trait").

15 Harris, p. 117 (the Clintons "just naturally assumed they were the smartest people in the room," quoting Donna Shalala).

16 Johnson and Broder, p. 10 ("sometimes employing as many as six hundred people"); Bruck ("six Cabinet secretaries and several top White House advisors").

17 Bob Woodward, *The Agenda* (New York: Simon & Schuster Paperbacks, 2005), p. 324.

18 Harris, p. 117.

19 Cooper later said of the meeting, "Maybe I was too up-front, but I wanted them to know that we were worried, that we could not support their plan, and that we would have to introduce our bill." Johnson and Broder, pp. 311–12.

20 Cooper later said of the meeting, "I think there was some shock and surprise that a junior member of Congress would presume to say there was trouble with one of the Administration's top priorities." Bruck.

21 Cooper later said of Hillary's reaction to his message at the meeting, "It was not a happy response." Bruck.

22 Months later, in a West Wing meeting, Hillary " 'kind of got this evil look and said, "We've got to do something about this Cooper bill. We've got to kill it before it goes any further." [Delivery Room manager Jeff] Eller suggested that he fly down to Tennessee and plant some stories. We put a couple people on the radio down there to beat up on the plan.' " Johnson and Broder, p. 315 (quoting an aide to Hillary Clinton).

23 Johnson and Broder, p. 36.

24 Johnson and Broder, p. 36.

25 David Segal, "The Real Leader of the Opposition," *Washington Monthly*, March 1, 1994, p. 38.

26 Howard Fineman, with Ginny Carroll, "Get Ready for Mr. Relentless," *Newsweek*, February 20, 1995, p. 28. ("He jokes about his homely

visage, which has been compared to a turtle without he shell, E.T.'s granddad and Darth Vader with the helmet off.")

27 http://www.nytimes.com/1993/09/23/us/clinton-s-health-plan-tran script-president-s-address-congress-health-care.html.

28 http://www.nytimes.com/1993/09/23/us/clinton-s-health-plan-tran script-president-s-address-congress-health-care.html.

29 Phil Gramm, "A Novel Idea," *Los Angeles Times*, April 11, 1993; "The Health Care Debate: Excerpts from Speeches by Senators on the Mitchell Health Care Proposal," *New York Times*, August 12, 1994 (quoting Phil Gramm).

30 Harris, p. 113; Nicholas Laham, *A Lost Cause*, pp. 29–31; Brock (quoting the CBO regarding alliances' functions); http://www.heritage.org /research/reports/1993/11/A-Guide-to-the-Clinton-Health-Plan.

31 http://www.heritage.org/research/reports/1993/11/A-Guide-to-the -Clinton-Health-Plan; Theda Skocpol, "The Rise and Resounding Demise of the Clinton Plan," *Health Affairs*, Spring 1995 (quoting Dick Armey).

32 http://ashbrook.org/publications/onprin-v2n1-kristol/ ("unprecedented intrusion into the American economy").

33 Johnson and Broder, p. 54. ("The President did have a plan. It had been almost two years in gestation. He understood it perfectly. The country [after his speech] understood it not at all.")

34 Paul Starr, "What Happened to Health Care Reform?" *American Prospect*, No. 20 (Winter 1995): pp. 20–31; Paul Starr, *Remedy and Reaction* (New Haven: Yale University Press, 2013), p. 118.

35 Johnson and Broder, p. 368.

36 Johnson and Broder, p. 36.

37 See Congressional Record—Senate, November 15, 2002, p. 22731. Gramm's conversation with McCain was described by Gramm in a speech to the Heritage Foundation. See Phil Gramm, "Freedom and Virtue," *Heritage Foundation Reports, Heritage Lectures*, No. 523, May 9, 1995, p. 1.

38 Bruck; Harris, pp. 111–15. The Harris book says Gergen, Emanuel, and Podesta were "warning against the ostentatious veto threat in January." The Bruck article describes a meeting with Bill and Hillary and advisors where Hillary argues for the veto threat. This scene draws an inference from the two sources to put Gergen, Emanuel,

and Podesta in the room for the meeting with the Clintons about the veto threat. Also, Gergen, as quoted in the Harris book, is the source for saying Bill Clinton was unusually deferential to Hillary Clinton in the weeks after the *American Spectator* article. Gergen attributes the president's decision on the veto threat in part to his reaction to the article.

39 Laham, p. 106.

40 Johnson and Broder, p. 363; Starr, p. 118.

41 Johnson and Broder, p. 363.

42 Starr, p. 118.

43 Ruth Shalit, "The Wimp-Out," *New Republic*, February 14, 1994, p. 19.

44 Laham, p. 100. Although this is an exact quotation by Gramm, he did not necessarily deliver this exact quotation in Annapolis.

45 Laham, p. 101. Although this is an exact quotation by Gramm, he did not necessarily deliver this exact quotation in Annapolis.

46 Laham, p. 99. Although this is an exact quotation by Gramm, he did not necessarily deliver this exact quotation in Annapolis.

47 Leslie Phillips, "GOP goes on road to sell its own plan," *USA Today*, October 13, 1993, p. 10A. Although this is an exact quotation by Gramm, he did not necessarily deliver this exact quotation in Annapolis.

48 Laham, p. 98. Although this is an exact quotation by Gramm, he did not necessarily deliver this exact quotation in Annapolis.

49 Johnson and Broder, p. 365.

50 Johnson and Broder, p. 366; Starr, p. 118.

51 Information about this meeting, including quotations from Hillary's speech, comes from Johnson and Broder, pp. 387–88.

52 Laham, p. 106.

53 Johnson and Broder, p. 456; Harris, p. 118

54 Johnson and Broder, p. 456.

55 Harris, p. 118.

56 This is a direct quotation from Harris, p. 118.

57 Harris, p. 118.

58 Johnson and Broder, pp. 460–63.

59 Johnson and Broder, p. 461.

60 Johnson and Broder, p. 465.

61 Johnson and Broder, p. 461.

62 Johnson and Broder, p. 461.

63 Johnson and Broder, p. 469.

64 Johnson and Broder, p. 462 (quoting Hillary).

65 Johnson and Broder, pp. 460–72.

66 Johnson and Broder, p. 475.

67 Johnson and Broder, p. 468.

68 Much of this epilogue comes from http://americanxt.org/wp-content
/uploads/2014/04/The-Freedom-and-Empowerment-Plan.pdf;
http://americanxt.org/america-next-letter-to-congress-on-obama
care/; http://www.politico.com/magazine/story/2015/02/gop-obama
care-alternative-114820.html. With regard to the entire chapter, in
addition to the sources listed in notes above, the following sources
were useful: Charles Jones, *Clinton & Congress: 1993, Risk, Restoration,
and Reelection* (Norman: University of Oklahoma, 1999); Adam Cly-
mer, Robert Pear, and Robin Toner, "What Went Wrong?" *New York
Times*, August 29, 1994.

7. A Party Divided: The Great Republican Crack-Up of 1912

1 James Chace, *1912: Wilson, Roosevelt, Taft and Debs—The Election That
Changed the Country* (New York: Simon & Schuster, 2005), p. 893.

2 Chace, p. 679.

3 Chace, p. 910.

4 Edmund Morris, *Colonel Roosevelt* (New York: Random House, 2010),
p. 159.

5 Chace, p. 199.

6 http://www.politico.com/magazine/story/2014/12/first-daughters
-alice-roosevelt-113302.html.

7 http://www.pbs.org/wgbh/americanexperience/features/interview/tr
-cooper/.

8 http://www.pbs.org/wgbh/americanexperience/features/transcript/tr
-transcript/.

9 http://www.heritage.org/initiatives/first-principles/primary-sources
/teddy-roosevelts-new-nationalism.

10 Chace, p. 952.

11 http://www.heritage.org/initiatives/first-principles/primary-sources /teddy-roosevelts-new-nationalism.

12 Max J. Skidmore, *After the White House: Former Presidents as Private Citizens* (New York: Palgrave Macmillan, 2004), p. 570.

13 Michael Wolraich, *Unreasonable Men: Theodore Roosevelt and the Republican Rebels Who Created Progressive Politics* (New York: Palgrave Macmillan, 2014), p. 230.

14 Doris Kearns Goodwin, *The Bully Pulpit* (New York: Simon & Schuster, 2013), p. 11.

15 Goodwin, p. 880 (large-print edition).

16 Louis L. Gould, *Four Hats in the Ring: The 1912 Election and the Birth of American Politics* (Lawrence: University Press of Kansas, 2008), p. 13.

17 Goodwin, p. 1130.

18 Chace, p. 1808.

19 http://www.claremont.org/article/why-the-election-of-1912-changed -america.

20 Wolraich, p. 230.

21 Morris, p. 196.

22 Goodwin, p. 1190.

23 Chace, p. 1808.

24 Gould, p. 74.

25 Morris, p. 210.

26 R. J. Pestritto, *Woodrow Wilson and the Roots of Modern Liberalism* (New York: Rowman & Littlefield, 2005).

27 Woodrow Wilson, *The New Freedom* (New York: Doubleday, Page and Company, 1913), p. 47.

28 http://www.archive.org/stream/crossroadsoffree007728mbp/cross roadsoffree007728mbp_djvu.txt.

29 Goodwin, p. 1230.

30 Goodwin, p. 1236.

31 Goodwin, p. 1238.

32 Gerald Helferich, *Theodore Roosevelt and the Assassin: Madness, Vengeance and the Campaign of 1912* (New York: Rowman & Littlefield, 2013), p. 192.

33 Goodwin, p. 1244.

34 http://www.inaugural.senate.gov/swearing-in/event/woodrow
-wilson-1913.

35 http://uselectionatlas.org/RESULTS/national.php?year=1912.

36 http://www.bartleby.com/124/pres44.html.

37 http://www.claremont.org/article/present-at-the-creation.

8. The Truman Afterthought: How Indecision and Recklessness Almost Lost the Cold War

1 Transcript of Churchill "Iron Curtain" speech. http://legacy.ford
ham.edu/halsall/mod/churchill-iron.asp.

2 Selected works of Henry Wallace. http://newdeal.feri.org/wallace
/haw28.htm.

3 Tim Tzouliadis, *The Forsaken* (New York: Penguin Press, 2008),
p. 220.

4 Tzouliadis, p. 221.

5 Varlam Shalamov, "Dry Rations," *Kolyma Tales*, (New York: W. W.
Norton & Company, 1980). Note: This acclaimed book contains fac-
tual stories and historical fiction based on real events and experiences
of the author.

6 The dialogue here, and elsewhere in this section, unless otherwise
noted, is from Tim Tzouliadis's *The Forsaken*.

7 Tzouliadis, p. 224.

8 John C. Culver and John Hyde, *American Dreamer: A Life of Henry A.
Wallace* (New York: Norton, 2000), p. 346.

9 David McCullough, *Truman* (New York: Touchstone, 1992), p. 299.

10 *American Dreamer*, p. 346.

11 McCullough, p. 299.

12 *American Dreamer*, p. 351.

13 *American Dreamer*, p. 346.

14 Robert H. Ferrell, *Choosing Truman* (Columbia, MO: University of
Missouri Press, 1994), p. 12.

15 *Choosing Truman*, p. 22.

16 *Choosing Truman*, p. 19.

17 *American Dreamer*, p. 348.

18 McCullough, p. 377.

19 Dennis Cashman, *America in the Twenties and Thirties: The Olympian Age of Franklin Delano Roosevelt*, (New York: New York University Press, 1989), p. 271.

20 McCullough, p. 379.

21 McCullough, p. 381.

22 *Choosing Truman*, p. 26.

23 *Choosing Truman*, p. 29.

24 *Choosing Truman*, p. 30.

25 McCullough, p. 381.

26 *Choosing Truman*, p. 24.

27 *American Dreamer*, p. 351.

28 Jean Edward Smith, *FDR* (New York: Random House, 2007), p. 619.

29 McCullough, p. 298.

30 McCullough, p. 299.

31 McCullough, pp. 382–83.

32 *Choosing Truman*, p. 37.

33 *American Dreamer*, p. 353.

34 *Choosing Truman*, pp. 32-33.

35 McCullough, p. 310.

36 McCullough, p. 307.

37 *American Dreamer*, pp. 355–59.

38 *American Dreamer*, p. 359.

39 McCullough, p. 394.

40 Smith, p. 620.

41 Tzouliadis, p. 227.

42 McCullough, p. 320.

9. Great Awakenings: Abolition and the Hidden Hand of God

1 Declaration of Independence, 1776.

2 Thomas Jefferson, Letter to the Danbury Baptists, 1802.

3 "Congress shall make no law respecting an establishment of religion, or prohibiting the free exercise thereof; or abridging the freedom of speech, or of the press; or the right of the people peaceably to assemble, and to petition the Government for a redress of grievances."

4 Edmund Clarence Stedman, Ellen Mackay Hutchison, ed., *A Library of American Literature*, Vol. IX (New York: Charles L. Webster & Company, 1888), p. 350.

5 Beecher, *The Bible a Code of Laws* (Andover, MA: Mark Newman, 1827), p. 37.

6 Beecher, p. 38.

7 Beecher, p. 40.

8 Daniel Walker Howe, *What Hath God Wrought: The Transformation of America, 1815–1848* (New York: Oxford University Press, 2007), p. 168.

9 Sharon Grimberg, "William Lloyd Garrison's Fight Against a 'National Sin' " *Huffington Post*, January 14, 2013. Last updated March 16, 2013. http://www.huffingtonpost.com/sharon-grimberg /william-lloyd-garrisons-fight-against-a-national-sin_b_2473779 .html.

10 Grimberg, "William Lloyd Garrison's Fight Against a 'National Sin.' "

11 Wendell Phillips Garrison and Francis Jackson Garrison, *William Lloyd Garrison, 1805–1879: The Story of His Life Told by His Children*, Vol. I (Boston, New York: Houghton, Mifflin and Company, 1894), p. 127.

12 Garrison and Garrison, pp. 127–28.

13 Garrison and Garrison, p. 136.

14 Garth M. Rosell, *Boston's Historic Park Street Church: The Story of an Evangelical Landmark* (Grand Rapids, MI: Kregel Publications, 2009), p. 114.

15 "Doctor Beecher's Address on Abolitionism & Colonization," University of Virginia, accessed March 6, 2015. http://utc.iath.virginia .edu/abolitn/abes38at.html.

16 "Doctor Beecher's Address on Abolitionism & Colonization."

17 "Doctor Beecher's Address on Abolitionism & Colonization."

18 "Doctor Beecher's Address on Abolitionism & Colonization."

19 Jone Johnson Lewis, "Harriet Beecher Stowe Facts," accessed March 6, 2015. http://womenshistory.about.com/od/stoweharriet/a /stowe_biography.htm.

20 "Harriet Beecher Stowe," *Encyclopedia Britannica* Online. Last updated May 8, 2014. http://www.britannica.com/EBchecked/topic/567810 /Harriet-Beecher-Stowe.

21 Annette Gordon-Reed, "The Persuader: What Harriet Beecher Stowe Wrought," *New Yorker,* June 13, 2011. Accessed March 6, 2015. http://www.newyorker.com/magazine/2011/06/13/the-persuader-2.

22 Ethan J. Kytle, *Romantic Reformers and the Antislavery Struggle in the Civil War Era* (New York: Cambridge University Press, 2014), p. 130.

23 "Uncle Tom's Cabin," Harriet Beecher Stowe Center. Accessed March 6, 2015. https://www.harrietbeecherstowecenter.org/utc/.

24 "Uncle Tom's Cabin," Library of Congress. Accessed March 6, 2015. http://memory.loc.gov/ammem/today/jun05.html.

25 "Uncle Tom's Cabin," Harriet Beecher Stowe Center.

26 Richard E. Ellis, *The Union at Risk: Jacksonian Democracy, States' Rights, and the Nullification Crisis* (New York: Oxford University Press, 1987), p. 78.

27 William Seale, "The Visit: A War Worker Calls for a Favor, Late 1862," White House Historical Association. Accessed March 6, 2015. http://www.whitehousehistory.org/presentations/waddell-artist-visits -white-house-past/president-abraham-lincoln-essay.html.

28 *Civil War Gazette*, "Lincoln Shocks His Cabinet with an Emancipation Proclamation."

29 *Civil War Gazette*, "Lincoln Shocks His Cabinet with an Emancipation Proclamation."

30 *Civil War Gazette*, "Lincoln Shocks His Cabinet with an Emancipation Proclamation."

31 "Notable Visitors: Harriet Beecher Stowe (1811–1896)."

32 "Notable Visitors: Harriet Beecher Stowe (1811–1896)."

33 Don E. Fehrenbacher and Virginia Fehrenbacher, *Recollected Words of Abraham Lincoln* (Stanford: Stanford University Press, 1996), p. 428.

34 Fehrenbacher and Fehrenbacher, p. 194.

35 Fehrenbacher and Fehrenbacher, p. 194.

36 Noah Brooks, *Lincoln Observed: Civil War Dispatches of Noah Brooks* (Baltimore: Johns Hopkins University Press, 1998), p. 16.

37 "Lincoln and His Marshal," U.S. Marshals Service, accessed March 5, 2015. http://www.usmarshals.gov/history/lincoln/united_states _marshals_service_2.htm.

38 "Downstairs at the White House: Vestibule and Corridor," Mr. Lincoln's White House, Lehrman Institute, Lincoln Institute. Ac-

cessed March 6, 2015. http://www.mrlincolnswhitehouse.org/inside
.asp?ID=70&subjectID=3.

39 Abraham Lincoln, letter to Horace Greeley, August 22, 1862. http://
www.nytimes.com/1862/08/24/news/letter-president-lincoln-reply
-horace-greeley-slavery-union-restoration-union.html.

40 "The Origins of the Republican Party," USHistory.org. Accessed
March 6, 2015. http://www.ushistory.org/gop/origins.htm.

41 Eric Foner, "The Emancipation of Abraham Lincoln," *New York
Times*, January 1, 2013. Accessed March 6, 2015. http://www.nytimes
.com/2013/01/01/opinion/the-emancipation-of-abe-lincoln.html?_r=0.

42 John Hope Franklin, "The Emancipation Proclamation: An Act of
Justice."

43 John Hope Franklin, "The Emancipation Proclamation: An Act of
Justice."

44 Louis P. Masur, "How the Emancipation Proclamation Came to Be
Signed," *Smithsonian Magazine*, January 2013.

45 Ralph Waldo Emerson, "Boston Hymn."

46 Fanny Garrison Villard, "How Boston Received the Emancipation
Proclamation," 1913. Accessed March 6, 2015, via the Antislavery Literature Project. http://antislavery.eserver.org/legacies/how-boston
-received-the-emancipation-proclamation/garrisonvillard.html.

47 Katherine Kane, "Lincoln and the Key to Uncle Tom's Cabin," *Connecticut Explored*, Winter 2012/2013. Accessed via Harriet Beecher
Stowe Center on March 6, 2015. https://www.harrietbeecherstowe
center.org/pdf/Lincoln-and-The-Key-to-Uncle-Tom.pdf.

48 "Beecher's Bibles," Encylopedia.com. Accessed March 6, 2015. http://
www.encyclopedia.com/doc/1G2-3401800402.html.

49 John Hope Franklin, "The Emancipation Proclamation: An Act of
Justice."

50 Debby Applegate, "Henry Ward Beecher," *New York Times*, "Times
Topics." Accessed March 6, 2015. http://topics.nytimes.com/top/ref
erence/timestopics/people/b/henry_ward_beecher/index.html.

51 Debby Applegate, *The Most Famous Man in America: The Biography of
Henry Ward Beecher* (New York: Doubleday, 2006), p. 264.

52 Debby Applegate, "Henry Ward Beecher."

53 http://www.huffingtonpost.com/rajiv-malhotra/bobby-jindal-race_b
_2588700.html.

10. Religion and the Schools: How Religious Bigotry Has Punished American Students

1 Steven Brill, "The Rubber Room," *New Yorker*, August 31, 2009.

2 Bobby Jindal and Bill Flores, *K–12 Education Reform: A Roadmap*, by America Next, with an introduction by Governor Jindal.

3 http://quod.lib.umich.edu/j/jala/2629860.0022.105/—nationalism-of -abraham-lincoln-revisited?rgn=main;view=fulltext.

4 Bobby Jindal and Bill Flores, *K–12 Education Reform: A Roadmap*, by America Next, with an introduction by Governor Jindal.

5 http://www.newenglandhistoricalsociety.com/fr-john-bapst-survives -tar-fathers-becomes-1st-boston-college-president/.

6 http://www.newenglandhistoricalsociety.com/fr-john-bapst-survives -tar-fathers-becomes-1st-boston-college-president/.

7 That Fr. John was pulled out of a confessional comes from http://www .newenglandhistoricalsociety.com/fr-john-bapst-survives-tar-fathers -becomes-1st-boston-college-president/. Sources conflict where he was when his attackers seized him. See, for example, http://www.forgotten books.com/readbook_text/Maine_A_History_v1_1000420752/345.

8 http://www.forgottenbooks.com/readbook_text/Maine_A_History _v1_1000420752/345.

9 Nell Irvin Painter, *The History of White People* (New York: W. W. Norton, 2010), pp. 148–49.

10 http://www.newenglandhistoricalsociety.com/fr-john-bapst-survives -tar-fathers-becomes-1st-boston-college-president/; http://www.for gottenbooks.com/readbook_text/Maine_A_History_v1_1000420752 /345. Some of the description of tarring and feathering comes from a general description of tarring and feathering. http://hortonsarticles .org/TarFeathering.pdf.

11 http://www.newenglandhistoricalsociety.com/fr-john-bapst-survives -tar-fathers-becomes-1st-boston-college-president/; Nell Irvin Painter, *The History of White People*, pp. 148–49.

12 http://www.forgottenbooks.com/readbook_text/Maine_A_History _v1_1000420752/345.

13 http://www.newenglandhistoricalsociety.com/fr-john-bapst-survives -tar-fathers-becomes-1st-boston-college-president/.

14 http://www.forgottenbooks.com/readbook_text/Maine_A_History _v1_1000420752/345.

15 http://www.newenglandhistoricalsociety.com/fr-john-bapst-survives
-tar-fathers-becomes-1st-boston-college-president/.

16 Neil Rolde, *Continental Liar From the State of Maine: James G. Blaine* (Gardiner: Tilbury House Publishers, 2007), p. 55.

17 Rolde, p. 55.

18 The description of the Serenade Speech comes from Rolde at pp. 140–41 and http://query.nytimes.com/mem/archive-free/pdf?res =9D06E2DE113EEE34BC4F52DFBE66838A669FDE.

19 *New York Times*, August 18, 1871.

20 http://query.nytimes.com/mem/archive-free/pdf?res=9D06E2DE113 EEE34BC4F52DFBE66838A669FDE.

21 Steven K. Green, "The Blaine Amendment Reconsidered," *The American Journal of Legal History*, Vol. 36, No. 1 (January 1992), p. 49, n. 73. See also Rolde, p. 164.

22 Steven K. Green, "The Blaine Amendment Reconsidered," *The American Journal of Legal History*, Vol. 36, No. 1 (January 1992), p. 44.

23 Steven K. Green, "The Blaine Amendment Reconsidered," *The American Journal of Legal History*, Vol. 36, No. 1 (January 1992), p. 50.

24 "[I]t was an open secret that 'sectarian' was code for 'Catholic.'" *Mitchell v. Helms*, 530 U.S. 793, 828 (2000).

25 Rolde, pp. 164–65; Steven K. Green, "The Blaine Amendment Reconsidered," *The American Journal of Legal History*, Vol. 36, No. 1 (January 1992), p. 54.

26 Steven K. Green, "The Blaine Amendment Reconsidered," *The American Journal of Legal History*, Vol. 36, No. 1 (January 1992), p. 53.

27 Steven K. Green, "The Blaine Amendment Reconsidered," *The American Journal of Legal History*, Vol. 36, No. 1 (January 1992), p. 50.

28 Steven K. Green, "The Blaine Amendment Reconsidered," *The American Journal of Legal History*, Vol. 36, No. 1 (January 1992), p. 67.

29 Steven K. Green, "The Blaine Amendment Reconsidered," *The American Journal of Legal History*, Vol. 36, No. 1 (January 1992), p. 67.

30 Steven K. Green, "The Blaine Amendment Reconsidered," *The American Journal of Legal History*, Vol. 36, No. 1 (January 1992), p. 67.

31 Rolde, pp. 178–81.

32 http://www.pfaw.org/issues/religious-liberty/religious-protection -laws-the-united-states; http://www.becketfund.org/blaineamend

ments/; https://www.ij.org/washington-student-teacher-policies-background.

33 Bobby Jindal and Bill Flores, *K–12 Education Reform: A Roadmap*, by America Next, with an introduction by Governor Jindal.

34 Bobby Jindal and Bill Flores, *K–12 Education Reform: A Roadmap*, by America Next, with an introduction by Governor Jindal.

35 *Zelman v. Simmons-Harris*, 536 U.S. 639 (2002).

36 Bobby Jindal and Bill Flores, *K–12 Education Reform: A Roadmap*, by America Next, with an introduction by Governor Jindal.

37 Bobby Jindal and Bill Flores, *K–12 Education Reform: A Roadmap*, by America Next, with an introduction by Governor Jindal.

38 Bobby Jindall and Bill Flores, *K–12 Education Reform: A Roadmap*, by America Next, with an introduction by Governor Jindal.

ACKNOWLEDGMENTS

I realize that the arts and the hard sciences are crucial to education. That said, I believe that our country's biggest educational deficit lies in our failure to understand and appreciate our history. Hopefully, this book can in some small way help address that.

Understanding our history is not looking backward. The only way that America can own the future is by understanding our past. President Reagan said it best—"Freedom is never more than one generation away from extinction. We didn't pass it to our children in the bloodstream. It must be fought for, protected, and handed on for them to do the same."

I fear that my generation has yet to lay claim to our freedoms. I believe that we will, but I also realize it is not inevitable. Here's to hoping and believing that we will.

This book was quite simply a blast to write. I hope that my agents and coauthors, Matt Latimer and Keith Urbahn, feel the same way about it. There would be no book without them. So if you enjoyed the book you can thank me, if you did not, it's their fault. I am grateful for the editorial wisdom of the fine publishing team at Simon & Schuster: Louise Burke, Mitchell Ivers, and Natasha Simons.

My good friends Curt Anderson and Timmy Teepell were also helpful, most of the time. My best friend, Supriya Jindal, on the other hand, was helpful all the time.

INDEX